HOW THINGS PERSIST

How Things Persist

KATHERINE HAWLEY

CLARENDON PRESS · OXFORD
2001

OXFORD

UNIVERSITY PRESS

Great Clarendon Street, Oxford OX2 6DP

Oxford University Press is a department of the University of Oxford.
It furthers the University's objective of excellence in research, scholarship,
and education by publishing worldwide in

Oxford New York

Athens Auckland Bangkok Bogotá Buenos Aires Cape Town
Chennai Dar es Salaam Delhi Florence Hong Kong Istanbul Karachi
Kolkata Kuala Lumpur Madrid Melbourne Mexico City Mumbai Nairobi
Paris São Paulo Shanghai Singapore Taipei Tokyo Toronto Warsaw
and associated companies in Berlin Ibadan

Oxford is a registered trade mark of Oxford University Press
in the UK and in certain other countries

Published in the United States
by Oxford University Press Inc., New York

British Library Cataloguing in Publication Data

Data available

Library of Congress Cataloging in Publication Data
Hawley, Katherine, Dr.
How things persist/Katherine Hawley.
p. cm.
Includes bibliographical references and index.
1. Space and time.   2. Ontology.   I. Title.
BD632.H29 2001   111—dc21   2001036727

ISBN 0–19–924913–X

1 3 5 7 9 10 8 6 4 2

Typeset in Minion
by Hope Services (Abingdon) Ltd.
Printed in Great Britain
on acid-free paper by
Biddles Ltd., Guildford & Kings Lynn

Preface

Chapters 1 and 3 draw upon my 'Why Temporary Properties are not Relations between Physical Objects and Times', *Proceedings of the Aristotelian Society*, 98/2 (1998), 211–16, by courtesy of the Editor of the Aristotelian Society: © 1998, and 'Persistence and Non-Supervenient Relations', *Mind*, 108 (1999), 53–67, by permission of Oxford University Press.

Much of this book was written whilst I was Henry Sidgwick research fellow of Newnham College, Cambridge, and I am very grateful to the principal and fellows of Newnham for the material and moral support I received during my time there.

It feels as if I have discussed persistence with everyone I have met during the last few years, in Cambridge, St Andrews, and elsewhere. I will not attempt to list them all, but acknowledge that I owe thanks to many people for their patience and interest. In particular, I have learned a lot from Joel Katzav, James Ladyman, Peter Lipton, Jonathan Lowe, Fraser MacBride, Hugh Mellor, Eric Olson, and Ted Sider. Finally, and especially, I am grateful to Philip Lakelin, who helped a great deal, and is very much missed.

Contents

Introduction

Why read this book? The book is about the metaphysics of persistence through time, about what it takes for a material object to last from one moment to another. But why suppose that we can discover some deep metaphysical fact about how things persist? And even if we can, why care? We certainly care a great deal about specific, concrete questions of persistence and identity, especially questions about people. For example, I am rather concerned about whether I will survive the night, and I would go to great lengths to ensure that I do persist until tomorrow. The death of a friend can occasion great sorrow, grief that the person no longer exists. And it means a lot to me that the friend I am meeting today is the person that I have known for the last ten years, not some impostor. Of course it rarely occurs to me to wonder whether I am meeting an impostor, but things might be different if I knew that my friend had an identical twin.

Issues of personal persistence and identity are of central importance to our practices of caring for and assigning responsibility to ourselves and others. Courts of law devote time and resources to adjudicating questions of personal identity: is the person in the dock the person who committed the crime? Our special responsibilities towards certain people are in part founded upon our past relationships to those people: they are our parents, our children, our oldest friends. I feel a certain pride or shame in thinking about my own past deeds which I do not feel about the deeds of others; similarly I have certain kinds of hope and fear about my own future life which I do not have about others' futures. Anyone who sacrifices part of her present income to invest for the future makes certain assumptions about persistence.

We also attach great importance to the persistence and identity of artefacts and of non-human organisms. The social institution of property relies on the fact that we are fairly good at keeping track of the objects we own. I paid for a book yesterday, took it home from the bookshop, and I have an extra possession today, unless I sell it or give it away, because I paid for that very book in the past. I don't own the books in your house, because I didn't pay for them or otherwise legitimately acquire them in the past. I thought it worthwhile paying for the book yesterday because I believed that doing so would entitle me to own that very book in the future, and I took care over my choice because I knew that my decision would affect my future, that which book I owned today would depend upon which book I paid for yesterday. All of this activity relies upon beliefs about the persistence of people (it was *me* who bought the book) and the persistence of books (*this* is the book I bought).

Our attitudes to objects often depend partly upon their histories, rather than their presently discernible properties. The very guitar Elvis played is worth a lot more money than its intrinsic duplicate, although both are equally useful for many guitar-related purposes. When Wembley stadium in London was rebuilt, pieces of the turf were sold as memorabilia. Fans were especially keen to buy 'significant' pieces of turf; one fan paid £2,000 for a piece of turf in the goalmouth, where a contentious goal was scored in the 1960s. It then emerged that the goalmouth turf was stolen by Scottish fans during a pitch invasion in the 1970s—had the fan really bought the piece of turf on which the famous goal was scored? Pride and money were at stake.

There is no denying that questions about persistence and identity through time are often of great legal, financial, and emotional importance. But why do we need metaphysics in order to address these questions? To discover whether I am speaking to my friend or to an impostor, I need to discover empirical facts about whether my friend has an identical twin, about what my interlocutor seems to remember about the past I shared with my friend, and so on. The same is true where ownership or responsibility for past actions is at stake: such questions are investigated with great thoroughness in courts of law, where neither defence nor prosecution is inclined to summon a metaphysician as expert witness.

Our methods of investigating specific, concrete questions of persistence rely upon various presuppositions, however, and it is here that metaphysics has a role to play. Metaphysical reflection can help us discover what kinds of empirical facts are relevant to questions about persistence and identity, what kinds of facts should be the focus of our investigation. For example, if I make sure that I am speaking to the same human organism that I have been encountering regularly for the last ten years, do I thereby guarantee that I am speaking to the same person, to my friend? Metaphysics alone cannot tell us whether I am indeed encountering the same organism: to establish that, I would need to make empirical investigations. But it can help us work out whether this question about the persistence of an organism is the same as the question about the persistence of my friend: might the same organism now 'house' a different person?

Or consider the prospect of entering an irreversible coma—would that be the end of you? One view is that you could not survive into such a state. A different view is that you could indeed survive into such a state—your continued existence might be of little value, but nevertheless you would continue to exist in that sorry position. These two views do not clash over the biological facts about how bodily functions are sustained during a deep coma. Rather, they disagree about the significance of those biological facts for the survival of a person. Less significantly, metaphysical reflection can help us discover what kinds of facts are relevant to the persistence of pieces of turf, at Wembley or elsewhere—does it matter whether the ground was dug over and reseeded at any point? Would it have mattered if there had been a landslide at Wembley?

One task, then, is to think about what it takes for people to persist, for organisms to persist, or for pieces of turf to persist—which sorts of empirical events can such entities survive, and which sorts of events spell doom? Thinking about persistence conditions can help us decide which sorts of empirical facts are relevant to practical disputes about persistence, identity and survival. We may well come up with different criteria for people, organisms and pieces of turf—perhaps an organism can survive a complete changeover of its parts, so long as the change happens gradually, whereas perhaps a piece of turf cannot survive so much change, and Elvis's guitar can survive even fewer changes. But we can also reflect at a more abstract level, thinking about the persistence of material objects in general, as opposed to the persistence of organisms, pieces of turf, or guitars in particular. For example, we might wonder why it is that certain kinds of object are more changeable than others: organisms, for example, must change in order to survive. What is the connection between change and persistence, and what determines whether an object continues to exist through a certain change? I discuss change in Chapter 1.

In settling practical questions about persistence and identity, we need to know what sorts of facts to look for, what changes are relevant. In establishing persistence conditions for different kinds of thing, it will help to know whether 'temporally local' facts always determine over-time facts about persistence. That's to say, do moment-by-moment facts determine all the facts there are, or are facts about persistence through time somehow more 'holistic' than this? For example, in discovering whether this guitar is the one Elvis played, is it enough to find out what happened at each moment, one at a time, and stick those facts together, or would we risk losing information if we only considered such moment-by-moment snapshots? Questions like these are addressed in Chapters 2 and 3.

In some cases—perhaps the row over the Wembley turf is such a case—it is tempting to say that there just is no deep fact of the matter about persistence. Perhaps it's simply indeterminate whether the piece of turf purchased by the gullible fan really is the very same piece of turf across which a certain goal was scored—there is no right answer to the identity question to be found, no matter how hard we think and how thoroughly we investigate. This view is certainly tempting—although the fan in question presumably believes that there is a definite fact about whether he now possesses the historically important piece of turf.

But in other cases, any verdict of indeterminacy has important consequences, and is, accordingly, contentious. How old are you? You know how long it is since you were born, but did you exist before that? Mostly we agree that people exist before birth, but often we disagree about how long people exist before birth. Have you existed since the moment of conception—were you once a bundle of four cells? Or did you begin to exist only when that bundle of cells developed its 'primitive streak', or when it started to look like a thumb-sucking baby? It is notoriously difficult to pinpoint an exact moment during pregnancy at which a person begins to exist.

On the assumption that there is no 'hidden' exact moment which we have so far failed to discover, we are left with two alternatives. One is to suppose that questions about identity through time are sometimes indeterminate. There may simply be no fact of the matter as to whether you were once a small bundle of cells—you began to exist during the period between conception and birth, but there is no precise moment at which you began to exist. If we reject this idea that persistence may be vague, or indeterminate, then we may be left with the idea that you began to exist either at conception or at birth, since there seems to be no exact moment between these events which could mark your beginning. These different views about whether persistence can be indeterminate—discussed in Chapter 4—have far-reaching political consequences, as the emotive, sometimes violent, debate about abortion illustrates.

A further metaphysical issue does not so obviously concern persistence, but we will see later that it is intimately connected with views about identity through time. Can there be two things occupying exactly the same place at the same time? Perhaps curled up purring by the fire are both a heap of biological matter, and also a cat, occupying the same location as each other without being identical to one another. One motivation for such a bizarre-sounding view is the thought that the heap of biological matter might out-last the cat—if the cat dies peacefully, the animal will cease to exist, yet the heap of matter will still be there. If this is the best description of feline expiration, then it looks as if the cat and the heap of matter are distinct objects—how else could one cease to exist and the other go on existing? Chapters 5 and 6 concern questions like these, about the possibility of coinciding objects.

We cannot avoid dealing with practical questions of persistence, and once we begin to reflect on these questions, we realize that our attempts to answer these questions depend upon various metaphysical assumptions. We need to take a stance on how facts about persistence relate to moment-by-moment facts, about the connection between persistence and change, about whether persistence is sometimes a vague or indeterminate matter, and about whether two things can occupy the same place at the same time. This book is an examination of the various stances we can take on these various questions, and an attempt to assess their relative worth—what should we really think about persistence?

Some may think, however, that such a project will inevitably prove fruitless. We clearly care a great deal about specific questions of persistence, affecting ourselves and other things. Our approaches to such specific questions may even embody some metaphysical attitude or other, some assumption about whether persistence may be a vague matter, for example. But is there really any hope of discovering metaphysical truths lying behind our practices? One line of objection here is that there really are no metaphysical facts to be discovered, and that we must simply choose a way of talking about persistence, in order to tackle the more pressing practical questions. A second line of objection is that, even if there are facts of the matter about how things persist, we cannot hope to discover what these are. I will discuss these objections in turn—I do not have a developed account of fact and method in metaphysics, but I can at least explain my own attitude to these matters, an attitude that informs this book.

First, let's consider the idea that there are no genuine objective facts to be discovered in this realm, that how things persist depends upon how we think about the world, rather than anything about the world itself. One idea is that questions of persistence in specific cases may be in some sense conventional. For example, it may simply be up to us to decide the persistence conditions for such objects as pieces of turf and guitars, and perhaps even for people. There is, perhaps, no objective fact of the matter about whether you would survive if you went into an irreversible coma—perhaps it is simply a matter for us to decide whether or not this would count as 'survival' for you.

To think that we can define, decide, or stipulate persistence conditions is to think that we can define, decide, or stipulate whether or not a certain object which exists right now also existed yesterday. Taken literally, this view attributes to us mystical, magical powers to affect the past, to create and destroy things by the mere power of thought, rather than through any physical manipulation, and for that reason I reject it, at least in so far as it applies to material objects. Yet this realism is an assumption that I will not attempt to justify; there is a rich and ancient debate about the ways in which mind may or may not play a role in constituting the world of material objects, and I will not engage with that debate here. Instead, I hereby advertise my assumption that we cannot in general alter facts about the persistence and existence of material objects, except by physically manipulating the world.

There is, however, a less radical way of spelling out the idea that the persistence conditions of material objects may be a matter of definition, decision, or stipulation. This is to suppose that it is at least partly a matter of definition, decision, or stipulation how we divide up the world into persisting objects, or which persisting things we choose to talk about. That's to say, perhaps it is to some extent 'up to us' whether by 'person' we mean a kind of thing which begins to exist at conception, or one which begins to exist at some later moment. To be interesting, this claim must not simply be that it is up to us what sense we attach to our words. It must also be that the world is densely populated, so that it is amenable to different classification systems, different ways of thinking about the world. If we can choose whether 'person' applies to objects which begin to exist at conception, or else to objects which begin to exist at some later date, then there must be objects of both sorts in the world.

If persistence conditions are in part a matter of stipulation, and yet mind does not constitute world, then material objects must be abundant: there are many ways in which we might have divided up the world into objects, and objects corresponding to those various schemes already exist. Are the objects abundant in this way? I believe that they are, whilst others believe that they are not. Either way, this is a substantive metaphysical question. So to suppose that persistence conditions are up to us, or a matter of convention, is not to remain apart from metaphysics, or neutral on metaphysical issues. It is to be committed either to the mind-dependence of the physical world (a metaphysical claim, if ever I saw one) or else to a mind-independent world with mind-boggling plurality of material inhabitants.

We cannot claim that metaphysics is superfluous because persistence conditions are a matter of convention. To suppose that persistence conditions are in some way conventional is to be committed to some sort of metaphysical view, not to avoid metaphysics altogether. What of the more general claim that there is no real, or no objective, difference between different metaphysical theories of persistence? This charge cannot be properly addressed in advance of a proper exposition of exactly what the different theories of persistence are—a task I undertake in Chapters 1 and 2. Indeed, I suspect that this charge cannot be properly addressed in advance of a full-scale investigation of the nature of truth, knowledge, and enquiry.

But, as this book will demonstrate, any theory of persistence is embedded in a network of broader claims—about the nature of vagueness, about wholes and parts, about time, about movement and change, about necessity and possibility, about language and reference. Moreover, different theories provide different contexts for our concern about certain concrete matters of persistence, and our views about self-interest and the future. Any claim that there is no fact of the matter as to which account of persistence is true will quickly spread outwards, committing us to conventionalism about a wide range of matters.

If there is a fact of the matter about how things persist, how can we find out what it is? As in many fields of human enquiry, claims in metaphysics are rarely susceptible to direct proof or disproof, and nor are they amenable to direct perceptual checks—we can't deduce how things persist from self-evident truths, nor can we just look and see. Instead, the best we can do is to examine the pre-suppositions and consequences of different accounts of persistence, to see how such accounts fit with beliefs we already hold—sometimes we may need to reconsider our existing beliefs, or examine the evidence for those beliefs.

This book focuses on two standard accounts of persistence—endurance theory and perdurance theory—and on a less well known view, stage theory. To assess the different accounts I will explore what they have to say about some of the issues I have already raised—how do things change, and what changes an object can survive? Is there more to the world than a collection of moment-by-moment facts? Can persistence sometimes be a vague matter, or a matter of convention? Can there be more than one thing in a place at a time? How do we manage to refer to and keep track of persisting things? No account of persistence is completely straightforward, or a perfect match to our pre-theoretical views—it would be surprising if our pre-theoretical views were so convenient and coherent. Here, as elsewhere, we will find that evidence underdetermines belief, that there is more than one reasonable view about persistence—I will set out what I take to be the best version of various accounts of persistence. Different readers will, inevitably, take different stances, but those stances should be considered, examined stances, which is why it is worth reading this book.

1

Sameness and Difference

1.1 How Things Persist

The world is a fairly stable place. Since picking up this book, you have changed its shape by opening it, you have warmed it slightly with the heat of your hands, and you might already have spilt coffee on it. Yet the book has survived these minor changes. You too have been changed by the encounter, yet you are still the person you were a few minutes ago. During your lifetime, you will undergo far more drastic changes—your cells will die and be replaced, your waistline will expand, your opinions will become more conservative and you will both acquire and lose both memories and skills. Yet these changes are all changes in *you*—you persist through momentous change, just as the book persists through less drastic change. Amidst the flux, persisting things are centres of stability.

How do things persist? To find out about the causal processes which sustain your life, enabling you to survive from day to day, we might consult a physiologist, who could tell us about the functioning of the human body, the metabolism and the processes of ageing. To find out how the book persists, we might consult a physicist, who could tell us about the physical forces which bind particles together, or we might consult a keeper of manuscripts, who could tell us which environmental conditions are favourable to the preservation of books, and which conditions will quickly prove disastrous. The processes that keep books intact are different from the processes that keep organisms functioning, which differ in turn from the processes that enable rocks to weather storms and persist for millennia. Things of different kinds persist through time in different ways—can we say anything purely general about what it is to persist rather than perish?

For a start, we can say that persistence occurs when something exists at more than one time—you existed a few minutes ago, and still exist right now. The same is true of the book you hold and the rock on the shoreline, and thus you have all persisted. So far, so good. We can go on to ask whether things persist through time in anything like the way in which they spread out through space. You, the book, and the rock all take up space—how do you manage this? Again, we could consult a physicist to find out what forces keep objects from imploding, or ask an evolutionary biologist how humans have come to stand erect, and be as tall as we are. But quite generally we can say that objects extend through space by having different parts in different places—your feet are down there and your head up here, your big toe is just there and your little toe just to the left. Perhaps the tiniest objects simply take up space without having different parts in different places. But a medium-sized object like you or me occupies a region of space by having its different parts occupy different parts of that region.

You occupy space by having parts down there in your shoes and parts up here under your hat; do you persist through time by having parts back then in bed and parts right now sitting in that chair? Many people resist this idea, believing that you are not spread out in time as you are in space; they think that the whole you is sitting right here right now, and the whole you was in bed earlier. To them, objects seem to 'move' through time in their entirety. But others are impressed by the analogy between space and time, and believe that you are indeed spread out through time as you are through space. Your little toe is merely a spatial part of you, and the whole you is not down there in your shoe. Similarly, say some, your current 'phase' or 'stage' is merely a 'temporal part' of you, and the whole you is not present right now. On this view, objects occupy temporal intervals in much the same way as they occupy spatial regions: they have different spatial parts in different parts of the spatial region they occupy, and they have different temporal parts in different parts of the temporal interval they occupy.

The first of these views, which sharply distinguishes persistence through time from extension through space, is *endurance theory*. The second view, according to which objects persist through time by having temporal parts, just as they extend through space by having spatial parts, is *perdurance theory*.[1] For many people, endurance theory is so close to their 'commonsense' or 'intuitive' picture of the

---

[1] Lewis (1986*a*: 202). Lewis attributes this terminology to Mark Johnston. Supporters of perdurance theory include Lewis (1976*a*; 1986*a*), Heller (1984; 1990), Jubien (1993), Armstrong (1980), Le Poidevin (1991), Noonan (1988), Quine (1950), and Robinson (1985). Supporters of endurance theory include Merricks (1994; 1995), Gallois (1998), van Inwagen (1990*a*), Haslanger (1994), Lowe (1988*b*; 1998), Mellor (1981; 1998), Oderberg (1993), Olson (1997), Wiggins (1980), Thomson (1983), and Simons (1987).

world that it can be difficult to see it as a theory at all, difficult to imagine why anyone would reject this picture, or adopt perdurance theory. After all, doesn't perdurance theory make the absurd claim that nothing persists at all?

Not quite. We agreed that things persist by existing at more than one time, and endurance theory interprets this in perhaps the most straightforward way: you, the whole you, are present at different times, yesterday, today, and tomorrow. That's what it is for you to persist. Yet perdurance theorists can agree that you are a single thing existing at more than one time. You exist yesterday, today, and tomorrow by having a temporal part yesterday, a temporal part today, and a temporal part tomorrow. You are a single object which exists at different times by having different parts at different times, just as a road exists at different places by having different spatial parts at those different places. Supporters of perdurance theory do not deny that objects persist, but they claim that persistence through time is much like extension through space. They challenge the 'commonsense' of endurance theory.

As we will see, perdurance and endurance theories account differently for many features of the world—how things change, how we refer to persisting things, and how and whether persistence can be a vague matter. Perdurance theory initially seems to be a strange alternative to down-to-earth endurance theory. But endurance theory, despite its image, must sometimes resort to far-from-commonsensical claims in order to explain what we see around us— as we will see, there is no straightforward, truistic account of how things persist. We can choose between different theories of persistence only by assessing their performance across a whole range of tasks. First, let's see how these theories account for change.

1.2 Change and Perdurance

Bananas ripen, your heart pumps, the book acquires a coffee stain. According to perdurance theorists, the way things change over time is very like the way they vary across space. The skin of the banana changes colour over time, from green to yellow, and the banana varies across its spatial extent right now. The banana is both tasty and bitter, because its flesh is tasty and its skin is bitter—its different spatial parts have different properties. And, according to perdurance theorists, the banana is first green all over then yellow all over because its earlier parts are green all over and its later parts are yellow all over—its different temporal parts have different properties, which means that the banana changes through time. On this picture, change over time is the possession of different properties by different temporal parts of an object.

There are two types of objection we might make to this perdurance account of change—objections of the first type are potentially good objections, but objections of the second type are bad. Good objections could be based on independent arguments for endurance theory, or against perdurance theory—for example, we might argue that spatial extension and persistence through time are not analogous in the way that perdurance theory supposes, or we might argue that perdurance theory cannot account for some aspect of the way things persist, or we might argue that endurance theory is clear and coherent, and should be accepted because it fits with our commonsense ideas about how things persist. We will encounter arguments of this kind later in the book.

The bad but tempting objection is that perdurance theory cannot account for change, because according to perdurance theory nothing really changes. According to perdurance theory, things 'change' by having a succession of different temporal parts with different properties. The objection is that, by definition, change consists in *one and the same object* having different properties at different times, not a succession of different things with different properties. As it stands, the objection is a bad one because it begs the question against perdurance theory. Any theory of persistence must account for ripening bananas, decaying books, and ageing people. But we cannot simply make the theoretical assumption that what we see around us are enduring objects with different properties at different times, rather than perduring objects, whose different temporal parts have different properties at different times.[2] Endurance theorists are not entitled to stipulate that perduring objects do not change—instead, they must provide an argument to the effect that the endurance account of change is the best one.

Perdurance theorists also have a duty to discharge. They must explain how their theory is compatible with our ordinary talk about changing things. According to perdurance theory, the banana changes

---

[2] I will return to this issue in section 3.7.

colour by having both a green temporal part and a yellow temporal part. Thus, bananas are pictured as multicoloured, having different parts of different colours. But often we can say truly that the banana is green, wholly green, green all over, not multicoloured—perdurance theorists must account for this way of talking. For perdurance theorists, talk about an object as it is at a time is made true or false by the temporal parts the object has at that time. When I speak about the banana as it is now, the present temporal part of the banana makes my utterance true or false.[3] If I say that the banana is now green all over, then what I say is true if and only if the present temporal part of the banana is green all over. If I say that the banana was green on Monday at 12 p.m., then what I say is true if and only if the temporal part of the banana which exists on Monday at 12 p.m. is green. And so on. Talk about the banana at different times is made true or false by the properties of the temporal parts that the banana has at those times.

Perdurance theory provides an account of our ordinary time-indexed talk about changing things, of what makes it accurate sometimes to say 'the banana is green all over'. The theory relies upon our also having an 'atemporal' perspective from which we can truly say that the banana *has* both yellow and green parts, where this 'has' is not in the present tense. Perdurance theory attempts to explain the metaphysical underpinnings of temporary predication and change, but to do so it needs to make claims like the following: the banana is three months long; the banana is not wholly present at any moment; the banana is not wholly green; the banana has a green temporal part and a yellow temporal part; the banana is not identical to its present temporal part.

These claims are not in the present tense. For if they were, then they ought to have the sorts of truth conditions which perdurance theory gives to present-tense utterances like 'the banana is now green'. Then the claims would become: the present temporal part of the banana is three months long; the present temporal part of the banana is not wholly present at any moment; the present temporal part of the banana is not wholly green; the present temporal part of the banana has a green temporal part and a yellow temporal part; the present temporal part of the banana is not identical to the present temporal part of the banana. But these do not capture the claims of perdurance

[3] Which temporal part is this? Is the part momentary, or a little longer? I will return to these questions in Chapter 2.

theory, and the last is self-contradictory: perdurance theory cannot be expressed straightforwardly in the present tense.

Nor are the atemporal claims of perdurance theory equivalent to conjunctive claims about how the banana is, was, and will be at every moment of its existence. Rendered like that, the claims would become: every temporal part of the banana is three months long; no temporal part of the banana is wholly present; no temporal part of the banana is wholly green; every temporal part of the banana has a green temporal part and a yellow temporal part; no temporal part of the banana is identical to the present temporal part of the banana. Again, these claims do not accurately represent the central claims of perdurance theory, claims which can be expressed only in an atemporal fashion. Perdurance theory requires an atemporal 'is', as well as an 'is' of the present tense.

Indeed, as we saw, perdurance theorists use atemporal locutions when explaining their account of temporary predication. If I say that the banana was green on Monday at 12 p.m., then what I say is true if and only if the banana *has* a temporal part which exists on Monday at 12 p.m. and is green. The 'has' which appears in this account of talk about how the banana is at a time is atemporal, not in the present tense. It might seem, then, that we could resist perdurance theory by resisting this atemporal way of talking—perhaps it is illegitimate to talk atemporally about ordinary persisting objects. But, as I will explain, this would be a dangerous strategy for those who wish to defend endurance theory against perdurance theory. Endurance theorists not only can but should permit atemporal talk about objects.

1.3 Change and Endurance

Endurance theorists believe that objects do not have temporal parts, and that persistence through time is quite different from spatial extension. What could be simpler than an endurance theory of change? Surely endurance theorists can say that objects persist through time by being wholly present at a succession of moments, and that they change by having different properties at different times? Thinking atemporally, matters are not so clear. The banana is green all over (on Monday), and is yellow all over (on Friday). Nothing can be both green all over plain and simple, and yellow all over plain and simple, because these states exclude one another—the colours in question are bright green and bright yellow, not an in-betweeny greeny-yellow. It is the qualifications '(on Monday)' and '(on Friday)' which prevent the banana disappearing in a puff of logical smoke.

Why can we say truly that the banana is green all over and yellow all over at different times, whilst we cannot say truly that it is green all over and yellow all over at the same time? What role do the different times play? According to perdurance theory, of course, when we talk about how the banana is at different times, our talk is made true or false by different objects (different temporal parts of the banana) and their different properties, whereas when we talk about how the banana is at a single time, our talk is made true or false by a single object—a temporal part—and its properties. The banana itself is neither green all over nor yellow all over, but it satisfies different predicates with respect to different times because of the different properties of its temporal parts. An earlier temporal part is green all over, and a later temporal part is yellow all over. Perdurance theory provides an atemporal description of the banana, and explains how our talk about how the banana is at different times fits with this atemporal description.

Endurance theorists reject this perdurance picture, for they believe that the banana is wholly present both on Monday and on Friday—they cannot ascribe different colour properties to different objects, for the only object in question is the banana itself. Endurance theorists might reject the whole project of giving an atemporal description of the reality underpinning our talk about how the banana is at different times. They might claim that the banana is green all over on Monday and yellow all over on Friday, that these states are compatible, and that there is no sense in asking what the banana is like without asking what it is like at a certain time. Although tempting, this move is ill-advised, as we will see, since endurance theorists need an atemporal way of talking about persisting objects, just as perdurance theorists do.

A better option is to supply an endurance-friendly atemporal description of the banana. According to perdurance theorists, the banana is extended through time, and talk about how the banana is at different times is made true or false by the properties of the banana's temporal parts. Endurance theorists might claim that the banana stands (atemporally) in different relations to different times—the *being green at* relation to times on Monday and the *being yellow at* relation to times on Friday—and talk about how the banana is at different times is made true or false by those relations between the banana and the times. Or they might claim that the banana has (atemporally) different instantiation 'connections' to different properties—the instantiates-on-Monday connection to *being green* and the instantiates-on-Friday connection to *being yellow*—and that talk about how the banana is at different times is made true or false by these various connections.

Of these two atemporal pictures, I think the former is more satisfactory: endurance theorists should claim that persisting objects satisfy different predicates with respect to different times because they stand in different relations to different times. I will examine this idea, and the alternative, in the sections which immediately follow this one. I will then return to the idea that we should not even attempt to give an atemporal description of persisting things, and that it is merely a confusion to think that there is some tension to be resolved between the banana's being green all over and its being yellow all over. We will need to look a little more closely at what time itself is, and at how things exist in time.

Discussions of objects and their changing features often mention the 'problem of temporary intrinsics', because it is supposed to be especially difficult for endurance theorists to explain how a single object can have different *intrinsic* features at different times. The label is misleading for, as we will see, intrinsic change is not inherently more problematic than change in extrinsic features, and thus I will simply refer to the 'problem of change'. But the underlying issue is not specifically about change. Rather, it is about what underpins our talk about objects as they are at different times—what, if anything, can we say about how a persisting object atemporally is, and how does this relate to our talk about how the object is at different times?

1.4 Properties as Relations to Times

The best endurance strategy involves the following claims.[4] The persisting banana does not have the conflicting properties of *being green* and of *being yellow*. Instead it bears the relation *being green at* to yesterday and the relation *being yellow at* to today. This is no more problematic than the fact that I bear the relation *being taller than* to

---

[4] e.g. Mellor (1981: 111–14) and van Inwagen (1990a). For a contrasting view, see Mellor (1998: ch. 8). See also Prior (1968a).

the Queen Mother and the relation *being shorter than* to Michael
Jordan. It is true that the banana is green on Monday if and only if the
banana stands (atemporally) in the *being green at* relation to times on
Monday. Let's call this the 'relations-to-times' response to the problem of change; it enables the endurance theorist to give an atemporal
description of the banana. The account has been attacked by an
important philosopher in an important book—by David Lewis in his
On the Plurality of Worlds (1986*a*; see also 1988*b*). But Lewis's attack
fails, as I will argue: it is not so easy to undermine the relations-to-
times account. Not every version of this account is viable, but if we are
careful, we can make the most of this idea.

First, Lewis's attack. Lewis objects that if he knows anything, he
knows that temporary properties like shape (his example) are intrinsic properties, not relations. It is 'simply incredible' (1986*a*: 204),
therefore, that all temporary properties are relations. This is too fast.
Lewis may know that a banana's shape is not a relation it bears to
material objects (other than its own parts, perhaps). It seems that a
banana is curved regardless of the existence or non-existence of other
material objects, since we can imagine it curved whilst alone in the
universe. But this doesn't tell us whether the banana's shape is a relation it bears to various times. Does the banana have its shape regardless of the existence or non-existence of times?

We simply cannot tell directly whether an object's shape is a relation it bears to a moment. What properties would a banana have if it
were alone in a world which did not contain any moments? Attempts
to imagine such a situation do not bring insight into the nature of
change, but instead show us the limitations of our intuitions about
these matters. We cannot proceed from the relatively straightforward
assertion that an object's shape is not a relation it bears to other
material objects to the assertion that an object's shape is not a relation
to anything at all.

The failure of Lewis's blunt objection to the relations-to-times
account is more obvious when we consider temporary relational properties. How can it be true on Monday that Joe is childless, and true on
Friday that the very same Joe is a parent? If temporary features are
relations to times, then *being a parent* is a relation to a time, as well
as being relational in the more obvious way. Opponents of the
relations-to-times account cannot deny that *being a parent* is a relational
property: instead, they must rather implausibly claim simply to know
that *being a parent* is not a relation to a time. The focus upon temporary

intrinsics leads the debate astray, and Lewis's straightforward rejection of the idea that temporary properties are relations to times is unconvincing.

It is worth exploring this relations-to-times account further, to see how it can best be defended. What should the account say about an object which satisfies a certain predicate throughout its lifetime, for example an apple which is green from start to finish? Although the apple is permanently green, other objects are, or could be, temporarily green, so the apple is permanently green because it stands in the *being green at* relation to every time at which it exists. We should not suppose that *being green* is an intrinsic property of the apple whilst supposing that it is a relation between the banana and certain times. This would be like claiming that *being taller than everyone* is an intrinsic property, whilst maintaining that *being taller than the Queen Mother* is relational. Although the apple is always green, its colour is a relation it bears to many times, if a banana's greenness is a relation it bears to a few times.

Very many features can be possessed temporarily. So the relations-to-times account entails that very many features of objects are relations between those objects and times. To some, this seems unacceptable: if the banana bears different mass-relations to different times, for example, then it seems really to have no mass of its own, which is absurd. The relations-to-times account seems to downgrade objects, picturing them as massless, colourless, shapeless, and so on. Lewis (1988*b*) may be expressing this idea when he suggests drawing circles around the 'contents' of distinct moments, the things which exist at those times. Things which exist at several times are placed in the intersection of several circles. Supporters of the relations-to-times account thus face the peculiar task of drawing a shapeless, massless object in that intersection if the object has different shape-relations and mass-relations to different times. But having different masses at different times, by having different relations to different times, is not the same as being massless, for the temporary is as real as the permanent, and relations are as real as non-relational properties. The banana has very few necessarily permanent properties, but this tells us nothing about the reality or robustness of the banana. Seeing the temporary features of things as relations to times does not in any way downgrade either the features themselves, or the objects which stand in those relations to times.

A different objection is that, although relations are real enough, an object must have *some* non-relational properties, and that this is not guaranteed on the relations-to-times picture. The idea that an object must have some non-relational properties arises naturally from the belief that an object is composed, somehow, of its properties, for it is hard (though perhaps not impossible) to make sense of the idea that an object is composed of the relations it bears to other things, or of those relations plus a very limited intrinsic nature. Objects seem to fade away if we combine the relations-to-times account with this 'bundle-of-properties' view of objects, and those who are tempted by this view of objects have a good reason to reject this account of change. Our views about persistence and change ought to cohere with our views on other matters.

Those who support the relations-to-times account need to say something about the relations in question—what are these relations between objects and times like, and what determines whether they hold? One thought is that the holding of these relations is determined by the intrinsic properties of the objects and times in question.[5] This would require that times—moments—have intrinsic properties. In fact, it would require that different moments have different intrinsic properties, since a single physical object with an unchanging intrinsic nature may stand in different relations to different times. This amounts to an extreme realism about moments, the claim not only that relations between times amount to more than relations between events, but also that times have intrinsic properties beyond their mutual relations. Perhaps times are like this.

Now consider the objects, rather than the times. If temporary features are relations determined by the intrinsic properties of objects and times, then an object's features at a particular moment are all determined by the intrinsic properties of the object on the one hand, and those of the moment on the other. But this goes for every object existing at that particular moment. Most of the features exemplified across the universe at a given moment are relations between the various objects and that single moment. But if temporary features are indeed relations, then most physical objects have very few intrinsic properties, not enough to sustain the great variety in these properties between objects. We should not, incidentally, rely upon 'individual essences' to do this work for us, else temporary features will all turn out to be essential. Thinking that temporary features are relations between objects and times which are determined by the intrinsic

---

[5] In terminology which I shall introduce in Chapter 3, such relations are 'supervenient'.

properties of the relata is hopeless—the limited intrinsic natures will not suffice to explain the vast differences between objects.

A better option is to suppose that relations between objects and times are not determined by the intrinsic properties of the objects and times. Relations of spatial separation are familiar examples of this kind: the distance between you and me at some moment is not determined by our intrinsic properties. There could be intrinsic duplicates of us which were separated by a different distance. Similarly, perhaps the relations between objects and times which constitute the temporary features of those objects are not determined by the intrinsic natures of the objects and times themselves. Can we say more? Lewis (1986*a*: 62) distinguishes between two types of non-supervenient relation, according as the relation in question is or is not determined by the intrinsic properties of the fusion or sum of the relata. But this taxonomy is too restrictive, for it supposes that any two things have a sum, are parts of a single larger object, and it is dubious whether a material object and a time really have a sum. There is no need to fit these relations into Lewis's taxonomy.[6]

The best version of the relations-to-times account, then, says that features which may be temporarily possessed by objects are relations between objects and times, relations which are not fully determined by the intrinsic natures of those objects and times. This account of change seems viable: we have seen no decisive objection to the account, and we have discovered more about the nature of these hypothetical relations. It is, however, worth emphasizing that this is not just an ontologically neutral way of saying that *of course* things satisfy different predicates at different times. In particular, the account entails that other possible accounts of change, like perdurance theory, are false. Moreover, we must take care not to picture the banana as located either outside of time or at some privileged time (in the middle of its lifespan?) from which it bears its relations to the various times. This picture would, of course, be untenable. Instead, the banana is at a different moment at each moment: perhaps it bears the relation of *wholly existing at* to many different moments? I will return to this issue after considering a rival view of change.

---

[6] I failed to appreciate this in my 1998*b*, where I was unduly critical of the relations-to-times account.

1.5 Adverbialism: Instantiation as Relative to Times

If we are to hang on to atemporal talk about objects, then we need a solution to the problem of change. Any such solution must make it clear how objects can satisfy apparently conflicting predicates at different times, by explaining what it is for an object O to satisfy a predicate 'is F' at a time t. The relations-to-times strategy relativizes properties to times, claiming that for O to be F at t is for O to bear (atemporally) the relation *F-at* to t. (A variant on this would be to claim that O has (atemporally) the time-indexed property *F-at-t*.) Perdurance theory, as we have seen, relativizes objects to times: for O to be F at t is for an object O-at-t to have (atemporally) the property *F*.[7]

Mark Johnston (1987), E. J. Lowe (1988*b*), and Sally Haslanger (1989) independently propose a third solution to the problem of change. They claim that instantiation—the possession or having of properties—is time-indexed, or relative to times, although properties themselves are not. This strategy, called *adverbialism*, says that for O to have F at t is for O to have-at-t the property *F*—for O to have *F* t-ly. Is there any reason for endurance theorists to prefer adverbialism over the relations-to-times account? It may well be true that taking temporal modifiers to be adverbial reveals the logical form of temporal predication—the deep structure of sentences like 'O is F at t'—but this is not enough to solve the present problem. As Trenton Merricks points out, adverbialism needs the 'further (plausible) claim that contradiction arises only when . . . complementary properties are exemplified *in the same way*' (1994: 169). The thought behind adverbialism is that the banana can be green in a Monday way and yellow in a Friday way, without fear of contradiction, whereas it *would* be contradictory for the banana to be both green in a Monday way and yellow in a Monday way.

Merricks says that it is 'plausible' that adverbial modification dissolves contradiction—why is this? Johnston draws a supportive analogy with modal adverbs: a banana can be both actually yellow and possibly green, in that it *is* yellow, but it *could have been* green. But analogy with more ordinary adverbs is not so encouraging. A person cannot be both quietly sitting and awkwardly standing, any more than

---

[7] This taxonomy of possible solutions to the problem of change is derived from Merricks (1994).

she can be both quietly sitting and quietly standing. Ordinary adverbs do not show how the adverbial interpretation of temporal predication can solve the problem of change. There is a precedent in our use of modal adverbs like *actually, possibly,* and *necessarily,* but the interpretation of these is as fraught, if not more fraught, than that of temporal adverbs. Modal and temporal adverbs do seem to dissolve contradiction, but pointing out that these words are adverbs does nothing to explain this. We need to understand what it is about time that allows temporal modifiers to dissolve contradiction.

Johnston explains modal modifiers in terms of abstract representations. For Sam to be thin in a possible world *v* is for the following to be true: 'The abstract representation, *v*, which corresponds to one way concrete reality might have been, has it that: Sam is thin.' (1987: 126.) Analogy to temporal modifiers would suggest that to have a property at a time is to be represented in a certain way by a certain abstract representation, yet the relations-to-times account shows that we can solve the problem of change without such radical revision of our notion of time.

Haslanger and Lowe have a more concrete proposal. They suggest that, although O's being F at t is not a relation between O, *being F,* and t, O's being F stands (atemporally) in the relation of *obtaining at* to t. So *being green* is a property, not a relation, but its particular instances can themselves stand in relations to times: the relation in question is that of *obtaining at.* It is true that the banana is green on Monday, because there is an instance of the banana's being green, and that instance stands in the relation of *obtaining at* to times on Monday. This suggestion avoids Lewis's objection that he simply knows that temporary features are not relations to times: according to Haslanger and Lowe, temporary features are (often) themselves intrinsic properties, whilst their instances bear different relations to different times.

But as we have seen, Lewis does *not* simply know that temporary features are not relations to times, so there is no compelling motivation here for adverbialism. As Haslanger says, 'There is a sense in which these responses to Lewis's concerns are simply a stubborn resistance to his intuitions about what it is to predicate an intrinsic property of an object.' (1989: 124.) But Lewis can be resisted without moving to adverbialism. Once we have rejected the idea that features like shape, mass, or colour must be intrinsic properties, adverbialism has no clear advantage over the claim that temporary features are relations between objects and times.

Moreover, the relations-to-times view provides a better account of the contrast between abstract and concrete than does adverbialism. Many people believe that there are abstract objects which exist without existing in time—perhaps numbers, propositions, or God are like this. Most properties can be possessed either by concrete objects or by abstract objects, but not by both—only concrete things like bananas can be green, and only abstract things like the number 5 can be prime. The relations-to-times account can explain why certain features, like colours, are possessed only by concrete objects, which exist in time— those features are relations between objects and times, and so *cannot* be possessed by objects which do not exist in time.

Admittedly, no explanation is forthcoming of why concrete objects cannot instantiate properties like *being prime*, which are not relations between objects and times. But the account can at least explain why properties which are shared by concrete and abstract objects—properties like *being self-identical* and *being an object*, if there are such properties—cannot be merely temporarily possessed by a concrete object. Such properties can be instantiated by abstract objects, so they are not relations between objects and times, which is why they cannot be possessed temporarily, even by concrete objects.[8] The relations-to-times account provides a neat explanation of why certain properties are instantiable only by concrete objects, and of why those properties which both concrete and abstract objects may possess cannot be possessed temporarily. And the account allows that instantiation is the same across the domains, that abstract things instantiate their properties and relations in just the same way as concrete things instantiate their properties and relations, even when the properties differ.

Adverbialism, in contrast, draws a metaphysical distinction between temporary and non-temporary instantiation, instead of between properties which may and may not be temporarily instantiated. Because of this, it fails to explain why certain properties can be instantiated temporarily, and others cannot: why is it that instances of *being green* cannot just obtain but must stand in the *obtaining-at* relation to times, whilst instances of being self-identical can just obtain? Moreover, the account relies upon an unfamiliar distinction between different modes of instantiation, instead of the more familiar distinction between

---

[8] Many sortal properties—like *being a banana*—must be possessed permanently if they are possessed at all, and yet are instantiable only by concrete objects. But such sortal properties are tied to more ordinary properties of concrete objects, which explains why they are instantiable only by the concrete. I will discuss sortal properties more fully in Chapter 2.

intrinsic and relational properties. Adverbialism avoids Lewis's objection to the relations-to-times account, but that objection was not a good one. And adverbialism has certain disadvantages—it claims that properties of abstract things or unchangeable properties of concrete objects are not instantiated in the sense that changeable properties are instantiated, it fails to explain why only certain properties are liable to change, and it fails to explain why certain properties cannot be instantiated by abstract objects.

1.6 Change, Parthood, and Being 'Wholly Present'

Endurance theorists should argue that properties which may be possessed temporarily are relations between persisting things and times; adverbialism is a less successful variant of the same basic idea. Endurance theorists can thus account for change whilst allowing us to speak atemporally about persisting things. Speaking atemporally, we can say that the banana bears different relations to different times—the *being green at* relation to Monday and the *being yellow at* relation to Friday. If I say that the banana is or was green on Monday, then what I say is true if and only if the banana bears (atemporally) the *being green at* relation to Monday. According to perdurance theory, what I say is true if and only if the banana has (atemporally) a temporal part on Monday which instantiates (atemporally) *being green*.

Although perdurance and endurance theories can both provide atemporal descriptions of persisting objects, there are important differences between the accounts. According to the relations-to-times account, to say that an object is green atemporally is to say something incomplete. It makes no sense to say that an object is green atemporally, just as it makes no sense to say that I am taller than *simpliciter*, for colours are relations between objects and times. Even an apple which is green throughout its existence cannot be described as green atemporally, just as the tallest person cannot be described as taller than *simpliciter*. Rather, the apple bears (atemporally) the *green-at* relation to every moment at which it exists, just as the tallest person bears (*simpliciter*) the *taller-than* relation to every other person. According to perdurance theory, in contrast, the claim that the apple is atemporally green is complete. Each of the apple's temporal parts is (atemporally) green, and so the apple itself is (atemporally) green.[9] The banana is not (atemporally) green, for it has (atemporally) both green parts and yellow parts, so it is (atemporally) multi-coloured.

Objects can change their parts as well as their colours or shapes—a boy loses his last milk tooth and later acquires a beard. We tend to think of parthood as a two-place relation between the boy and his tooth, or between the boy and his beard, but according to the relations-to-times account, we should accept that parthood is a three-place relation, between a whole, a part, and a time. We cannot claim atemporally that the boy has his tooth as a part, for this claim would be incomplete, just like the claim that the banana is (atemporally) green, or that I am taller than. Rather, we should claim atemporally that the boy, the tooth, and a certain time stand in the *has-as-a-part-at* relation, and so do the boy, the beard, and a different time.

Theodore Sider (1997) argues that, because they must adopt something like the relations-to-times view of changeable properties and relations, endurance theorists have difficulty even articulating their own thesis. I characterized endurance theorists as claiming that persisting objects are wholly present whenever they exist. This is naturally understood as the claim that the whole object is present whenever it exists, that all of the object's parts are present whenever it exists.[10] But Sider points out that, if parthood is time-relative, then this claim is either trivial or false. Either it is the trivial claim that, whenever the object exists, all of the parts which the object has *at that time* are then present—if the milk tooth is a part of the boy on his seventh birthday, then the milk tooth is present on the boy's seventh birthday. Or else it is the false claim that, whenever the object exists, all of the parts which the object has *at any time* are then present—if the beard is ever a part of the boy, then the beard is present on the boy's seventh birthday.

After exploring various options, Sider concludes that the best the endurance theorist can do is to deny that, for any way of dividing a persisting object O's lifespan in two, there is an object which exists for exactly the first period, and which has exactly the same parts as O at any moment during the period, and there is a second object which

---

[9] In contrast, perdurance theorists cannot atemporally attribute shape properties to persisting things, even to things which have the same shape at all times, because a four-dimensional thing cannot instantiate *being spherical*. I will expand this argument in Chapter 2.

[10] Sider has a stronger reading: an object is wholly present whenever all of its parts exist and are parts of it. But the weaker reading is enough for the present point.

performs the corresponding role during the second period of O's lifespan. Roughly speaking, the best the endurance theorist can do is to deny that the world is full of short lived objects which coincide with persisting objects. But this is an unsatisfactory formulation of endurance theory, for two reasons. First, an endurance theorist might not want to deny the existence of all those short-lived things. One version of endurance theory would have it that ordinary objects endure whilst the world also contained vast numbers of short-lived things—an unattractive position, but still a version of endurance theory. Second, as Sider notes, a perdurance theorist might also deny that, for any arbitrary period of an object's life, there is an object which coincides with the persisting thing throughout exactly that period; this perdurance theorist might believe that there are only instantaneous temporal parts, plus a few extended four-dimensional things, just enough to correspond to our ordinary ontology of bananas, apples, and people.

To explain how change in parts is possible, endurance theorists must deny that we can speak atemporally about whether an object has another as a part; such claims are supposed to be incomplete. Sider argues that, given this, endurance theory is not satisfactorily articulable. Perdurance theorists, in contrast, believe that atemporal talk about parthood is complete, without reference to specific times. Thus they can articulate their thesis that at any time at which a persisting object exists, not all of its parts are present. The object has (atemporally) parts which are not present at that particular time. In effect, endurance theorists cannot make sense of the notion of a temporal part, because they cannot accept atemporal talk about parthood.

But we need not see this as a failing of endurance theory. Rather, we can take the rejection of atemporal talk about parthood to be a defining feature of endurance theory. According to endurance theory, a claim that something is a part of a persisting object only makes sense if it is made relative to a certain time, just as a claim that I am taller than must be made relative to some other person or thing.[11] According to perdurance theory, in contrast, atemporal claims that something is a part of a persisting object are perfectly complete. We may also make claims about parthood at particular times, and those claims are made true or false by the relevant temporal parts of the relevant objects: if I

---

[11] This is not a specific commitment to the relations-to-times view. For example, adverbialists would agree that talk of whether one object is a part of another is incomplete without reference to some time or other.

say that the tooth is a part of the boy on his seventh birthday, then what I say is true iff temporal parts of the tooth which exist only on that day are (atemporally) parts of temporal parts of the boy which exist only on that day.[12]

I propose to characterize endurance as follows: an object endures if and only if (i) it exists at more than one moment and (ii) statements about what parts the object has must be made relative to some time or other. Then endurance theory is the claim that ordinary material objects—animals, fruit, furniture, and the like—endure. First, I will explain how this fits with the more standard characterization of endurance theory that I have already been using. Second, I will explain the advantages of this characterization.

Previously, I characterized endurance theorists as believing that persisting things are wholly present whenever they exist—that, at any given time, no persisting object has parts which are not then present. This is entailed by the claim (ii) that statements about what parts a persisting object has must be made relative to some time or other. A persisting object is wholly present whenever it exists, because there is no sense in which it has (as opposed to will have or has had) parts which do not then exist. Characterizing endurance theory by its claim that atemporal talk about the parts of persisting objects is incomplete captures the standard idea that enduring objects are wholly present whenever they exist.

If something endures in the sense I have characterized, then it endures in the standard sense—it is wholly present at each moment at which it exists. But does the converse hold? Could there be an object which endured in the standard sense but not in my sense? There might perhaps be an object which endured without changing its parts—atemporal statements about this object's parts would not be contradictory, since the object has the same parts at all times. Nevertheless, there may be a deeper reason for endurance theorists to accept the second clause of my definition—that statements about an enduring object's parts must be made relative to some time or other— even with respect to objects which do not change their parts over time.

The disagreement between perdurance and endurance theorists is often glossed as a disagreement about whether ordinary persisting objects have temporal parts. But at a more fundamental level, it is a

---

[12] Compare Thomson (1983).

disagreement about whether ordinary persisting objects are temporally extended (as perdurance theorists believe) or whether they occupy times in a rather different way (as endurance theorists believe). The claim that an object is temporally extended—that it perdures—is not analytically equivalent to the claim that it has temporal parts, for it is not trivial that an extended object must have parts (Markosian 1998). It is at least conceivable that an object could be spatially extended without having spatial parts—and it ought to be equally conceivable to a perdurance theorist that an object could be temporally extended without having temporal parts. The contrast between an enduring mereological atom and a temporally extended mereological atom is analogous to the contrast between an immanent universal, wholly present at each of many spatial points, and a spatially extended mereological atom.

So what is it for an object to endure, to be wholly present at each moment of its existence? There seem to be two options—either simply to characterize endurance as persistence without temporal extension, or else to go on and offer some analysis of what it is for an object to be temporally extended, as opposed to being wholly present at each of a series of times. Although being extended need not be equivalent to having parts, it seems that the best way of explicating extension (as opposed to multiple location) is in terms of parthood. An object is temporally extended just if the appropriate basic notion of parthood for that object is an atemporal notion; an object persists without being temporally extended if there is no atemporal notion of parthood appropriate for that object. This characterization is not entirely satisfactory—I am attempting to avoid the issue of what makes a parthood relation 'appropriate' for an object which has no parts. But nevertheless I think it is significant that more standard perdurance theory requires an atemporal notion of parthood, and that more standard endurance theory must reject just such a notion. Moreover, there are various advantages to characterizing endurance theory in terms of a claim about what notion of parthood is appropriate to ordinary persisting objects.

First, the characterization excludes those hypothetical perdurance theorists who do not believe in arbitrary temporal parts of things. Such theorists believe that there can be atemporal parthood; they simply believe that perduring objects have fewer parts than is commonly believed, just as the more extreme theorists believe that perduring objects have no temporal parts at all. And the characterization includes those hypothetical endurance theorists who also believe in a plenitude of short-lived objects. Such theorists believe that there are multitudes of coinciding things, but that these objects cannot be thought of atemporally as parts of one another.

A second advantage of this characterization is that it sets endurance theory firmly against an important motivation for perdurance theory. Perdurance theory pictures persisting objects as sums of different things existing at different times. Analogously, we think of spatially extended objects as sums of different things existing at different places. We use an 'aspatial' notion of parthood, and can say that your little toe is a part of you *simpliciter*, without specifying that it is a part of you down there rather than up here. Perdurance theory draws an analogy between spatial extension and temporal persistence, but this is compelling only if we accept an atemporal as well as an aspatial notion of parthood, and can say that objects existing at different times are parts of a persisting object, *simpliciter*. Characterizing endurance theory by its rejection of atemporal parthood thereby highlights the theory's rejection of the space-time analogy which motivates perdurance theorists.

A third advantage of the characterization is that it allows endurance theorists to distinguish between persisting objects and processes. Although they deny that persisting objects have temporal parts, endurance theorists are often happy to allow that processes, like meals and lectures, have temporal parts or phases—the lecture has an exciting early part, a boring middle part, and a surprising final part. Moreover, it may be that processes cannot change their parts—the lecture does not change from having an exciting to having a boring part, as an animal changes its parts: instead it simply *has* its exciting, boring, and surprising parts. These ideas can be captured in the claim that, although there is no atemporal notion of parthood appropriate to persisting objects (or 'continuants'), there is a perfectly good atemporal notion of parthood which is appropriate to processes (and, perhaps, to abstract objects). The sense in which persisting things have parts is quite different from that in which processes have parts. Endurance theorists need not suppose that all persisting things change their parts, only that to be a persisting thing is to have parts in a time-relative way, even if in fact those parts are constant.

Finally, the characterization captures the spirit of a very common initial reaction to the problem of change, the reaction that there simply is no such problem. I tried to draw out a tension between the banana's being green all over and its being yellow all over, but one response is to claim that we simply cannot talk about the colour of an object, *per se* or atemporally, as opposed to its colour at some given time. An over-strong version of this response is to claim that we cannot talk atemporally about persisting objects at all, but this response leads to trouble, as we will shortly see. A better version of the response is just to claim that, although we can indeed talk atemporally about what objects are like, what we can say is mostly that objects stand, atemporally, in relations to times, and that to say simply that an object is green (or that it has another as a part) is to say something incomplete. Thus the natural reaction to the problem of change is directly captured by endurance theory, when the theory is characterized by its refusal to accept atemporal talk about the parts of persisting things, without reference to specific times.

So I will continue to characterize endurance theory as the claim that ordinary objects are such that (i) they exist at more than one time and (ii) statements about what parts they have must be made relative to some time or other. But we should bear in mind that this is intended to embody the more fundamental idea that ordinary objects exist at more than one time, but without being temporally extended. Perdurance theorists accept the first claim, that ordinary objects exist at more than one time, but they reject the second. We may note that there is space for another view—stage theory—according to which it makes perfect sense to talk about parthood atemporally, but ordinary objects do not exist at more than one time. I will return to stage theory in Chapter 2.

1.7 Time and Persistence

Both perdurance theory and endurance theory can provide an atemporal description of persisting things, along with an account of what makes our talk about how things are at different times true or false. According to perdurance theory, objects are stretched out in time, with different temporal parts at different times. According to endurance theory, objects stand in different relations to different times. In particular, a persisting object can stand in the *has as a part at* relation to a certain object and time without standing in that relation to that object and every time. Although we cannot just say, atemporally, that a persisting thing has a certain part, we can talk atemporally about the properties and relations of persisting things, including the relations which underpin legitimate talk about the parts that things have at different times. But why attempt to preserve this atemporal mode of description—why not just accept that the only way to speak about persisting objects is to speak about how they are at various times?

If we give up the possibility of an atemporal description of persisting objects, then perdurance theory is unavailable, but endurance theory becomes unformulable, as I will explain, so this cannot constitute a defence of endurance theory against perdurance theory. Moreover, giving up the possibility of atemporal description commits us to a certain view of time, one which many reject. However, neither of these consequences is fatal: some accept the requisite view of time, and may even be pleased to find that they need not engage in the debate about how things persist. The task of this book is to explore the debate about persistence, not to convince those who believe that there should be no such debate, so my engagement with sceptics will be limited. In this section, I will merely explain why the endurance–perdurance disagreement dissolves if we abandon atemporal description, and show what theory of time would be needed to support this move.

If we accept that we can speak atemporally about persisting things, then we can characterize the disagreement between perdurance and endurance theory as a disagreement over whether there is an atemporal notion of parthood appropriate to ordinary persisting things (or, more fundamentally, about whether ordinary persisting things are temporally extended). Perdurance theorists affirm and endurance theorists deny that we can say that one object has another as a part, atemporally.

If, on the other hand, we give up the possibility of atemporal description, then *a fortiori* there can be no saying atemporally whether one object has another as a part, for there can be no saying *anything* atemporally. But this does not spell automatic victory for endurance theorists.

According to endurance theorists, it is one and the same object—the banana—which is first green all over then yellow all over. The definition of endurance had two clauses—to endure, an object must exist at more than one time. Now, if we give up atemporal talk, how can we assert that the green banana and the yellow banana are identical? We must talk about identity at particular times. We might say that the yellow banana is on Friday identical with the green banana, which is to say that the yellow banana is on Friday identical with something which was the green banana. But it is common ground between many accounts of persistence that the yellow banana used to be the green banana. Both endurance and perdurance theorists will accept that the yellow banana used to be the green banana, although the theories can give different atemporal descriptions of the under-lying reality so long as atemporal talk is permitted. Even stage theor-ists, who deny that any single object exists at more than one time, have an account according to which it is true that the yellow banana used to be the green banana.[13] If we are only permitted to talk about how things are at various times, then the most we can do in speaking of persistence is to speak of the histories and futures of objects at times. We cannot assert or deny claims of identity between objects existing at different times, and thus endurance theory is unformulable.

Some might welcome this 'resolution' of the debate, believing that we cannot really make sense of questions of identity between things existing at different times, because this requires an unachievable atemporal perspective. In contrast, we *can* make sense of questions of identity between things existing at different places at the same time. Usually we think that objects wholly located at different spatial loca-tions at the same time cannot be identical. Nevertheless, this standard claim of distinctness seems to be a substantial one, which could be coherently denied. Those who believe that properties are universals often believe that universals wholly located at different spatial loca-tions at the same time can be identical.

If we are to dissolve the debate about persistence by denying that questions of identity can even be posed regarding objects existing at different times, then we shall need to explain how time is importantly different from space. Views about time are often divided into 'tensed' and 'tenseless' views, as Quentin Smith explains:

Philosophers who claim that all successively ordered events have the same ontological status . . . [are] proponents of the tenseless theory of time. They hold that the nature of time can be captured completely by tenseless sen-tences, such as 'The birth of Plato is earlier than the birth of Russell.' Philosophers who hold that there is temporal becoming are . . . proponents of the tensed theory of time. They believe that tensed sentences, such as 'Plato

---

[13] I will offer a full exposition of stage theory in Chapter 2.

was born a long time ago', are necessary if the complete nature of temporal reality is to be described.[14]

Tenseless theorists believe that events are related by being earlier than, later than or simultaneous with one another; tensed theorists believe that an important further feature of an event is whether it is past, present or future. How does this dispute connect with the debate between endurance and perdurance theories? The tenseless view of time is compatible with both perdurance and endurance theories, provided endurance theorists are willing to accept either the relations-to-times or the adverbial response to the problem of change. An object may have different temporal parts at different times, or bear different relations to different times, without there being any inherently 'tensed' aspect to the world.[15]

Matters are less straightforward for tensed theories of time. According to one type of tensed theory, we can talk tenselessly about the world if we are content with a partial picture, but we must take tense into account if we are to give a complete picture of the world. Both perdurance and endurance theories are compatible with this view of time: an object has different temporal parts at different times, or bears different relations to different times, and moreover to tell the full story about an object we must say what time is the present, and thus which temporal part is present, or which relation of the object is a relation to the present, what the object is like *now*.

But according to a more radical tensed theory we cannot speak tenselessly about objects existing in time, not even to give a partial picture. According to this view, it is illegitimate to write that the banana has different temporal parts at different times, or bears different relations to different times, because this atemporal language is appropriate only for describing objects which exist outside of time. This is the view of time which is required if the debate between perdurance and endurance theorists—as to which is the better atemporal description of persisting things—is to be dissolved. If we *only* have a tensed idiom in which to talk about objects in time, then we cannot express the difference between endurance and perdurance theorists.

---

[14] Smith (1994: 1). There is a large and lively debate between tensed and tenseless theorists, and several versions of each position. I will not attempt to survey this debate here. Useful starting points include Oaklander and Smith (1994), Le Poidevin (1998), and Mellor (1998).

[15] In claiming that endurance theory and the tenseless view of time are compatible, I disagree with Lowe (1998) and with Oaklander (1992), and agree with Smith (1992).

Finally, there is presentism—the view that only the present is real. According to presentism, there can be no atemporal talk about things existing in time, because the present moment is the whole of temporal reality. We cannot then ask whether objects present at different times are identical, as opposed to distinct, for there are no objects existing at times other than the present. Adopting presentism solves the problem of change, since it means that, once the banana is yellow, there just is no green banana, and the question of the relationship between yesterday's green banana and today's yellow banana therefore does not arise (Merricks 1994, 1995; Prior 1970).

Where does this leave us? Those who adopt an irreducibly tensed view of the temporal world, and do not accept that a tenseless description can ever be even partially adequate need have no truck with the debate between endurance and perdurance theories. I will not attempt to undermine that view of time here, though it is one that I myself reject. Instead, I will take it as an unargued assumption that we can speak atemporally about the world (even if tensed talk is also required) and thus that the debate about persistence is a live one.

1.8 Conclusions, and Personal Persistence

We have seen that endurance and perdurance theories can both account for the facts of change. I have already remarked that endurance theory is very close to most people's pictures of the world—we do tend to think of time and space rather differently, and to think of objects as spread out through space yet somehow 'moving' as a whole through time (although prolonged exposure to physics lectures often seems to undermine these habits of thought). So why should we even consider perdurance theory? One quite general reason is that, if we are interested in whether our beliefs are true—even our most obvious-seeming beliefs—then it is good policy to consider alternatives to those beliefs, to consider ways in which our beliefs might turn out to be false. If our beliefs survive this process, then we can have greater confidence in those beliefs. As I argued in the introduction, questions about persistence—of ourselves and other things—are of central importance to us, and so it is worth examining the grounds of our beliefs about persistence.

More particularly, we have already seen that endurance theory cannot simply be a plain piece of commonsense, for it must somehow address the problem of change—it may be that one of the solutions already discussed in this chapter is satisfactory, but in any case, some theoretical framework or other is required. Endurance theory is not just a default 'no-theory' theory, for it must incorporate a sophisticated account of properties and instantiation, and requires a certain view of time if it is even to be formulable. One positive aspect of perdurance theory is that it offers us a neat solution to the problem of change, by introducing the notion of variation between temporal parts. This neatness may not be enough to justify our adopting perdurance theory, but it does provide an incentive for exploring further.

I will conclude this chapter—and other chapters—by considering how the material we have encountered applies to questions about the persistence of people. People change, just as material objects do. This will come as no surprise to those who think that people are material objects, perhaps that they are living organisms, just like banana trees are. If people are physical things, they are subject to the same kinds of arguments as I have explored with respect to bananas in this chapter.

But similar arguments apply, I think, even if people are immaterial things, or have immaterial parts, so long as those immaterial things exist in time. Right now I am hungry, grumpy, and thinking about Vienna, whilst yesterday I felt well fed, cheerful, and concerned with Budapest. How can this be explained? Perhaps my immaterial self (or my immaterial part) bears different relations to different times; perhaps my (or my part's) instantiation of a given property stands in different relations to different times; perhaps only the present exists; perhaps I (or my immaterial part) have different temporal parts at different times (Lewis 1983*a*: 76). These are peculiar notions but no more peculiar than the idea of an *unchanging* immaterial thing.

Or people may be immaterial things existing outside of time. If such things are unchanging, then there will be no need to explain how it is they can change, and thus the questions addressed in this chapter will not arise for people. But then urgent questions arise about how my beliefs, feelings, and desires can change, if that is not because I myself change: when I have a change of mind, or a change of heart, what is it that changes? Change is inescapable, and needs accounting for in the case of people as it does for other objects. Is any of the theories of persistence peculiarly attractive or unattractive as it applies to people? One question is whether perdurance theory can account for the special concern we feel for our own future selves. According to endurance theorists, this concern is underwritten by the fact that each of us is identical to our future selves, whereas according to perdurance theory, the thing which is losing spending power right now, in order to provide for a future pension, is not strictly identical to the thing which will collect the pension. I will revisit this issue at the end of Chapter 2, once I have developed perdurance theory more fully, and introduced a further rival, stage theory.

2

Parts and Stages

2.1 Wholes and Parts, Properties and Predicates

In later chapters I will put endurance and perdurance theories to the test, looking at how they can handle a variety of problems. Before doing so, I want to develop the theories further, and to introduce a third contender, stage theory. According to endurance theory, we can speak atemporally about persisting objects, but when we do so we cannot attribute shapes, colours, or parts to those things, for such talk is incomplete without reference to some time or other. The most we can do when speaking atemporally about persisting things is attribute properties like *being self-identical*, or else discuss the relations in which such objects stand to times, the *obtaining-at* relations in which their property instances stand to various times, or the like. Talk about how things are at times is made true or false by the relations between objects and times, or perhaps by the obtaining-at relations between property instances and times.

As we have already seen, perdurance theorists permit—indeed, require—atemporal talk about what parts a persisting object has. And, atemporally, persisting things have properties like *being self-identical*. What other properties do persisting objects have, atemporally speaking? Do they, for example, have colour, mass, or shape? According to perdurance theory, a persisting thing O is F at t if and only if O has a temporal part existing at t which has the corresponding property (or cluster of properties) *being F*. The banana is first green then yellow, so, according to perdurance theory, it has (atemporally) both green and yellow temporal parts. It is natural to conclude that, atemporally speaking, the banana is multicoloured: a thing which has differently coloured parts is itself multicoloured. Similarly, the apple is, atemporally, wholly green, because every temporal part of the apple is green.

So far, so good. What about mass? At various times, it is true that the banana has a mass of 100g. So, according to perdurance theory, the banana must have various temporal parts, each of which has (atemporally) a mass of 100g. Ordinarily, we think that, if we divide an object into non-overlapping parts, the mass of the object is the sum of the masses of those parts: the mass of the table is equal to the mass of the table top plus the masses of the four legs. What mass does a persisting banana have, atemporally speaking? Analogy would suggest that its mass is the sum of the masses of all the 100g temporal parts— a worryingly large figure. Perdurance theorists may prefer to claim that persisting objects do not have mass, atemporally speaking.

When it comes to shape, matters are even stranger. Consider a persisting tennis ball. There are many times at which we can say truly that the tennis ball is then spherical. According to perdurance theory, the tennis ball satisfies 'is spherical' with respect to a time t if and only if it has (atemporally) a temporal part at t which instantiates the property *being spherical*. This property of the temporal part at t entitles the whole persisting object to satisfy (atemporally) the corresponding predicate, 'is spherical at t', and to satisfy at t the predicate 'is spherical'. So the persisting tennis ball has many spherical temporal parts.

Now, things do not automatically have the same shape as their parts—we do not have to find house-shaped bricks if we want to build a house. But the persisting tennis ball *cannot* instantiate the property *being spherical*, because it is a four-dimensional object. To instantiate the property *being spherical*, an object must be three-dimensional, just as an object must be two-dimensional in order to instantiate *being a plane circle*, and just as an object must be one-dimensional in order to instantiate *being a straight line*. A plane cannot be a straight line, nor a solid a plane circle, nor a four-dimensional thing a sphere. Persisting objects can be green, they may perhaps have mass, but they cannot be spherical, if perdurance theory is true. Moreover, the tennis ball must have three-dimensional temporal parts if it is to satisfy 'is spherical' at various times in virtue of the properties of its temporal parts.

Consider a spatial analogy, a pipe which has differently shaped cross-sections at different points along its length. We might say that the pipe is circular at one place, and that it is triangular at another place, and what we say is true if and only if the pipe has appropriately shaped cross-sections at the relevant places. But nevertheless, the pipe itself is neither circular nor triangular—it has an irregular three-dimensional shape. Even if every cross-section of the pipe were circular, then the pipe itself would be cylindrical, not circular. Similarly, the tennis ball is not, atemporally speaking, spherical, even if each of its three-dimensional parts is spherical.

According to perdurance theory, persisting things atemporally satisfy various theoretical predicates—predicates like 'is four-dimensional'. Indeed, it is because the use of such predicates requires atemporal talk that the debate between endurance and perdurance theories presupposes the viability of some atemporal talk. Moreover, according to perdurance theory persisting four-dimensional things satisfy sortal predicates.[1] Sortal predicates include 'is a tennis ball', 'is a banana', 'is a cat', and 'is a finger'. They contrast with non-sortal predicates like 'is yellow', 'is purring', 'is hungry', and 'is spherical'. According to David Wiggins (1980: 8, n.1), when we know what sortal an object falls under, we know what the object *is*, as opposed to what it is *like*, or what it is *doing*.[2] An object's sort determines what types of change it can survive (its persistence conditions), what it takes to bring an object of that sort into existence (its existence conditions), and what it would take for the object to be identical to some 'other' object of the same sort.[3] For example, we know that cats cannot survive radical changes of shape. We cannot make such general pronouncements about yellow things, for the yellow things are not a sort in the relevant sense: some yellow things can survive radical changes in shape, whilst others cannot.

Are there sortal properties, as well as sortal predicates? That's to say, are there properties corresponding to predicates like 'is a cat' and 'is a banana'? I will remain neutral on this question, since I believe it can be answered only by developing a general account of properties and predicates, both sortal and non-sortal. But it is evident that if there is a property *being a banana*, then it is instantiated only when certain other, non-sortal properties are instantiated. And if there is no such property, then satisfying the predicate 'is a banana' is a matter of instantiating certain non-sortal properties. That is to say, being a banana usually involves growing on a banana tree, having a characteristic shape, colour, and taste, and perhaps instantiating a certain pattern of genes, even if we can give no exhaustive, exceptionless characterization of what it takes to be a banana. Perdurance theorists

---

[1] Helpful discussions of sortals include Hirsch (1982: ch. 2), Hirsch (1993), Wiggins (1980), Strawson (1959), and Lowe (1989*a*).

[2] Wiggins attributes the distinction to Aristotle.

[3] According to Strawson, 'A sortal universal supplies a principle for distinguishing and counting individual particulars which it collects.' (Strawson 1959: 168.)

claim that it is not, after all, characteristic of bananas that they instantiate properties like *being banana-shaped* and *tasting of banana*. Rather, it is characteristic of bananas that they have banana-shaped, banana-tasting temporal parts. We are, however, provided with a translation manual, which explains why it is true to say that the banana is banana-shaped, yellow, banana-tasting, and so on, at particular times.

Not everything with banana-shaped, banana-tasting temporal parts can be a banana, however. The first month-long temporal part of the banana is not itself a banana, even though it has suitable temporal parts. It is not a banana because it is itself a proper temporal part of a banana.[4] For perdurance theorists, sortal predicates are *temporally maximal*. That is to say, nothing can satisfy a given sortal predicate if it is a proper temporal part of something which satisfies that predicate—no proper temporal part of a banana can be a banana. In this respect, sortal predicates contrast with non-sortal predicates like 'is green'. Something can be green even if it is a proper part of a green thing. As we will see in Chapter 5, many philosophers believe that sortal predicates are spatially maximal—for example that no cat can be a proper spatial part of a cat. But temporal maximality has stranger consequences than does spatial maximality.

Recall the perdurance translation manual: a persisting thing is F at t if and only if it has a temporal part existing at t which instantiates the F property. We now have a new question for the perdurance theorist: can *every* four-dimensional thing join this game, satisfying predicates at times in virtue of the properties of its temporal parts? Take a cat, Margaret. According to the perdurance theorist, Margaret is purring at t if and only if she has a temporal part at t which purrs.[5] So far so good. But consider Daisy, the temporal part of the cat which lasts throughout the first year of Margaret's life. Although Daisy is very cat-like, she is not a cat, for she is a proper part of a cat. Does Daisy purr at *t*, where *t* is during the first year of Margaret's life? After all, Daisy has a temporal part at *t* which is purring, and it is this feature which qualifies the cat itself as purring at *t*.

Perdurance theorists have two options. They can accept that Daisy is also purring at *t*, along with all the hordes and hordes of other temporal parts of Margaret which exist at *t* (although somehow the noise level is not determined by how long Margaret lives). Or they can say

---

[4] A proper part of an object is a part that is not identical to the object itself.
[5] Can a brief temporal part really purr? More on this below.

that only Margaret the cat is purring at *t*, because the business of satisfying predicates in virtue of the properties of temporal parts is also
maximal—only the *largest* suitable candidate qualifies as purring at *t*.
The latter option seems preferable—not only is the satisfaction of
sortal predicates determined by temporal maximality (no proper
temporal part of a cat is a cat), but the satisfaction of non-sortal predicates at times is determined by temporal maximality (the purring of
the brief temporal part of the cat makes it true that the largest cat-like
thing is purring at t, but nothing else counts as purring at t).

2.2 Stage Theory

According to perdurance theory, persisting objects like bananas and
tennis balls are four-dimensional, and they satisfy certain predicates
with respect to certain times because of the properties of their temporal parts. Alongside perdurance theory, there is space for an
alternative account of persistence, one which retains the four-
dimensional metaphysics of perdurance theory whilst rejecting perdurance claims about predication. Following Theodore Sider, who
proposes such an account, I will call this position *stage theory* (Sider
1996). According to stage theory, nothing is wholly present at more
than one moment, so endurance theory is false. But stage theory also
claims that the satisfiers of sortal predicates like 'is a banana' and 'is
a tennis ball' are momentary things, the very things which instantiate ordinary properties like *being yellow*, *being spherical*, or *being
banana-shaped*.

Consider the series of momentary stages whose sum is what
perdurance theorists think of as the tennis ball. According to stage
theory, when we talk about the tennis ball with respect to different
times, we talk about different stages in that series, and each of those
stages is a tennis ball. The tennis ball at one moment is spherical, and
the squashed tennis ball at another moment is not spherical: the
spherical tennis ball and the non-spherical tennis ball are different
objects. Here is a spatial analogy to stage theory. Imagine a row of
houses, each with a front door. As we walk down the street, or simply
move our focus of attention down the street, we can use the phrase
'the front door' with respect to different houses, and thereby talk
about different doors. The front door at number 73 is green, and the
front door at number 77 is yellow: the green thing and the yellow

thing are different objects, though each can be referred to as 'the front door', when we are talking with respect to different houses.

The analogy is not perfect, for the various front doors are not causally connected in interesting ways—we cannot change the colour of one door, for example, by changing the colour of another. In contrast, there are intimate causal connections between each of the stages which is the tennis ball—if we damage an early stage, that damage will be transmitted to later stages. This causal connection between stages will be discussed in Chapter 3. Nevertheless, the analogy is a useful one: according to stage theory, when we talk about the tennis ball with respect to different times, we talk about different objects, each of which is a tennis ball. Similarly, when we talk about the front door with respect to different houses, we talk about different objects, each of which is a front door.

Perdurance and stage theories share a common metaphysical picture—the world is full of very short-lived objects existing in succession. Atemporal talk about the parts of material objects makes perfect sense, just as it makes sense to claim 'aspatially' that my nose is a part of me. Perdurance and stage theorists can even agree that there are plenty of perduring objects in the world—that the short-lived objects make up longer-lived ones—although this is not a central claim of stage theory. But the two accounts differ over what we talk about when we use phrases like 'the tennis ball', and about which objects satisfy sortal predicates like 'is a tennis ball'. According to perdurance theory, it is long-lived sums of stages which are tennis balls, whereas according to stage theory, it is the stages themselves which are tennis balls (or bananas, or human beings, as the case may be).

Why on earth should we take stage theory seriously? One general reason for considering alternative accounts is that by comparison we may arrive at a more accurate assessment of our established beliefs. But of course in considering endurance, perdurance, and stage theories I am not thereby conducting an exhaustive test of all possible accounts of persistence—there are many stranger yet coherent-seeming alternatives that I will not even mention.[6] Why consider this particular account? The remainder of this book will demonstrate that stage theory is a successful, plausible account of persistence, that the theory holds up well against both endurance and perdurance theories when it comes to explaining various familiar features of the persistence of material objects.

---

[6] See MacBride (2001) for some of these.

In brief, however, the story is this. Endurance theory is a seemingly attractive and seemingly simple account of the way in which material things persist through time. But the central claim of endurance theory—that things wholly present at different times can be identical—creates problems for the theory, requiring sophisticated adjustments and complications. The root cause of these problems is the inflexible nature of the identity relation—as we have already seen, it is the insistence on *identity* between objects wholly present at different times which gives rise to the problem of change, the question of how one and the same thing can be both green all over and yellow all over. We will see further problems as the book progresses.[7]

This reliance on identity is a severe constraint, and I think we ought to give up the central endurance claim that things wholly present at different times can be identical—that objects can exist at more than one time without being temporally extended. We should adopt the four-dimensional metaphysical framework shared by perdurance and stage theories. But we are then faced with the question of how our ordinary thought and talk about material objects—which seem to embody something like endurance theory—can be successful in a four-dimensional world. What is it we are talking about when we talk about bananas, tennis balls, and human beings? Perdurance theory offers one account of the semantics of ordinary talk; stage theory, I believe, offers a more attractive account, though one rooted in the same basic metaphysical picture as that of perdurance theory. In particular, I think that stage theory avoids some of the objections commonly raised against perdurance theory by endurance theorists. I cannot justify these claims without further argument—this is part of the task of the rest of the book. First I must say more about how stage theory differs from perdurance theory.

Stage theory has it that sortal predicates like 'is a tennis ball' are satisfied by the same brief objects as instantiate properties like *being spherical*. Does stage theory thereby differ metaphysically or merely semantically from perdurance theory? It rather depends. I intend to make my account of stage theory compatible with a wide range of views about properties, so far as I can, and to avoid commitments about the existence of universals or tropes. I will also try to avoid taking a stance on whether the properties are sparse or abundant, whether the world contains just a few basic properties, or whether

---

[7] For example, reliance upon identity makes endurance theory vulnerable to the Evans–Salmon argument against vagueness in the world (see Chapter 4).

there are lots of different properties. But in the present context, I need to discuss these possibilities, because I am discussing what it takes for something to satisfy a predicate.

First, let's consider the view that properties are universals or classes of tropes.[8] One version of this view has it that there is a single universal or class of tropes which corresponds to the property *being a banana*. Each banana instantiates that universal, or possesses one of those tropes, which is why it satisfies the predicate 'is a banana'. Stage theory claims that it is brief stages which satisfy predicates like 'is a banana'. So if there is a universal or class of tropes which is the property *being a banana*, then it is stages which instantiate that universal, or possess those tropes. In this case, the contrast between stage and perdurance theories is clear: the theories differ over which objects instantiate the relevant universals or possess the relevant tropes.

A different realist about universals or tropes would say that the predicate 'is a banana' does not correspond to a single property, but that an object satisfies the predicate if and only if it possesses (enough of) a certain range of simpler properties. According to stage theory, it is brief stages which possess ordinary properties like shape, colour, internal structure, and so on. Then an object satisfies 'is a banana' in virtue of its having enough of those ordinary properties. In contrast, perdurance theory has a different account of the connection between possessing certain properties and satisfying the related sortal predicates. Stage theory claims that an object must instantiate various ordinary properties in order to satisfy a sortal predicate. Perdurance theory claims that an object's temporal parts must instantiate various ordinary properties in order that the object itself satisfy the sortal predicate.

What if there are no universals or tropes at all? Nominalists have to give some account or other of the workings of predicate-satisfaction and property-attribution talk. And stage theory can take advantage of whatever account is thereby given. If predicates are satisfied in virtue of certain resemblances between particulars, then it is momentary stages which enter into the resemblances underpinning the predicate 'is a banana', as well as those underpinning the predicates 'is spherical' and 'is green'. On this more low-key metaphysical picture, the differences between perdurance theory and stage theory look more semantic than metaphysical. But that is to be expected. Stage theory and

8 Entry points for the debate about the nature of properties include Mellor and Oliver (1997) and Armstrong (1989).

perdurance theory differ about what sort of things are bananas, tennis balls, and human beings. What sort of disagreement this is will partly depend upon other questions about the nature of ordinary objects and properties, about what it takes to be a banana, a tennis ball, or a human being. Simply put, stage theorists claim that whatever it takes to be a banana, stages have what it takes. The strength of this claim depends upon what it takes to be a banana.

One difference between the two theories concerns maximality. As we have already seen, perdurance theorists must claim that if an object is to satisfy a sortal predicate (or instantiate a sortal property), then that object must not be a proper part of something which falls under the sortal. Moreover, if a persisting object is to satisfy predicates at times in virtue of the properties of its temporal parts, then it must not be a proper part of another such predicate-inheritor. But none of this applies to stage theory. According to stage theory, a stage satisfies a sortal if and only if it has the appropriate intrinsic properties and stands in suitable qualitative relations to other stages—I will say more about these properties and relations in the chapters that follow. But in the competition to fall under a sortal there can be many winners—any suitably qualified candidate will do.

Another distinguishing feature of stage theory is that it comes close to satisfying the endurance theory intuition that we cannot speak atemporally about the changeable properties and parts of persisting objects. Recall that, according to perdurance theory, we can think and talk atemporally about the changeable properties of persisting things—for example we can say that the apple is wholly (since permanently) green, and that the banana is multi-coloured, part yellow and part green. (We can also, of course, talk about the banana in a time-indexed way; such talk is made true or false by the properties of the temporal parts of the banana.) Endurance theorists resist this, as they must. They argue that we cannot talk about an object's parts or colour atemporally, but must index this to times—an object is green at one time, yellow at another, and the boy has his milk tooth as a part at one time, his beard as a part at another. Even things which are permanently green, like the apple, are not green atemporally, but green at every moment of their existence.

According to stage theory, we can speak atemporally about perduring objects, as perdurance theorists say we can, and we can make atemporal claims about parthood. But we cannot speak atemporally of 'the tennis ball' or about 'Tony Blair', for these terms do not refer to perduring four-dimensional things; rather, they refer to different objects when used with respect to different times. We cannot just ask whether the boy has the tooth as a part, not because we cannot ask about parthood atemporally, but because we have failed to pick out any individual if we do not speak about the boy at a certain time. We may legitimately make claims about how the boy is at all times, but this is not to speak about him atemporally.

Recall that there were two clauses to my definition of endurance: an object endures iff (i) it exists at more than one time and (ii) statements about what parts the object has must be made relative to some time or other. Stage theory comes close to accepting that ordinary objects satisfy the second of these clauses: when using the words and phrases we think of as designating ordinary objects, we cannot speak atemporally about parthood. This is because atemporal use of such words and phrases fails to pick out any particular individual. But stage theory emphatically rejects the idea embodied in the first clause, that ordinary objects exist at more than one time. When speaking about the boy with respect to different times, we talk about different objects. Endurance theorists must endorse the first clause if they are to be distinguished from stage theorists—this is why, as I argued in section 1.7, endurance theorists must allow us to speak atemporally about ordinary objects, to make atemporal identity claims about ordinary things.

2.3 Developing Stage Theory

Is stage theory genuinely a viable account of persistence? Some readers may already have their doubts, which I will now begin to address. One worry concerns 'sameness' over time. According to stage theory, many present stages are bananas, and many stages tomorrow are bananas. But this seems to omit the important fact that some of those stages are intimately linked, that certain stages today are the *same* banana as certain stages tomorrow. In Chapter 3 I will address the metaphysical question of what that intimate linkage is. This is a question that arises equally for perdurance theory: what is the relation which holds between temporal parts of a single banana? In stage theory terms, the question is: what relation holds between bananas which are 'the same' banana?

A second worry is that there are far too many bananas in the world on this account: if every instantaneous banana-like stage is a banana, then throughout history the number of bananas is enormous. Stage theory does give exactly the right answer to the question of how many bananas there are at any one moment, but diachronic counting, counting over time, is a major problem for the theory. Below, I will explain how stage theory can attempt to deal with the problem, but the problem cannot be entirely dissolved.

A third worry is about stages themselves: surely momentary stages are just too thin to populate the world, and too thin to be the objects of reference? A related worry concerns predicates which seem to take time to be satisfied, like 'is digesting', 'is conscious', 'is growing', 'is thinking of Vienna', and so on. How can such 'lingering' predicates, as I shall call them, be satisfied by momentary stages? Similarly, how can a momentary stage instantiate 'historical' predicates? What makes it true that the banana used to be green although it no longer is?

Stage theorists need accounts of the nature of stages and their temporal extent, of the properties of stages (and the predicates they satisfy), of how we refer to stages, and of our talk of identity and number, and I will provide such accounts in the sections which follow. A recurring theme is a reliance upon the notion of 'suitable' relations between stages which are stages 'of' the same object: this notion will be more fully explored in the following chapter. Endurance theory is barely mentioned in the remainder of this chapter, for my present aim is to show that stage theory is viable, not that endurance theory is false. In contrast, perdurance and stage theories share a background metaphysical picture, and so it will often be appropriate to compare the two accounts—sometimes stage theory can draw upon perdurance theory in answering metaphysical questions, and sometimes a challenge to stage theory is also a challenge to perdurance theory.

On balance, I prefer the stage theory of persistence to either endurance or perdurance theory, and I will be explaining why during the course of this book. But I do not think that the evidence is conclusive, or even overwhelming; interesting, valid arguments with obviously true premises are as rare in metaphysics as they are elsewhere. Moreover, the kinds of arguments needed to arbitrate the metaphysical dispute between endurance theory on the one hand, and perdurance or stage theory on the other, are different from the kinds of arguments required to settle the mainly semantic dispute between perdurance and stage theories. Endurance and perdurance theories are well-developed in the philosophical literature, and, I believe, neither theory is obviously false. But stage theory is a less familiar

position, and some work is required in order to establish that it is a
viable account of persistence. I undertake that groundwork in this
chapter—here the aim is not to demonstrate that stage theory is the
most satisfactory account of persistence, but simply to show that it is
a contender, that it is not obviously or trivially false.

2.4 How Long are Stages?

According to endurance theory, material things do not have temporal
'length'; rather a thing exists for a certain period of time, different
periods in different cases. According to perdurance theory, material
things have temporal lengths, different lengths in different cases: I
hope that my temporal length is at least three score years and ten. But
according to stage theory, when we talk about material objects
(including our bodies, ourselves), we talk about brief stages. Exactly
how brief are these stages? I have already argued that the briefest
stages or temporal parts must be three-dimensional, since they must
be capable of instantiating three-dimensional shape properties like
being spherical. But I will now approach the same question from
another angle, by considering how stage and perdurance theories
must account for change. I will argue that stages must be as fine-
grained as possible change, and then that this means that stages must
be as fine-grained as time.

Any account of persistence must explain how change is possible—
we saw a range of such explanations in Chapter 1. Both perdurance
and stage theories explain change by claiming that incompatible
properties are instantiated by different objects—different temporal
parts or stages. The banana ripens from green to yellow, because earlier things are green and later things are yellow. To account for change,
stages and temporal parts must be as fine-grained as change: a material thing must have as many stages or parts as it is in incompatible
states during its lifetime. If it were in more incompatible states than it
had stages or parts, then at least one of its stages or parts would be in
incompatible states without itself having parts or stages, and the
problem of change would re-emerge.

Stages must be as fine-grained as change, which is to say that stages
must themselves be unchanging. This leaves us with two options.
Perhaps stages are as fine-grained as possible change: even if a material thing persists unchanging for millennia, it nevertheless has very

very many brief stages (or temporal parts), corresponding to all the incompatible states it could have instantiated. Or perhaps stages are only as fine-grained as actual change: an unchanging thing has but a single stage, and thus different stages last for different periods of time. Either option is compatible with stage theory, but I prefer the first option, according to which stages are of uniform temporal extent, as fine-grained as possible change. Moreover, I believe that perdurance theorists should adopt the same attitude towards temporal parts—the briefest temporal parts of things are all equally brief.

Consider a spatial analogy; imagine a spatially homogeneous object, one which does not vary in any way across its spatial extent. Some take it that the object has as many spatial parts as there are spatial regions which it completely fills: its left half and its right half, its top half and its bottom half, the part which exactly occupies the cubic inch at its centre, and so on and so on. Others would contend that the homogeneous object is partless, that objects (including parts of objects) must in some way be distinguished from their surroundings, and that objects do not have 'arbitrary undetached parts' (van Inwagen 1981). Suppose, however that the object is not *essentially* homogeneous, and that if it had varied across its spatial extent, it would have had spatial parts—different parts to instantiate the complementary properties in which it would have varied.[9] Does the homogeneous object, which could have had spatial parts, actually have spatial parts?

If the homogeneous object does not actually have spatial parts, we face a problem. The object could have become inhomogeneous midway through its career—someone might have painted stripes on it. Then, presumably, it would have had parts. But would it have had parts before the painting, because of the later painting, or does painting the object create its parts? Neither option is attractive, and both can be avoided if we accept that the homogeneous object actually has spatial parts. Moreover, if the object actually has spatial parts, this explains why it *could* have been inhomogeneous—its different parts *could* have had different properties. Similarly, if stages are as fine-grained as possible change, not merely as fine-grained as actual change, this explains how an actually-unchanging object could have changed—its different stages could have had different properties. The

[9] Could it have varied without having different parts? Only by creating a spatial version of the problem of change: how can one and the same object instantiate incompatible properties? (MacBride 1998.)

same goes, of course, for perdurance theorists—they should believe that temporal parts are as fine-grained as possible change.

I have argued that stages are as fine-grained as possible change, and I will write as if I have demonstrated this conclusion. But the argument is not watertight, especially since it relies upon considerations about explanatory priority, and the relation between the actual and the possible. Those readers who insist that stages or temporal parts are merely as fine-grained as actual change will disagree with the letter of my exposition of stage theory (although they will also need to address the argument that stages must be three-dimensional if they are to instantiate three-dimensional shape properties). But they may nevertheless agree with the spirit of the account, for the viability of stage theory does not depend upon the success of arguments about the fine-grainedness of stages. Those who believe that stages (or temporal parts) are only as fine-grained as actual change could read what follows as an exploration of stage theory as it applies to (actual or possible) constantly changing things. An account of persistence ought, after all, to apply to such things, even if most things are not constantly changing.

2.5 Time and Change

Stages must be as fine-grained as possible change, but how rapidly can things change? I will argue that possible change is as fine-grained as time, and thus that stages must be as fine-grained as time. How fine-grained can change be? Someone who thought that there was no time without change would have an excellent reason to think that change can be exactly as fine-grained as time, that there is no extended interval of time so short that nothing could change in that time.[10] But is there a more neutral way of arguing that change can be exactly as fine-grained as time?

There might perhaps be essentially temporally homogeneous material things, which last through an extended interval without changing. Then the possibility of qualitative change would not require us to posit that such things have temporal parts or stages. But even such an unchanging thing is at different times—different temporal locations—at different times: if different temporal locations are

---

[10] See Shoemaker (1969) for a discussion of time without change.

incompatible, then the problem of change would lead us to posit a stage for each moment at which the object exists. Moreover, temporally extended things, even if they are homogeneous in other respects, might move during their existence, and thus might occupy different spatial locations at different moments. So if locations are features of things, and things are not essentially stationary, then there are no necessarily homogeneous yet temporally extended things: possible change is as fine-grained as time itself.

How fine-grained is time? There seem to be three possible ways that time could be at the micro-structural level. The ordering of the instants could be discrete, dense, or continuous. If the ordering is discrete, then it is like the ordering of the integers, and every instant is followed by a unique next instant. In that case, finite stretches of time are not infinitely divisible, but are made up of discrete smallest units. If the ordering is dense, it is like that of the rational numbers (the fractions), and instants are not followed by unique next instants or successors. Between every two instants there is another instant. If the ordering is continuous, then it is like that of the real numbers (the rationals together with the irrationals), and, again, between every two instants there is another instant. So if time is discrete, it is not infinitely divisible, and if time is either dense or continuous, then it is infinitely divisible.

There are empirical arguments to the effect that time is not discrete. Current physical theories are extremely successful, and the mathematics of such theories uses continuously varying time and space variables. Wesley Salmon remarks that 'continuity is buried deep in standard mathematical physics', since velocity and acceleration are defined as derivatives of the 'motion function', which gives position as a function of a continuous time variable (W. Salmon 1975: 63). Newton-Smith, however, argues that, although the success of physics provides good evidence that space and time are not discrete, it fails to distinguish between the competing hypotheses that time and space are continuous, and that they are merely dense (Newton-Smith 1980: VI.3).

I will take it, then, that any finite interval of time is infinitely divisible (that time is either dense or continuous), and develop stage theory on that basis, although I believe that stage theory could also be made compatible with the claim that time is discrete. Indeed, such a theory would be easier to develop: to suppose that time intervals are infinitely divisible is to work with the hard case. I will claim that stages

Parts and Stages

have the same structure as the instants, which, I take it, means that the nature of this structure is an empirical matter, one which I cannot settle here. It seems that space and time are real, and so whatever structure they turn out to have must be a possible structure; what is possible for time is possible for stages.

So what are stages like? They are like instants. Stages need to be as fine-grained as possible change, and thus they must be as fine-grained as instants, in order to account for possible change in position: henceforth I will refer to the briefest material things as 'instantaneous stages'. Indeed, an argument we have already encountered also leads to this conclusion. If material things can have three-dimensional shape properties, like *being spherical*, then there must be material things which are three-dimensional, having no temporal extension. Those three-dimensional things are either tennis balls, as stage theory (and endurance theory) claims, or else temporal parts of tennis balls, as perdurance theory has it. Perdurance theory has as much need of instantaneous things as stage theory does, although the theories disagree about whether those brief things are ordinary objects, or just parts of ordinary objects.

Moreover, perdurance theory takes on extra commitments that stage theory need not. Perdurance theory is committed to the existence of sums of temporal parts, for it is these very sums which are supposed to be the ordinary objects of everyday life. But, given that perdurance theorists are also committed to the existence of instantaneous temporal parts, they must therefore explain how instantaneous things can have a sum of finite but extended size, as extensionless instants can make up finite but extended intervals of time. Stage theory can remain neutral here. If it makes sense to think of instantaneous stages as having extended fusions, or sums, then stage theorists can recognize those sums. But if not, then no problems arise, since, according to stage theory, sums of stages play no significant role in our everyday ontology. Perdurance theorists, on the other hand, must establish the existence of such fusions, for those very fusions are supposed to be familiar objects.

Before moving on to semantic issues concerning stage theory, I will very briefly discuss the impact of the theory of special relativity on the debate about persistence. According to special relativity, simultaneity is frame relative, which is to say that whether or not two events are simultaneous depends upon the frame with respect to which they are measured. This is sometimes taken to be a problem for presentism, the view that only the present exists. For if simultaneity is frame relative, then what is present—what is simultaneous with now—is a frame-dependent matter. And many believe that whether or not a thing exists should not be a frame-dependent matter.[11]

Now, stage theorists are not committed to anything like the frame-dependence of existence. An instantaneous stage is composed of things which exist simultaneously. So whether or not some things compose a stage depends upon the frame of reference. Thus whether some things compose a banana depends upon the frame of reference, according to stage theory. This is, of course, a strange consequence of special relativity, but we are by now used to the idea that special relativity has strange consequences. Stage theorists need not claim that whether some things compose *anything at all* depends upon the frame of reference, merely that whether they compose a *stage* is frame-dependent—for stages are made of simultaneously existing things. Stage theory makes being a stage frame-dependent, but there is no sense in which stage theory makes existence frame-dependent.

2.6 Lingering and Historical Predicates

Both stage and perdurance theories are committed to the existence of material objects that are as fine-grained as time itself, but so far we have seen no reason to think that this commitment is problematic. The basic ontology of stage theory is coherent. But can instantaneous stages really be what we are talking about when we talk about ordinary things, about tennis balls, bananas, and human beings? Two main questions need to be answered. First, can instantaneous stages instantiate the properties and satisfy the predicates we associate with ordinary objects? Second, can we refer to instantaneous stages at all, given their brevity?[12]

According to stage theory, it is instantaneous stages which satisfy sortal predicates like 'is a banana', and instantiate sortal properties like *being a banana*, if there are such properties. But some might doubt whether such predicates can really be satisfied by instantaneous things, or whether such properties can really be instantiated by

---

[11] Mellor (1998: ch. 5), Putnam (1967), Weingard (1972). For responses, see McCall (1994: 33–4) and Tooley (1997: ch. 11).

[12] I am indebted throughout this and the following sections to Sider (1996), although our versions of stage theory do not agree on every point.

instantaneous things. For example, it might be that nothing could be a banana unless it grew on a banana tree. Similarly, perhaps nothing could be a tennis ball unless it was designed to be a tennis ball, and perhaps nothing could be a human being without going through the normal developmental processes of human beings. How could an instantaneous thing have such a history?

To avoid prejudging questions about what properties there are in the world, I will talk in terms of predicate-satisfaction, rather than property-instantiation. Two sorts of predicate seem to be problematic for stage theory. The first sort I will call 'historical'. At any time, a persisting thing satisfies predicates which describe its past and its future states, rather than its present states. These are predicates like 'grew on a banana tree', 'was an unpleasant child', and 'will marry young'. How could an instantaneous stage satisfy any of these predicates? The second sort of problematic predicate I will call 'lingering': these are predicates which seem to take some time to be satisfied, predicates like 'is thinking of Vienna', 'is travelling to Vienna', 'is photosynthesizing', and 'is alive'. Stage theory must be concerned with both historical and lingering predicates because stage theory claims that ordinary objects like tennis balls are stages. And tennis balls satisfy lingering and historical predicates, like 'is travelling across the court' and 'is six months old'. If stages cannot satisfy predicates like 'is six months old', then it is hard to see why we should identify tennis balls with stages.

But stages can satisfy both lingering and historical predicates. True, an *isolated* stage could not satisfy such predicates: an instantaneous tennis ball-like thing could not be travelling across a tennis court, or be six months old. Nor, for that matter, could an extremely short-lived perduring or enduring thing be travelling across a tennis court or be six months old. But an instantaneous stage *can* satisfy such predicates if it is suitably surrounded by and related to other stages with appropriate properties. Roughly speaking, the stage satisfies 'is travelling across the court' if and only if it is embedded in a series of stages which are appropriately located at points across the court. And the stage satisfies 'is six months old' if and only if it is preceded by an appropriate sequence of stages which stretches back over six months.

Very many predicates turn out to be relational, according to stage theory. If there are properties corresponding to lingering and historical predicates, then they are relational properties of stages, but they are properties of stages nevertheless. The same is true of sortal predicates like 'is a tennis ball' and 'is a banana', and the corresponding

sortal properties, if there are any. The satisfaction of most sortal predicates requires the satisfaction of some lingering and historical predicates, so no isolated stage could satisfy such predicates. No stage can
be a banana unless it is suitably related to other stages which are
bananas, and which themselves have appropriate properties. An isolated instantaneous stage could not be a banana. But this is to be
expected, on any account of persistence—no isolated stage, no
momentary and isolated perduring thing, no miraculous flash of an
enduring object could be a banana. Instantaneous stages need not be
isolated stages.

Do these considerations indicate that, contrary to stage theory, it is
not instantaneous stages which satisfy sortal predicates, but rather collections, series, or sums of such stages? No. According to stage theory,
what it takes for a stage to satisfy the predicate 'is a banana' is a little
like what it takes for a person to satisfy the predicate 'is a sibling' on
any account of persistence. I am a sibling if and only if I am suitably
related to at least one other sibling. I could not be a sibling without the
existence of at least one other sibling. Nevertheless, I am a sibling in
the most direct way in which anything can be a sibling; neither the
collection nor the sum of me and my siblings is in any sense itself a
sibling. Analogously, the stage itself is a banana in the most direct way
in which anything can possibly be a banana. If there is a property *being
a banana*, then the stage instantiates it. The claim is simply that any
such property is a relational property (Sider 1996: 449).

Recall that, according to perdurance theory, an extended four-
dimensional tennis ball can satisfy the predicate 'is spherical' with
respect to a certain time in virtue of the fact that a different object, a
part of the ball, instantiates the property *being spherical*. Moreover, it
is only certain, temporally maximal things which satisfy predicates at
times in this way in virtue of the properties of their parts. Thinking
atemporally, it is the four-dimensional thing which satisfies the sortal
predicate, whilst the part satisfies the non-sortal predicate. Stage
theory turns this picture around: it is one and the same thing which
satisfies both sortal and non-sortal predicates, but many predicates of
both kinds turn out to be relational.

There are two possible worries about this stage theory account of lingering and historical predicates. The first concerns the question of what
these 'suitable' or 'appropriate' relations between stages are. Exactly
what relation must a stage bear to other banana stages in order to qualify as a banana? Must it simply be spatio-temporally continuous with

such stages, or is something more (or less) required? These questions about the relations between stages 'of' the same object are equivalent to standard questions about persistence conditions or criteria of identity through time, questions which also arise for perdurance theory, and, perhaps, for endurance theory. I will defer this important issue to Chapter 3. The second worry concerns circularity: to be a banana it is necessary to be suitably related (whatever this amounts to) to other stages which are bananas. But those other stages qualify as bananas only because they themselves are suitably related to bananas, and so on. Is this a vicious circle?

No. Granted an advance on my account of suitable relations, there is no reason to think that the characterization is circular. The type of characterization I have in mind is this: for a stage to be a banana it is necessary (and perhaps sufficient) that it be yellow, curved, edible, and suitably related to other yellow, curved, edible, stages. 'Yellow, curved, and edible' is, I take it, neither sufficient nor necessary—it is difficult to give a reductive definition of what it is to be a banana, and this is the business of the scientist, not the philosopher.[13] But this is not a peculiarity of stage theory. Whatever it takes to be a banana will be a matter both of having appropriate non-relational properties, and of being suitably related (whatever that amounts to) to other things with appropriate non-relational properties. The account is schematic, but it is not circular, and we have no reason to suspect that it would be viciously circular if it were spelled out in more detail.

Whether or not a stage satisfies a predicate like 'is a banana' turns out to be a relational matter, but this does not undermine stage theory: that *isolated stages* could not satisfy sortal predicates does not entail that *stages* do not satisfy sortal predicates. How isolated is too isolated? How many stages must be gathered together in order for each of them to have a chance of qualifying as a banana, or a tennis ball? An isolated stage could not be a banana, but nor, presumably, could just two suitably related instantaneous stages. This is an interesting question to which I do not have the answer, but exactly analogous questions arise on any account of persistence. How short-lived might a banana or a tennis ball be? The (vague) answers will be different for different kinds of thing. For example, it might be that nothing could be a person unless it had a certain sort of origin and perhaps a certain developmental history. Perhaps a science-fictional swamp

---

[13] If it is anyone's business, that is. Dupré (1993: ch. 3) argues that this would be a fruitless project.

creature intrinsically indiscernible from a human person would not be a person, or perhaps it would. Perhaps miraculously created adult cat-doppelgangers would be cats, or perhaps they would not. But one thing is clear: there are no problems for stage theory here which do not also arise for endurance and perdurance theories. Stage theory can offer a general account of how it is that instantaneous objects can be the subjects of ordinary, historical, lingering, and sortal predicates. Substantive questions about the nature of different kinds of material objects remain, but these questions arise for every theory of persistence, and do not trouble stage theory in particular.

2.7 Reference and Reidentification

Two issues about reference need to be addressed, if I am to show that stage theory is viable. One is the question of how we can ever refer to ordinary objects at all, if they are mere fleeting stages. The second question is how reidentification can work according to stage theory, how we can introduce names or descriptions of objects at one time and then use them to talk about other times. In dealing with these questions, I will not offer a comprehensive account of the ways in which we refer to material particulars. Rather, I will show how stage theory can fit with whichever account of reference the reader prefers. Stage theory does not make special demands on theories of reference: it creates no more problems than do perdurance and endurance theories.

First, then, how can we refer to instantaneous things? The task here is to explain how we manage to refer to one instantaneous thing rather than another: can we really achieve this level of precision? A glib response would be that we manage to talk about individual stages in the same way as we manage to talk about individual moments like the present—whatever way that is. The response is dangerous, however: some might suspect that in fact we never do talk about particular moments, and thus that there is no model here for stage theory. So I will explore this issue further.

How does present-tense predication work? As we saw in Chapter 1, philosophers of time disagree about the truth-conditions of tensed sentences, like 'the banana is now yellow'. According to tenseless theorists, the utterance is true if and only if the banana's being yellow is simultaneous with the time of the utterance. According to tensed theorists, on the other hand, the utterance is made true by the *presentness*—at the time of utterance—of the banana's being yellow. On either account, present-tense predications single out a time—the time of utterance—with respect to which they should be assessed. Likewise, past and future tense predications single out times with respect to which they should be assessed. For example, consider the utterance 'the banana was green'. According to tenseless theorists, the utterance is true if and only if the banana's being green is earlier than the time of utterance; according to tensed theorists, the utterance is made true by the *pastness*—at the time of utterance—of the banana's being green.

How do the various accounts of persistence account for such predication? I will work an example for a tenseless theory, but the example can easily be adapted to fit a tensed theory of temporal utterances. According to endurance theory, 'the banana is now yellow' is true iff the enduring banana is yellow at the time of utterance. According to perdurance theory, the utterance is true iff something which is a temporal part of the perduring banana at the time of utterance is yellow. And according to stage theory, the utterance is true iff the stage which is the banana at the time of utterance is yellow.

But of course it takes time to make an utterance, and there is no unique moment of utterance. Exactly which stage must be yellow if the utterance is to be true? This is a tricky question, but endurance and perdurance theories face equally tricky questions. Exactly which temporal part of the banana must be yellow if the utterance is to be true? At exactly which moment must the banana be yellow if the utterance is to be true? I can think of three alternative answers to these questions, whichever theory of persistence we adopt. Each requires that there be a domain of moments at around the time of utterance, moments which might feasibly count as present moments for the purpose of evaluating the utterance. How large this domain is, and how vague its boundaries are will vary from case to case.[14]

The three possibilities are to interpret a given present-tense predication as an existential claim over a domain of moments, temporal parts, or stages, to interpret it as a universal claim over a domain of moments, temporal parts, or stages, or to be supervaluationist and take a present-tense predication as concerning a single, but vaguely specified, moment, temporal part, or stage within a certain domain.

[14] This domain of moments which could be 'the present' need not have anything to do with the notion of 'the specious present' sometimes invoked in the philosophy of mind.

These are alternative ways of accounting for the truth-conditions of such predications, rather than alternative hypotheses about content or meaning. Let's see how these proposals could work.

First, the existential reading of 'the banana is now yellow'. For endurance theorists: there is a moment in the present short interval at which the enduring banana instantiates *being yellow*. For perdurance theorists: there is an instantaneous temporal part of the perduring banana in the present short interval which instantiates *being yellow*. For stage theorists: there is some instantaneous stage in the present short interval which is the banana and which instantiates *being yellow*. Is there a special problem here for stage theorists? For both endurance and perdurance theorists, it is clear how we might have established *which* banana is in question, thus allowing us to quantify over the moments through which it endures, or to quantify over its temporal parts. But I have not yet discussed the stage theory account of reident-ification. For now, let us say that, according to stage theory, on this existential reading we invoke the most salient series of stages, each of which is a banana, as our domain, and we say that one of those stages is yellow.

Second, the universal reading of 'the banana is now yellow'. For endurance theorists: at every moment in the present short interval the banana instantiates *being yellow*. For perdurance theorists: every instantaneous temporal part of the banana which exists in the present short interval instantiates *being yellow*. (In the case of *being yellow*, this amounts to the claim that the temporal part of the banana which lasts exactly through the interval is yellow. But this will not be the case for non-cumulative properties like *being spherical*.) Finally, for stage theorists: every one of the salient series of banana stages which exists in the present short interval instantiates *being yellow*.

Third, the supervaluationist reading of 'the banana is now yellow'. This treats the issue as one of vagueness in reference (to moment, part, or stage). It is indeterminate which one of a range of moments, parts, or stages enters into the truth conditions of the present-tense predication. But we can count the utterance as true if the predicate in question is satisfied by every member of that range, by every potential referent. So for endurance theorists: the enduring banana is yellow at every moment in the salient period, so it is true that the banana is now yellow, despite the fact that it is indeterminate which moment is 'now'. For perdurance theorists: each of the instantaneous temporal parts of the banana in the salient period is yellow, so it is true that the banana is now yellow. For stage theorists: each of the salient bananas is yellow, so it is true that the banana is now yellow. The supervaluationist approach locates vagueness in which moment is the present, but there will be higher-order vagueness here too: vagueness in which moments are within the salient period.

On all three readings, and on all three accounts of persistence, context plays a large role in determining how wide the salient interval is taken to be, and thus what the relevant domain or range of candidates is (whether these are moments, parts, or stages). The predicate in question surely plays a role. And, in a rapidly changing situation, I take it that we usually and charitably take the speaker to pick out an interval during which her utterance comes out true. I don't know how to decide between the three possible accounts of present-tense predication, and, indeed, I don't know how to decide whether there is a fact of the matter as to which reading is correct. Indeed, if there *are* genuine differences between existential, universal, and supervaluationist readings, different readings might be most appropriate for different sentences in different contexts. But I need not settle these questions about reference and logical form, for all I need establish is that, however present-tense predication operates, it can operate just as well according to stage theory as it does on either of the alternative accounts of persistence. There is nothing inherently problematic about referring to instantaneous stages.[15]

The other pressing semantic question concerns reidentification. So far I have been discussing the question of how we can refer to a thing at a time, whether that involves picking out a certain moment, temporal part, or stage. But I only discussed how we pick out one moment rather than another, or a stage or part at one moment rather than a stage or part at another moment. I assumed that, once the moment was determined, it would also be determinate *which* of the many bananas existing at that moment enters into the truth conditions of the utterance. I have explained how a particular moment in the life of a persisting banana can enter into the truth conditions of an utterance, but I have not explained how one persisting banana rather than another gets picked out—what determines that we are talking about this banana here, rather than that banana over there?

Now, the mechanisms of reference to particulars are a matter of much debate. I do not undertake to explain how reference works, but

---

[15] Accounts of past- and future-tense predication could be developed from any of the three alternatives I have proposed.

again I hope to show that stage theory faces no particular problems here. Why might someone think that stage theory would have diffi-culty accounting for reference to persisting things? As an example, I'll discuss proper names as Kripke sees them (Kripke 1972). A name is attached to a persisting object at some time, either by ostension, or by a reference-fixing description. The name is passed on from one language-user to the next, and this 'causal chain' somehow ensures that in its future uses, the name refers to the object it was first attached to, more or less independently of the states of mind of the subsequent users.

The name can be used to talk about the object as it is at the moment of dubbing, but it can also be used to talk about the object as it is at moments other than the dubbing moment. This is fortunate, other-wise proper names would be of limited use. For endurance and per-durance theorists, this flexibility is easily explicable; the object which was initially dubbed with the name continues to exist, and is thus available to be referred to at later times. For stage theorists, things might look trickier, for the instantaneous stage which was dubbed no longer exists. How then can we use the name to talk about what goes on at later times?

Stage theorists claim that the name refers to different things—dif-ferent stages—when it is used to talk about different times. Let's say we dub a banana on Monday with the name 'Billy'. When we use the name to talk about what's going on in the fruitbowl on Tuesday, what do we refer to? According to stage theorists, we talk about a stage which stands in a suitable relation to the stage which was initially dubbed.[16] This suitable relation, of course, is the very same as that relation between stages which accounts for lingering and historical predication. Certain series of stages are connected by such relations (which I will discuss at greater length in Chapter 3), and certain series are not. What counts as a suitable relation may depend in part upon the sort of object we are talking about: suitable relations for bananas may be different from suitable relations for soap bubbles.

Stage theory is in no important respect different from perdurance theory here. According to perdurance theorists, no banana is wholly present at the dubbing event. A name gets attached to the persisting banana because later parts of the banana are suitably related to the

---

[16] The claims that we refer to a single stage in the fruitbowl, and that we dub a single stage, are both subject to a caveat: they must be understood in the existential, universal, or supervaluationist ways I outlined above.

temporal part which is present at the dubbing event. (That temporal part is, after all, a part of all sorts of peculiar gerrymandered things, as well as being a part of the banana (Quine 1950).) So according to stage theory, proper names (and definite descriptions, and other referring devices) have many different referents, at many different moments. Each of the stages suitably related to the initially dubbed stage is a potential referent of the name 'Billy'. The initial stage thus plays a role in attaching the name to the series of stages.[17] The schematic account of reference I have given here will be fleshed out by the discussion of 'suitable relations' in Chapter 3, but, again, the strategy has been to show how, although stage theory is involved with deep and complex philosophical issues, it faces problems which are neither more difficult nor even significantly different from the problems faced by perdurance theory (and, sometimes, by endurance theory).

2.8 Sameness, Identity, and Counting

Endurance theorists claim that the green banana is identical to the yellow banana. Perdurance theorists claim that the four-dimensional green banana is identical to the four-dimensional yellow banana, although neither actually instantiates either *being green* or *being yellow*. Stage theorists say that in no sense is the green banana identical to the yellow banana—persistence is not a matter of identity over time. Stage theorists can, however, talk about sameness through time: the green banana is the same banana as the yellow banana. The relational predicate 'is the same banana as' does not invoke the relation of identity.[18] It is satisfied by a pair of things if and only if they are bananas which stand in appropriate relations to one another.

The word 'same' does not always mean the same as 'numerically identical' in English: two people on opposite sides of the world can be wearing the same outfit and reading the same book. We might try to understand this locution in terms of the numerical identity of types, and thus preserve the notion that 'same' means the same as 'numerically identical': the Australian is reading a book whose type is identical to the type of the book being read by the Scot, and she is wearing an outfit of a type identical to the type of outfit worn by the Scot. But this

---

[17] In Chapter 6 I will discuss modal issues concerning names and stage theory.
[18] Sider develops his stage theory using a different account of talk about identity through time. See his 1996.

interpretation is problematic, since it supposes that our talk of outfits commits us to the existence of abstract outfit-types. Stage theorists can claim that, when we talk of sameness over time, of the green and yellow bananas being the same banana, this is another example of 'same' not meaning the same as 'numerically identical' (Armstrong 1993). A possible version of stage theory would have it that we talk about abstract types, of which stages are tokens, but this is unattractive: if it is difficult to believe in abstract outfit-types, it is even harder to believe that bananas are abstract objects. (Simons (2000) develops a view of this sort.)

Stage theory accounts for our talk of 'sameness' between things existing at different times by divorcing this notion of sameness from that of numerical identity. But this creates problems concerning diachronic counting. Stage theory seems massively to overestimate the number of bananas in the world. For every banana posited by perdurance and endurance theory, stage theory posits an enormous number of bananas: every instantaneous stage is a banana. Exactly how many bananas there are will depend upon empirical questions about the structure of time, as we saw earlier in this chapter, but even on the most conservative estimate, the numbers are huge.

Perdurance theory has a related but less serious problem—if we ask how many spherical things have been in the room today, strictly speaking perdurance theorists should count every instantaneous temporal part of the tennis ball, for each of those things instantiates *being spherical*. But this problem is less serious because we have weaker intuitions about counting spherical things than we do about counting tennis balls. Stage theory must at least offer some explanation of our habits of diachronic counting—strictly speaking there have been enormous numbers of bananas in the fruitbowl today; nevertheless when we are not speaking strictly, it is better to say that there has been one banana there than to say that there have been fifty-seven.

There are various options available. One is to claim that when we say we are counting how many bananas have been in the fruitbowl all day, we are counting something other than bananas, or counting things which would not count as bananas in other contexts. Theodore Sider is a stage theorist who makes a suggestion of this type. He says that, although in general it is stages which satisfy 'is a banana', in contexts concerning diachronic counting, it is after all sums of stages which satisfy 'is a banana', as perdurance theorists claim. It is those sums of stages which get counted (Sider 1996: 448). A variant on this is to suppose that when counting diachronically we count certain classes of stages, classes whose members are appropriately related. The disadvantage of the class suggestion is that it entails that we are not really counting bananas, in any sense of 'banana', for there is no sense in which a banana is a class. A disadvantage of Sider's suggestion, on the other hand, is that it commits us to the existence of sums of stages, thus sacrificing one of the positive advantages of stage theory. Moreover, in either version, this proposal commits us to the ambiguity of ordinary terms like 'banana'.

A different option is to claim that when we count how many bananas have been in the fruitbowl today, we do not count bananas 'by identity', because we count many bananas as one.[19] Given that stage theory can supply a semantics for 'is the same banana as' which does not depend upon the identity relation—the green banana is the same banana as the yellow banana, although they are not identical—it seems natural to extend this semantics to diachronic counting. We do not count by identity when counting diachronically; instead we count 'by sameness', counting as one all those bananas which are the same banana as each other. In ordinary cases this strategy will work, despite feeling rather contrived.[20] Whichever approach we take, stage theory is bound to say something fairly peculiar about diachronic counting. This issue highlights perhaps the least attractive feature of stage theory, one which must be weighed in the balance when we come to compare the overall advantages and disadvantages of the various theories of persistence.

2.9 Personal Persistence

The issues under discussion here have striking consequences for personal persistence. As elsewhere in this chapter, I will focus upon contrasts between stage theory and perdurance theory, between the idea that instantaneous stages satisfy ordinary sortal predicates, and the idea that long four-dimensional things satisfy those predicates. According to stage theory, very many properties of stages turn out to be relational. A stage satisfies many predicates partly in virtue of its standing in certain relations to other stages with the right properties;

[19] Lewis (1976a) discusses counting which is not 'by identity'.
[20] Non-ordinary cases include those where an object divides, becoming two objects of the same kind. I will discuss such cases of fission in Chapter 5.

in particular this is true of lingering and historical predicates, none of which could be satisfied by an isolated stage. But an instantaneous stage need not be an isolated stage, and it is single, non-isolated stages which satisfy those predicates, and instantiate the corresponding properties when there are such properties. The same goes for predicates typically instantiated by people, including lingering and historical predicates like 'is thinking about Vienna', 'was born on the 4th of July', 'likes chocolate cake', and so on. A single stage can satisfy such a predicate, if it has the right intrinsic properties and stands in the right relations to other stages and to its environment. Both critics and advocates of perdurance theory often assume that very brief things cannot have mental states, just because they are too brief. But this seems to be a mistake.

For example, David Brink (1997) argues that temporally minimal person-slices cannot be agents or bearers of reasons, on the grounds that they are just too short to have the requisite complex mental states, to have interests (in any but a rudimentary sense), or to perform actions.[21] If he were right, then stage theory would be false, at least concerning people, because no stage could be a person. But Brink's argument succeeds only if having mental states, having interests, or acting must be intrinsic properties of slices, and we have no reason to think this. My present stage has interests and acts, partly because it is appropriately related to other stages which have appropriate properties. In the same way, this piece of wood is a table-leg partly because it is appropriately related to other pieces of wood. It is no less a table-leg for all that.

Brink is concerned to establish that, if perdurance theory is true, seventy-year-long four-dimensional objects are agents and bearers of interests, because he is concerned to establish that it is the same thing (me) which both sacrifices and benefits when I act in my future interests. What turns on this? Brink considers three different theories of rationality and practical reasoning, and the consequences of these theories for issues about the distribution of benefits and harms across time and across persons.

Neutralism is both temporally neutral and person-neutral; it holds that an agent has reason to do something just in so far as it is valuable, regardless of whom the value accrues to or when it occurs. Presentism, on the other hand,

---

[21] Judith Jarvis Thomson makes a similar claim in the same volume: 'For example, can one really think that point-duration temporal slices of bodies believe things or want things?' (Thomson 1997: 211.)

is both temporally biased and person-biased; it holds that an agent has reason to do something just in so far as it is in his own present interest. (Brink 1997: 98.)[22]

Neutralism and presentism contrast with a mixed theory, rational egoism. 'Rational egoism claims that an agent has reason to do something just in so far as doing so contributes to her own overall happiness or welfare.' (Brink 1997: 97.) '[R]ational egoism is not present-biased, because it assigns equal importance to benefits and harms of equal magnitude at different times in the agent's life.' (Brink 1997: 98.)

Defenders of rational egoism must defend its asymmetrical treatment of time and persons. Why do I have more reason to make a sacrifice now for the benefit of my future self than to make a sacrifice now for your present benefit? Brink argues that this asymmetry can be justified by a 'compensation principle', the principle that it is unreasonable to make uncompensated sacrifices. If I make a sacrifice for you, then I may receive no compensation. But if I make a sacrifice for my future self, I receive the benefits of that sacrifice (eventually) and so I am fully compensated for making the sacrifice. It is crucial to this defence of rational egoism that the sacrificer is the beneficiary of the sacrifice. According to stage theory, one stage makes a sacrifice for the benefit of another, and appears to receive no compensation for doing so. In contrast, if the extended four-dimensional thing is the agent and bearer of reasons, then she is both sacrificer and beneficiary, and rational egoism looks safe. If Brink is correct, then stage theory is incompatible with rational egoism.

But is he correct? It rather depends upon the formulation of the compensation principle, the claim that it is unreasonable to make uncompensated sacrifices. We might claim that it is unreasonable for a person to make a sacrifice unless that same person receives compensation. This principle supports rational egoism even if stage theory is true, because stage theory allows that distinct stages can be the same person as one another. Alternatively, we might claim that it is unreasonable for a person to make a sacrifice unless the very stage which makes the sacrifice receives compensation. Then, given stage theory, this principle would not support rational egoism, the idea that it is rational for me to make present sacrifices for my future interests.

---

[22] This doctrine of presentism is entirely distinct from the ontological doctrine of presentism about time which I mentioned briefly in Chapter 1.

But only the first version of the compensation principle is at all plausible. Drawing on Henry Sidgwick (1907: 418–19 and 498), Brink defends the compensation principle by citing considerations about what it is to be a person, about the essentially forwards- and backwards-looking elements of being a person, and of personal desires, intentions, and so on.

[P]art of what it is for me to be a distinct, temporally extended person is for me to have a particular perspective on the world that displays a concern for my past and future self that is not proportional to the impersonal value of my activities. But then part of what it is for me to be a separate person is for me to be unwilling to sacrifice my interests without appropriate compensation. (Brink 1997: 105.)

The compensation principle is based upon considerations of persons and their persistence through time, a phenomenon which stage theorists explain by invoking relations between distinct stages. So it is appropriate to frame the stage theory version of the compensation principle in terms of being the same person, instead of identity, where these come apart. Stage theory does not undermine rational egoism (nor does it lend extra support to that view).

We have seen that, contrary to what is usually assumed, there are no particular problems for the view that it is instantaneous stages which satisfy both ordinary predicates and the predicate 'is a person'. Moreover, stage theory can explain the rational nature of concern for one's future self as well as any other theory of persistence can. Indeed, the fact that, at any moment, my present properties, including my goals and interests, are determined in part by the properties of my past and future selves, may reinforce the special nature of my concern for myself, at least in the near future (Shoemaker 1999). It is time now to investigate what makes certain things my past and future selves, to ask what binds stages together.

3

Sticking Stages Together

Here I am again, sitting on the very same chair as yesterday, looking through the very same window at the very same trees. According to stage theory, when I talk about the chair at different times, I am talking about different objects, different stages. Even perdurance theorists think that, although the chair exists at different times, it does so not by reappearing in its entirety but by having different temporal parts at different times. Both stage theory and perdurance theory contrast with endurance theory, according to which the chair and I are wholly present whenever we exist.

Perdurance and stage theorists populate the world with stages, and with collections or sums of those stages. Some collections correspond to the careers of everyday objects: there is the (I hope) long series of stages which corresponds to my life, and the fairly long series of stages which corresponds to the 'life' of this chair. What's special about those series? According to perdurance theory, I am identical to the sum of the stages in 'my series', and the chair is identical to the sum of the stages in 'its series'. According to stage theory, each of the stages in 'my series' is a person, each of them is me at a different moment. Similarly, each of the stages in 'the chair's series' is a chair, partly because it is surrounded fore and aft by stages which are chairs.

What goes for me and my chair goes for you too. According to perdurance theory you are identical to the sum of your stages; according to stage theory each of your stages is a person, is you. But what, if anything, binds your stages together to make a person? According to perdurance theory, each of *your* stages is a temporal part of a person, and each of *my* stages is a temporal part of a person. Yet we don't think that a random assortment of your stages and mine together form a person. Consider the collection made up of your stages at weekends, together with my stages on week days. The sum of *that* collection of stages isn't a person. Moreover, the sum of your weekend stages (you-at-weekends) isn't a person, either.

According to perdurance theory, some series of stages form persisting people, some series form persisting chairs, and some series don't form anything interesting, like the mixed-up collection of your stages and mine. Similarly, stage theory has it that some stages are 'the same person' as each other, like the members of 'my' series, other stages are 'the same chair' as each other, whereas other stages, the members of other more mixed-up series, do not stand in any such interesting relations to one another. What distinguishes the interesting, chair-forming, or person-forming collections of stages from the less interesting, mixed-up, or incomplete collections?

This is a pressing question—I have already invoked the notion of 'suitable relations' between stages in my exposition of stage and perdurance theories. Without some such notion, the theories would be seriously incomplete. For example, I needed to explain how a brief stage could satisfy a lingering predicate like 'is conscious', or 'is travelling to Vienna', or a historical predicate like 'originated on a banana tree'. I said that stages satisfy such predicates by standing in suitable relations to earlier and later stages which instantiate appropriate properties, like *being on a banana tree*. The restriction is crucial: the properties of the past stage have implications only for a certain restricted class of later stages, those which are suitably related to it.

I also invoked suitable relations between stages when accounting for diachronic counting, and when discussing names; the name 'Katherine' is inherited by those stages which are the same person as my present stage, stages which stand in suitable relations to my present stage. Which stages those are, which stages were me, and which will be me, is a matter of practical interest to me—I go to the supermarket today, to ensure that certain future stages will not go hungry, whilst I make no provision for the vast majority of future stages.

A restricted notion of 'suitable relations' is crucial if stage theory is to be plausible, and the same goes for perdurance theory—only suitably related stages can form an ordinary perduring thing. Endurance theorists, on the other hand, face no equivalent challenge. The transtemporal relation in question, according to endurance theorists, is just the relation of identity. Past and future objects are relevant to past- and future-tense predications about this tennis ball just in case they are identical to this very tennis ball. Nothing else needs to be said, and in this respect endurance theory is simpler than either stage or perdurance theory. Perdurance and stage theorists have extra work to do. In the present chapter I will discuss the nature of the suitable relations between stages, relations which underpin our talk about persisting objects, including ourselves. In doing so I will rarely distinguish between stage and perdurance theories, since most of what I say applies equally to both theories. Moreover, the reader will find few criticisms of endurance theory in this chapter. The main role of the chapter is to show that perdurance and stage theories are adequate theories of persistence, genuine rivals to endurance theory.

So what relations hold between the temporal parts of a single perduring object? In stage theory terms, what relations hold between stages which are the same object? A naïve response would be that the most important relations are those of similarity. The tennis ball tomorrow is the same ball as the tennis ball today because of the similarity between the two objects. But of course there are many tennis balls tomorrow which are qualitatively very similar to this present tennis ball, even though most of them are not the same ball as this ball. Indeed, if I dunk the tennis ball into a can of paint, then relying solely upon qualitative similarity would lead an observer to make the wrong judgement about the persistence of the ball. Tomorrow's purple tennis ball is less like its earlier green self than are many other green balls tomorrow.

Introducing a requirement of spatio-temporal continuity helps. A certain ball tomorrow is spatio-temporally continuous with the tennis ball I have in my hand right now. We could in principle trace out a continuous tennis ball-filled region between the present object and the future object. But such continuity will not always guarantee the persistence of a single object. Consider a cauldron of porridge. We could trace out a continuous porridge-filled region, moving from one side of the cauldron to the other over time. But this does not guarantee that we have been following the career of a single blob of porridge, instead of highlighting different blobs at different times.

What relations underpin the persistence of a single object may depend upon what kind of object is in question. Debate is intense about whether the relations which hold between two stages of the same person are always the same as the relations which hold between two stages of the same human organism, for example. To investigate such relations is to search for 'persistence conditions' or 'criteria of identity through time' for things of various kinds. I will not undertake this detailed task; instead, in this chapter I will discuss various more abstract questions about suitable relations between stages.[1]

---

[1] Important work on these issues includes Hirsch (1982; 1993) and Wiggins (1967; 1980).

In earlier sections of the chapter, I will discuss a thought experiment—the rotating disc—which is supposed to tell in favour of endurance theory, for it has been thought to show that persistence through time cannot be reduced to relations between stages or temporal parts. I will argue that the 'suitable relations' which underpin the persistence of ordinary things are non-supervenient, which is to say that whether or not two stages are suitably related is not entirely determined by the intrinsic properties of those two stages, nor even by those intrinsic properties plus spatio-temporal relations between the stages. But non-supervenient relations are unmysterious, and the rotating disc does not favour endurance theory.

Stages which are stages of the same ordinary object stand in special relations to one another. What about series of stages which do not stand in such relations to one another, like the series which is made up of your weekend stages together with my weekday stages? Does such a collection have a sum, does it form a larger, temporally extended object, or is it merely a collection of individual stages? In later sections of this chapter I will be investigating the status of 'unnatural' series of stages, from both a stage theory and a perdurance theory point of view.

So this chapter has two main aims. One is to address the rotating disc argument, and thereby to say something about the suitable relations which are crucial to perdurance and stage theories of persistence. In these earlier sections, I will treat perdurance and stage theories on a par, for the target argument is perceived to be a threat to both theories equally. Because of this, I will help myself to talk about stages *of* persisting objects. But this should not be taken too literally: the stage theory view is that stages are bananas, tennis balls, and so on, not parts of those things.

The second aim of the chapter is to consider the distinction between ordinary and 'mixed-up' or 'incomplete' series of stages, and to explore some differences between stage theory and perdurance theory on this issue. In particular, I will ask whether the difference between ordinary and non-ordinary series of stages is merely a difference in our attitudes to different series, or whether our attitudes reflect some deep distinction in the world. This returns us to questions about conventionalism and realism like those I raised in the introduction—in what sense is it up to us and our concepts whether or not a person can survive into an irreversible coma?

3.1 Non-supervenient Relations

What sorts of relations hold between stages of the same object? Many relations are wholly determined by the intrinsic properties of the relata. If height is an intrinsic property, then relative height is one of these relations: whether Jill is taller than Jack is wholly determined by their heights. Other relations seem at first not to be wholly determined by the intrinsic properties of the relata, but can in fact be analysed in terms of intrinsic properties once additional places in the relation are recognized. Whether Jill is closer to average human height than Jack is not wholly determined by their intrinsic properties, but it seems likely that it *is* wholly determined by the intrinsic properties of Jill, Jack, and the other human beings.

Other relations, however, are not wholly determined by the intrinsic properties of the relata, not even when we include 'hidden' relata. The relation of being a certain distance apart is like this. The distance between Jill and Jack is not wholly determined by their intrinsic properties: there could be exact intrinsic replicas of Jill and Jack who were further apart. Their separation is not determined by purely intrinsic properties even if we take space–time points to be 'hidden' relata, for Jill's being located at point P is not wholly determined by the intrinsic properties of Jill and of P. So facts about such spatio-temporal relations between objects are not determined by facts about the intrinsic properties of their relata: such relations are 'non-supervenient'.[2]

Paul Teller suggests that non-supervenient relations of a different kind can explain otherwise mysterious connections between quantum objects (Teller 1986, 1989). More-or-less simultaneous measurements on pairs of spatially separated photons give results which cannot be explained by the intrinsic states of the particles just before measurement. This might be evidence of a near-instantaneous causal connection between the intrinsic properties of the two photons. Teller prefers to account for the correlations by positing a relation between the particles which is non-supervenient, in the sense explained above. Unlike the relation of separation, this is not a straightforward spatio-temporal relation, and in what follows I shall use the term 'non-supervenient relation' to refer to non-spatio-temporal non-supervenient relations,

---

[2] We have already encountered non-supervenient relations, in Chapter 1, where I considered the different relations which might hold between objects and times according to the relations-to-times solution to the problem of change.

like those Teller discusses. I will argue that there are non-supervenient relations between stages which are stages of the 'same' object, or, in perdurance theory terms, between temporal parts of persisting objects.

3.2 The Homogeneous Disc Argument: Exposition

Imagine a perfectly homogeneous disc, made of smooth stuff not atomistic matter.[3] For every moment, record all the information about the state of the world at that moment, but without recording information about relations between objects which are wholly present at different moments. Call this record the 'holographic representation' of the world.[4] Now, the holographic representation will reveal that at every moment there is a homogeneous disc in a particular spot, but it will not reveal whether that disc is rotating about a vertical axis through its centre. Yet its rate of rotation seems to be an intrinsic property of the disc. So the persisting disc seems to have an intrinsic property which is not determined by the intrinsic properties of its instantaneous stages. I think that the best response to this homogeneous disc argument is to accept that there are non-supervenient relations between stages. There are other possible responses to the argument, and I shall discuss these below.

If the homogeneous disc argument is successful, then it tells against the doctrine of Humean Supervenience, according to which 'all there is to the world is a vast mosaic of local matters of particular fact, just one little thing and then another', together with spatio-temporal relations between these 'local qualities' (Lewis 1986c: ix–x). If, as I suggest, there are non-supervenient relations between the stages of a single persisting object, these non-supervenient relations hold independently of the local matters of particular fact and spatio-temporal relations which are supposed to determine what goes on in the world. Humean Supervenience is at stake in the rotating disc argument, and for this reason there have been various attempts to resist the argument. Before considering different non-Humean responses to the argument, I will first defend the argument against a variety of Humean objections.

---

[3] The argument is published in Armstrong (1980) and was the subject of lectures by both Kripke and Armstrong during the 1970s.

[4] The term 'holographic' is supposed merely to indicate the richness of the representation; no closer analogy to real holograms is intended.

3.3 The No-difference Objection

The argument supposes that there are two possible worlds, discernible only in that one contains a rotating homogeneous disc, whilst the other contains a stationary homogeneous disc. The argument is that a certain kind of record, a 'holographic representation', could not capture the difference between these two possible worlds. The holographic representation records all and only the information about the world as it is at every moment, without recording information about relations between objects existing at different moments. The argument is supposed to establish that there are facts about the world which cannot be captured by such a moment-by-moment representation.

The no-difference objection to the homogeneous disc argument is the claim that, contrary to supposition, there *is* no difference between these two possible discs, and thus, *a fortiori*, there is no difference which goes uncaptured by the holographic representation. The claim is not that both discs are stationary, for it would be arbitrary to pick out zero as the common value of angular velocity. Rather, the claim must be that, for a homogeneous disc in such circumstances, there can be *no fact of the matter* as to whether it is rotating. This option—biting the bullet—is perhaps the most attractive for the defender of Humean Supervenience. The holographic representation records all the Humeanly acceptable facts; if those facts do not determine facts about rotation in such peculiar situations, then there are no facts about rotation in such situations. There is nothing incoherent, I think, about this response, but it has some peculiar consequences.

If there is no fact of the matter about whether a given disc is rotating, then there is no fact of the matter about what would have happened if someone had touched the disc, or had splashed paint onto it. For each disc, it is true that if someone had measured the angular velocity of that disc, then she would have obtained some determinate result. But in neither case is there some determinate result that would have been obtained had someone measured the angular velocity of the disc. The result of any possible measurement of angular velocity is undetermined.

The same goes for counterfactual measurements of indeterministic-ally evolving quantities (Redhead 1987: 92–5). Wearing green trousers, I record the determinate time, t_1, at which an atom indeterministically decays. If I had performed the experiment in red trousers, I would also have obtained a determinate result, but there is no fact of the matter as to what it would have been, despite the apparent irrelevancy of my trousers. The class of possible worlds indiscernible up until t_1 from the actual world, except in the matter of my trousers, contains worlds in which the atom decays at t_1, but also worlds in which it does not. The time of decay is an indeterministic matter, so nothing which happens before t_1 makes the atom decay at t_1 or prevents it from decaying at t_1.

Where there is indeterminism, such indeterminacy about counter-factual measurements is unmysterious. But what of the discs? The no-difference objection supposes that, for any homogeneous disc, a measurement of angular velocity *would* give a determinate result, but that there is no fact of the matter as to what that result would be. Yet neither rotation nor measurement of the disc is supposed to be an indeterministic process. This indeterminacy is rather peculiar, to say the least.

Moreover, the no-difference objector must allow that if the disc *had* been measured, then it *would have had* a determinate angular velocity, even before the measurement. If she denies this back-tracking counterfactual, and supposes that measurement would have created new determinacy, then she produces a bizarre classical analogue of the quantum measurement problem. So whether a homogeneous disc has a determinate rate of rotation at a given moment counterfactually depends upon whether that rate is measured at any time in the future. Recall that, in this context, a 'measurement' need not involve any con-scious observer, or special apparatus. Any event which makes the disc slightly inhomogeneous—the landing of a speck of dust on the disc, for example—would give the disc a determinate rate of rotation for all time.[5]

I have been considering this strange indeterminacy for the disc, but matters are even worse for wedges or segments of the disc. A segment has determinate rotation or rest if and only if the others do too. Whether or not a particular segment has a rate of rotation at all, whether or not there is a fact of the matter as to where that segment is in the future, depends upon whether the rate of rotation of any *other*

---

[5] Kripke argues that the same problems arise even for inhomogeneous discs: why should we suppose that the disc and speck are both rotating, rather than just the speck? I shall ignore this complication, which reinforces the rotating disc argument which I am presently defending.

segment is measured, upon whether a speck of dust ever falls upon another segment.[6]

What is the appeal of Humean Supervenience—what makes it worth denying that there are facts of the matter about rotation for homogeneous discs? One motivation is parsimony, the thought that if it is unnecessary to believe in anything beyond the Humean facts, then we should not do so. Of course, we cannot use this familiar form of argument unless we agree about what it is necessary to believe in. I have suggested that it is necessary to believe in something beyond the Humean facts, in order to avoid the odd consequences of supposing that there are no facts about rotation for homogeneous discs, but any such argument is hostage to the possibility that someone will simply accept the 'odd' consequences of the position.

3.4 Holographic Difference Objections

The homogeneous disc argument attempts to show that there can be differences between worlds without differences in their holographic representations. I have just rejected the suggestion that there is no real difference between the two worlds in question, that there could be worlds which simply failed to determine facts about rotation. The second type of objection is that there *is* a difference between the two holographic representations after all, one which underpins the difference in facts about rotation. I will consider, in turn, the suggestions that the representations can capture differences in angular velocity, differences in causes of rotation, and differences in effects of rotation between the two discs.

3.4.1 *Differences in Angular Velocity*

The difference in angular velocity between the two discs allegedly goes unregistered by the holographic representations, but why not simply include instantaneous angular velocities in the representations?[7] The holographic representation, as I defined it, includes all and only those

---

[6] Craig Callender (2001) suggests that a suitably Humean account of laws of nature can account for the way in which facts about rotation can depend upon facts about other objects, or about the future.

[7] Dean Zimmerman's discussion of this issue is detailed and helpful (Zimmerman 1998).

facts which can be recorded without recording facts about relations between objects wholly existing at different times. Can't we include the instantaneous velocity of a disc-segment without entailing anything about objects existing at other moments?

Prima facie, angular velocity is excluded from the holographic representation on the following grounds. To say that something is stationary, for example, is to say that at the next moment it will be in the same place. To say that a disc-segment is rotating at a certain rate is to say something about where it will be at future moments. Wesley Salmon cautions us that

[i]t is important to note . . . that this notion [of instantaneous velocity] is defined by a limit process, so the value of the velocity at an instant depends logically upon what happens at neighboring instants . . . Although instantaneous velocity does characterize motion at an instant, it does so by means of implicit reference to what goes on at neighboring times. (Salmon 1970: 24.)

To include angular velocity in the holographic representation is to reject Salmon's claim that attributions of velocity involve 'implicit reference to what goes on at neighboring times'. There are two main motivations for rejecting Salmon's claim, but I shall argue that neither is compelling. The first concerns Zeno-type paradoxes, the worry that if we cannot attribute instantaneous velocity to objects considered as they are at a moment, then we cannot explain how motion is possible. The second thought is that the possession of a certain instantaneous angular velocity by a segment at a moment does not entail anything *categorical* about objects at other times, for there may be all sorts of accelerations and forces at play. To say that something has zero velocity is to say only that it will be in the same position a moment later *if* no net forces act upon it. I shall deal in turn with these motivations for including instantaneous angular velocity in the holographic representation.

The Zeno worry is as follows. We must be able to attribute instantaneous velocity to objects regardless of what goes on at other times, else we could never distinguish between stationary and moving objects, which would be absurd. I agree that this result would be absurd, but I *can* distinguish stationary from moving objects: I allow that we *can* attribute instantaneous velocity to objects, and I certainly do not claim that things are always instantaneously at rest. The existence of instantaneous angular velocity is not at question here, merely its admissibility to the holographic representation.

Perhaps this seems disingenuous. After all, I claim that to attribute angular velocity to a disc-segment at a moment is to say something about other times. Were a stage of the segment not surrounded before-and-after by other stages, then there would be no fact of the matter as to whether it was rotating. But this does not entail that 'really' the stage has no determinate rate of rotation when it *is* surrounded by other stages. Were this table-leg not appropriately connected to other legs and to a table-top, it would not be part of a table. But this does not entail that 'really' the leg is not part of a table when it *is* thus connected. To think otherwise is mere prejudice against relations, a prejudice which begs the question in this context. My claim that velocity is a matter of relations between objects existing at different times does not downgrade or ignore velocity. Nor does it entail that everything has an instantaneous velocity of zero.

We have seen something like this already, in Chapter 2. Recall that, according to stage theory, satisfying a sortal predicate like 'is a banana' is partly a relational matter. A single isolated stage could not be a banana, because in order to be a banana a stage must be suitably related to other stages with appropriate properties. Discovering something about the nature of that 'suitable relation' is the business of this chapter. According to stage theory, what it takes to be a banana, and what it takes to have an instantaneous velocity are both relational matters, but no less real for all that.

The second argument for including angular velocity in the holographic representation runs as follows. An instantaneous angular velocity, of course, has effects on displacement, consequences for later stages of the object. But we should not *identify* an instantaneous angular velocity with its effects on displacement, since these effects will depend upon whether any net forces are acting. An instantaneous velocity, angular or linear, is a disposition, which produces different behaviour under different circumstances. We should not mistake the disposition for its particular, contingent display, and the disposition itself may be included in the holographic representation.

I agree that there is both less and more to instantaneous angular velocity than the actual spatio-temporal relations between successive stages. Less, because these relations are a function of applied forces as well as initial velocity. More, because the instantaneous angular velocity also grounds counterfactual conditionals of the form 'if a net force F had been applied to the disc then . . .' But these conditionals concern what goes on at other times, even if they say nothing categorical. Classical mechanics is the device we use for establishing such conditionals, which relate locations at different times to net forces applied, given initial velocity. Take a particular disc-segment stage. The positions of various future stages depend upon the position of that initial stage, in a way conditioned by net forces acting and by the initial velocity. To attribute instantaneous velocity to the present stage is to say something partial and conditional about certain future stages, and not about others. It is to say something about how future states of a persisting object will vary according to the forces which apply.

Michael Tooley (1988) has an interesting alternative account of instantaneous velocity, but even Tooleyan velocities are ineligible for inclusion in the holographic representation.[8] He surveys different possible accounts of velocity, and concludes that there are two principal contenders. The first is a Russellian view, according to which velocity is a limit notion, the rate of change of position of an object. This is the kind of account towards which Salmon gestures in the quotation I gave above. It is clear that the Russellian view makes instantaneous velocity inadmissible to the holographic representation. Tooley offers an alternative account of velocity, according to which velocity is a theoretical quantity. It is whatever plays the role accorded to velocity by the laws of motion. This account is 'in a sense, along Russellian lines, *except that* it treats velocity as a theoretical property of an object at a time, and one that is *causally related* to an object's position at different times, rather than as a logical construction out of them' (Tooley 1988: 237). Could this kind of instantaneous velocity be included in the holographic representation?

I am sympathetic to the idea that velocity is something that interacts with applied forces and initial position to determine future position, that velocity thus has a causal role. Nevertheless, as I argued above, velocity is not an intrinsic property of stages. Velocity interacts with applied forces to determine future positions, but future positions of what? The velocity of a given stage helps determine the positions of certain future stages, and not of others. Certain futures stages are such that *those very stages* would have had different locations had the present stage had a different velocity. Zimmerman makes a related point when he says that the fact that Tooley's velocity is abstracted from the laws of motion makes it unsuitable for inclusion in the holographic

---

[8] See Zimmerman (1998) for further discussion.

representation, for those laws of motion presuppose facts about persistence (Zimmerman 1998, 1999; Lewis 1999*b*).

Again, it helps to imagine an isolated stage. Such a stage could not have a Tooleyan velocity, even though Tooleyan velocity is not identified with rate of displacement. In such a case it would be undefined what the Tooleyan velocity was, since the laws of motion for persisting objects would not apply to the isolated stage. Angular velocity cannot be included in the holographic representation, for it is not an intrinsic property of stages, whether we see it in Russell's way, or in Tooley's way. So neither the Zeno worry nor the dispositional nature of velocity gives us reason to suppose that instantaneous angular velocity is admissible to the holographic representation. A specification of the angular velocity of a segment at a moment entails something about what goes on at other times, albeit something conditional, and thus is inadmissible to a holographic representation.

3.4.2 *Differences in Causes of Rotation*

There are, however, other ways of differentiating the holographic representation of the spinning-disc world from that of the stationary-disc world, by including either the causes or the effects of rotation. Both Harold Noonan and Denis Robinson remark that there must have been some cause of the difference between the two discs (Noonan 1988: 96; Robinson 1989: 405–6). This interaction between the disc and some other object could be included in the holographic representation and could thus distinguish the representations of the two worlds.

There are two things to be explained: that each disc has a determinate rate of rotation, and that they have different rates of rotation. The latter may be explained by the fact that one disc was shoved when the other was not, *provided* we can assume that before the shove both discs had some determinate angular velocity. Shoving and dampening do not cause rotation or rest *per se*, just changes in rate of rotation. What, in the holographic representation, can explain the determinacy of the pre-shove state? It cannot be the subsequent shove, since only one of the two discs is shoved.[9]

Ultimately, something about the way in which the discs first came into existence must have made their initial angular velocity determinate,

---

[9] And recall my earlier objections to the idea that earlier velocity is made determinate by later measurement.

and thus amenable to change by subsequent applied forces. So, to be effective, the objection from causes must be that a homogeneous disc *could not* simply appear, or always have existed, but must rather have been produced by some holographically recordable process which determined its initial angular velocity.

Understanding the real form of the objection from causes makes it less plausible. It may seem obvious that if one disc were not given a distinguishing shove, then the two discs would have the same angular velocity. It is less obvious that, as the objector from causes must claim, a homogeneous disc could not simply appear or always have existed. But let us accept the objection, and suppose that there must have been some holographically recordable aspect of the production of the discs which gave them *determinate* initial angular velocities, and some simultaneous or subsequent difference in applied forces which gave them *different* angular velocities.

So the two worlds have different holographic representations. Nevertheless, there are facts about these worlds which go uncaptured even by these enriched holographic representations: we cannot identify the difference between the discs with the cause of that difference. Robinson makes a similar point, noting that, if we suppose everything to be captured in the holographic representation, then we must suppose that the result of any later measurement of angular velocity would be a direct causal consequence of the initial shove, since there are no intervening differences between the two discs. He calls this 'action at a (temporal) distance' (Robinson 1989: 406). 'Initial shove' differences do not capture the full difference between rotating and stationary discs. They make a historical difference between the discs at any moment, and a difference in counterfactual measurement results, but they leave an explanatory gap, since the former cannot explain the latter in any unmysterious way. If we accept the demand for explanation—and the Humean might not—then there is still something missing from the picture.

If we posit non-supervenient relations between the stages of a segment then we *can* explain how the results of any measurement performed on the disc right now are a direct consequence of the present state of the disc, not of its historical properties. The successive stages of a segment stand in non-spatio-temporal non-supervenient relations to one another. In conjunction with applied forces, spatiotemporal relations between these 'specially related' stages—and not those between other stages—determine the rate of rotation of the segment and thus the disc. So far as the holographic representation tells us, there are no present differences between the discs at any moment. But there are relational differences which do not show up in the representation. These differences are direct causes and explanations of the actual and counterfactual differences in measurement results. I can feel the disc moving because the stage I am touching is specially related to an earlier stage which was elsewhere, rather than to one which was here.

Teller introduced non-supervenient relations between distant elements of a quantum system instead of positing mysterious causal influences between these elements. Such influences would be mysterious principally because they appear to travel faster than light. Direct causal connections between the initial shove and the present measurement of rotation would not be mysterious in this respect. But there is a second, lesser mystery in the quantum case: any causal influence between the distant elements of the system appears to be transmitted directly, without any intervening disturbance. This mystery has a direct parallel in the homogeneous disc: if the holographic representation is complete, there is a direct causal influence between the initial shove and the later measurement result, without any intervening differences between the rotating and the stationary discs. Non-supervenient relations provide the required intervening differences.

The objection from causes is less plausible than it seemed, since it must suppose that differences in the holographic representation can explain why the discs have any determinate rate of rotation at all, as well as the difference in their rates of rotation. But even if we accept that there are such differences between the holographic representations of the two worlds, these alone cannot explain the direct consequences of, for example, touching the discs. I have shown how non-supervenient relations can be of assistance here. In a later section I will argue that, given that the holographic representation is incomplete, positing non-supervenient relations is not just one way of completing the picture, it is the best way.

3.4.3 *Differences in Effects of Rotation*

I am considering possible objections to the homogeneous disc argument, objections which attempt to differentiate between the two holographic representations. I have dismissed the suggestion that angular velocity be included in the representation, and I have limited the role of initial causes. Finally I want to consider differences in the holographic representations brought about by the effects, rather than the causes, of the rotational differences between the two discs.

There are differences between an object rotating and the same object stationary. If the coffee in a cup is rotating, it has a concave surface; stationary coffee is flat. Such differences in shape are admissible to the holographic representation, and might seem to distinguish the rotating from the stationary coffee without any need for non-supervenient relations or the like. The main problem with this response is that not all objects fit this pattern. We may take it that a concave cup of coffee is rotating, but an oblate object might be stationary or might be a rotating, bulging spherical object. Even regarding the coffee, we might think that there is nothing inconceivable about a stationary cup of coffee with a concave surface, nor, indeed, about rotating coffee with a flat surface. The difference between concavity and flatness happens to be correlated with the difference between rotation and rest, but this is a contingent matter, and should not be taken as constitutive of the difference between rotation and rest.

The adequacy of this response hinges upon the value of considering worlds unlike our own. In our world, concavity of coffee and rotation go along together: need we be concerned about possible worlds in which they come apart? I skirted a similar question above, when I agreed that we need not be concerned about perpetually existing or instantaneously created discs. More simply, we might question the relevance of stories about homogeneous discs to our actual atomistic world. The more we focus upon possible worlds very like our own, the less successful the homogeneous disc argument seems, and thus the less compelling non-supervenient relations may seem.

The defender of Humean Supervenience against non-supervenient relations cannot take this line, however. David Lewis acknowledges that the quantum situations Teller discusses may provide an empirical refutation of Humean Supervenience, but announces his determination to defend Humean Supervenience from attempted philosophical, or *a priori*, refutations (Lewis 1986c: xi ; 1994: 474). It would be *ad hoc* to invoke empirical considerations when they favour Humean Supervenience, whilst ignoring those which undermine the doctrine. Explanatory considerations provide another reason to take notice of other possible worlds, and to avoid identifying rotation with its contingent causes and effects. Otherwise, as we saw above, we are unable

to explain those effects, except by imagining that the result of measurement today is a direct causal consequence of a shove many years
ago. Part of what we hope for from a *measurement* result is that it be
correlated with some present feature of the object measured.

There is a third reason for acknowledging worlds in which rotating
coffee is flat, worlds in which discs appear out of thin air, or worlds in
which there are homogeneous discs. Although these worlds differ
from our own in various ways, they are nevertheless worlds in which
there is rotation and rest. The 'coffee' world is odd precisely because
coffee *rotates* there without becoming concave. Similarly, an object's
being atomistic is not a pre-condition of its rotating, and a disc's origins do not, in general, affect whether it can have a determinate rotation. So these worlds are relevant to our discussion of rotation. An
atomistic disc rotates in the same way as a smooth disc, although rotation is more easily detected in the former case, if we have a powerful
microscope to hand. If we agree that rotation is not determined by
intrinsic properties of stages in non-atomistic worlds, then we should
also accept this for our own world.

Craig Callender objects to this line of argument, saying that
although our notion of rotation may not tie it to any single effect of
rotation, we cannot reasonably suppose that there could be rotation
without any of the effects of rotation (Callender 2001). Not, at least,
without begging the question against Humean Supervenience, for
bare facts about rotation are inevitably non-supervenient. It is true
that those who have a prior commitment to Humean Supervenience
cannot accept that there could be differences in rotation without any
Humean differences. But for those who are undecided, it is perfectly
reasonable to suppose that there could be such differences in rotation.

First, such rotation need not be *undetectable*, rotation which cannot show up in Humeanly acceptable ways. The argument depends
only upon the possibility of *undetected* rotation. Second, the argument does not presuppose that there could be a single object which
was unaffected by whether or not it is rotating. Instead it supposes
only that there could be indistinguishable objects one of which was
rotating and the other not. That's to say, we need not accept that there
could be a sphere which did not bulge when it rotated. All we need
accept is that there could be a stationary oblate object and an oblate
object which would be spherical if it were not rotating, without there
being any non-Humean difference between these two things. The

presupposition of the rotating disc argument, though it rules out Humean Supervenience, is not so science-fictional as it might first seem.

3.5 Non-supervenient Relations, and Alternatives

The homogeneous disc argument is powerful, and is relevant to the actual world. In this section I want to show how non-supervenient relations can explain the phenomena highlighted by the homogeneous disc argument. I will also argue that these relations provide the best explanation of the phenomena, better than a range of alternatives. I claim that there are relations between the distinct stages of a persisting object which are not determined by the intrinsic properties of those stages. What motivates my claim? Opting for non-supervenient relations is the natural 'least move' in response to the homogeneous disc argument, since the holographic representation captures exactly those properties of the stages which underdetermine these relations.

Series of stages which are stages of the same object are distinguished from other series as follows. The state of a later stage depends, counterfactually and causally, upon the state of earlier stages, in a way in which it does not depend upon stages of other objects. Non-supervenient relations ground these dependencies. Seeing this allows us to spell out the connection between the rate of rotation of the disc and the nature of its segments. Any given stage of a disc segment is linked by special relations to some later stages, and not thus linked to others. If a stage is thus linked to stages in the same place at later moments, the disc is at rest; if it is not, the disc is rotating.

We saw earlier that an instantaneous velocity does not guarantee any later position, but that it entails certain conditionals about the relation of later position to applied net forces. I talked of an instantaneous velocity as a disposition of a persisting object, one which could be displayed in different ways under different conditions. We can now see non-supervenient relations between stages as determining *which* later stage is conditionally dependent upon the position and velocity of a given earlier stage. In short, I claim, non-supervenient relations account admirably for the phenomena highlighted by the homogeneous disc argument.

What are these non-supervenient relations? They are the relations, whatever they are, which underpin the relation of 'immanent causation' which holds between stages of the same object, and we can pick them out by their theoretical role. Do the relations necessarily underpin persistence and immanent causation, or could they play a different role in a world governed by different laws? There are two parts to this question. First, could the actual relations of immanent causation have held between stages of different objects? Second, could the non-supervenient relations have failed to underpin the relations which are actually the relations of immanent causation?

It certainly seems possible to imagine the relations of immanent causation holding between stages which are not spatio-temporally continuous—to imagine, for example, a banana's disappearing in one location and a qualitatively identical banana appearing in a different location. Would this be a world in which objects could move discontinuously, or a world in which the actual relations of immanent causation held between stages of different objects? I don't know what we should say about such a world: in the actual world we are guided by both spatio-temporal continuity and immanent causation (which takes in qualitative continuity and the like), so there is no clear answer about what we ought to do, or would do, if these came apart.

The second question was whether the non-supervenient relations necessarily underpinned the relations of immanent causation which transmit qualitative similarity, velocity and so on. Again, there seems to be no clear answer here, but this time because to get a clear answer we would need a clear account of causation, and the reducibility or otherwise of causal relations to non-causal relations. Indeed, this raises the question of why I have insisted upon non-supervenient relations, instead of merely saying that there are special causal relations between the different stages of a persisting object. I agree that there are 'special' causal relations between the earlier and later stages of a persisting object. But I claim that non-supervenient relations are needed in order to account for these causal relations. Consider, for example, some standard accounts of causation.

Regularity theorists claim that causation is nothing more than constant conjunction, in this case that the state of an earlier stage causes that of a later stage if and only if there is a regular correlation between states of these types. But our central problem is that, so far as intrinsic properties go, there *is* no correlation between the earlier and later stages of a particular segment which does not also hold between any arbitrary pair of stages of different segments. We accepted this when we accepted that rate of rotation was not captured by the holographic description.

The same problem arises for universals-based accounts of causation, at the other end of the metaphysical spectrum. Without non-supervenient relations, there are no universals exemplified by pairs of stages of a single segment that are not also exemplified by stages of different segments. Counterfactual accounts of causation say that a causal connection is exhausted by the counterfactuals it appears to ground. One advantage of non-supervenient relations is that they relieve any discomfort we may feel at the thought of 'bare' counterfactuals, grounded in no regularity or property of the object in question (Noonan 1988: 97). Furthermore, taking the 'special connection' between stages of a single object to be a matter of counterfactual dependence seems to get things the wrong way round. The later stage depends for its state upon that of the earlier *because* they are stages of the same object; because, according to me, they stand in a non-supervenient relation to one another.

Zimmerman argues that Humean accounts of causation are inadequate to account for the rotating disc (Zimmerman 1998). An account of causation is 'Humean' in the relevant sense if it says that there can be no causal difference without a non-causal difference. A Humean account need not be an austere regularity analysis of causation. The non-causal differences required for a causal difference may include differences in laws of nature, where laws of nature are construed in a metaphysically heavyweight manner, perhaps involving relations between universals. As we have seen, there are causal relations between certain pairs of stages (those which are stages of the same disc segment) which do not hold between other pairs of stages. And, unless we posit non-supervenient relations, there is no non-causal difference between these different pairs of stages. So, unless we posit non-supervenient relations, there seem to be causal differences without non-causal differences, and thus causation must be non-Humean.

If the rotating disc argument is sound, we face a dilemma: either there are non-supervenient relations between stages, as I have argued, or else causation is non-Humean. There are three reasons to favour the former option. First, I think we should be reluctant to draw general conclusions about the Humean or non-Humean nature of causation based upon consideration of the rather peculiar case of 'immanent' causation, causation between earlier and later stages of the same object. I prefer to conclude that *non*-causal relations between earlier and later stages of the same object are importantly different from the relations between distinct objects, or between stages of distinct objects. Second, the existence of non-supervenient relations *explains* why some stages are linked by immanent causation whilst others are not. In effect, this is just to reiterate the fact that if we posit non-supervenient relations, we can retain a Humean view of causation, the idea that causal facts should be explicable in terms of non-causal facts of one kind or another.[10]

Third, non-supervenient relations can account for the possibility of uncaused, or indeterministic rotation. I will explain this point by considering Denis Robinson's notion of 'second-order quasi-qualities having the character of vectors' (Robinson 1989: 406). These qualities guide the propagation of ordinary first-order qualities, yet they are allegedly intrinsic properties of stages, and are thus eligible for inclusion in the holographic representation. This differs from the suggestion that we include instantaneous angular velocity in the holographic representation. Robinson's qualities expand the holographic representation, supposedly filling the explanatory role I reserved for non-supervenient relations.

Douglas Ehring has a powerful objection to Robinson (Ehring 1997: 111–12). He considers a homogeneous disc which rotates indeterministically: its velocity and position at one moment are not fully determined by its previous velocity and position, and by applied forces. Then the actual velocity of the disc, the question of where a given segment is from one moment to the next, is underdetermined by Robinson's vector qualities, which have only a probabilistic influence on these quantities. Yet the disc still has a determinate angular velocity. So there is a further fact of the matter about velocity, over and above the vector qualities.[11]

Ehring's scenario distinguishes velocity from its causes, by supposing it to have an uncaused element. Robinson attempts to capture velocity by attributing extra intrinsic properties to stages, but at most these can capture the causes of velocity. Non-supervenient relations, on the other hand, escape Ehring's criticism. If a homogeneous disc were moving indeterministically, non-supervenient relations would still hold between earlier and later stages of a single segment, and not

---

[10] Zimmerman might argue that positing non-supervenient relations amounts to a refusal to give an informative criterion of identity over time for persisting objects. I will deal with this objection towards the end of this chapter.

[11] Tooley (1988: 244) denies that objects would have velocities at all under such circumstances.

between stages of different segments. These relations would ground probabilistic conditionals relating the earlier and later stages, just as they ground non-probabilistic conditionals in the deterministic case.

As we have seen, it is the intimate connection between earlier and later stages which explains measurement results whilst escaping objections from indeterminism. This may suggest the closest connection of all, that of identity. Perhaps the segment persists by enduring through time. This is certainly a possible response to the homogeneous disc argument, but not one we are forced to adopt. If objects have stages (or temporal parts), then those stages stand in non-supervenient relations to one another, but this is not to say that those stages are identical, either 'wholly' or 'partly'. Consideration of the rotating disc does not provide evidence either in favour or against endurance theory, because the disc can be accounted for either by accepting endurance theory, or else by rejecting endurance theory and accepting non-supervenient relations.

Some have thought that the rotating disc provides a metaphysical argument against perdurance theory. By extension, the disc might be perceived as a threat to stage theory, which shares many metaphysical presuppositions with perdurance theory. We have now seen that, provided we posit non-supervenient relations between stages, there is no reason to opt for endurance theory after consideration of the rotating disc.[12] Non-supervenient relations provide an alternative both to belief in Humean Supervenience, and to endurance theory. It is perfectly possible to believe in temporal parts or stages whilst rejecting Humean Supervenience.[13] Just as Teller's non-supervenient relations give an unmysterious sense to 'holism' in quantum mechanics, my use of non-supervenient relations provides an unmysterious sense in which different stages of a single object are connected without being identical. Notice that, although I have rejected Humean Supervenience in Lewis's sense, I have not denied that causation is Humean in Zimmerman's sense—I have not claimed that the causal does not supervene upon the non-causal. Instead, I have argued that the causal does not always

---

[12] Ehring's response to the homogeneous disc argument is to suppose that tropes persist without having temporal parts, and that this grounds rotation and so forth. Like scepticism about temporal parts of physical objects, Ehring's response is not forced upon us by the homogeneous disc (Ehring 1997).

[13] Sally Haslanger argues convincingly that the doctrine of Humean Supervenience does not entail that objects have temporal parts (Haslanger 1994). I have tried to show that objects may have temporal parts even though Humean Supervenience is false. If I have succeeded, then the link between Humean Supervenience and theories of persistence is broken.

depend upon non-causal *intrinsic* properties of stages, together with
the laws relating those properties.

3.6 Natural Objects

Stage theory focuses upon instantaneous stages, but, as we saw in
Chapter 2, we need a notion of 'suitable relations' between stages in
order to account for various features of our experience, and for our
ways of talking about objects. The historical and lingering predicates
satisfied by an instantaneous stage will depend upon the properties
of other stages to which it is suitably linked. It should by now be
apparent that these suitable relations will partly involve the non-
supervenient relations I have been discussing in this chapter. Take a
present banana; some past and future stages are more relevant to it
than others are. So some series of stages are in a sense more cohesive
than others, and these are series of stages linked by non-supervenient
relations. The rotating disc argument shows that, if rotation is an
objective matter, then there are objective differences between series of
stages which correspond to ordinary objects, and those which do not.
In the remainder of this chapter I will explore some consequences of
recognizing this objective difference.

   In his *Dividing Reality*, Eli Hirsch considers the differences between
apparently 'natural' and apparently 'unnatural' ways of dividing up
the world, at the level of individual objects, and also at the level of
properties (Hirsch 1993). His primary interest is in whether, if there
are natural divisions in reality, then our language and classification
systems *ought* to reflect those divisions. This is an interesting question, and Hirsch's discussion is impressive and subtle, but it is not my
main focus here. I will, however, borrow his taxonomy of different
approaches to divisions in reality.

   First, consider properties. We can think of properties as (at least)
associated with classes of particulars. Some classes seem to us to be
cohesive: the class of all green things, for example. Others seem less
cohesive: the class of all things which are either green or circular. Others
seem less cohesive still: the class which just contains this piece of paper,
my left ear, and the number 2. What, if anything, is the difference
between these more and less cohesive classes? Hirsch distinguishes
three different types of answer to this question, which he calls 'ontological inegalitarianism', 'elitist inegalitarianism', and 'egalitarianism'.

Ontological inegalitarianism is the idea that cohesive, or natural classes are associated with an extra kind of entity, one which unnatural classes simply lack. An ontological inegalitarian, then, might claim that certain natural classes correspond to universals, whilst unnatural classes do not. But ontological inegalitarians have difficulties with the fact that naturalness seems to come in degrees. Not every class of particulars is either perfectly natural or perfectly unnatural. The class of all things which are either green or circular, for example, does not seem to be perfectly natural, but it does seem more natural than the class which contains just this piece of paper, my left ear, and the number 2. Ontological inegalitarians claim that natural classes are associated with certain entities (universals) whilst unnatural classes are not. But either a class has a universal associated with it, or it does not, which seems to leave no space for a sliding scale of naturalness for classes.[14]

At the other end of the metaphysical scale, egalitarianism is the claim that there is no objective difference between natural and unnatural classes, that any perceived differences are grounded in human interests or the like. Finally, elitist inegalitarianism is a middle position, according to which natural and unnatural classes are objectively different from one another, but not because a natural class corresponds to an extra entity to which an unnatural class does not correspond. Perhaps naturalness is a primitive feature of certain classes and not of others. Or perhaps we can analyse naturalness in terms of similarity: if two objects are members of the same natural class, then this makes for a genuine similarity between them, whilst co-membership of an unnatural class adds nothing to their similarity.

Hirsch also discusses three analogous approaches to individual objects. Consider four-dimensional regions of space–time. Some of these seem to be the paths, or histories of objects, and others do not. Regions of the first kind we can call 'natural', and regions of the second kind 'unnatural'.[15] Ontological inegalitarians would claim that a natural region corresponds to an entity of some kind, whilst no unnatural region corresponds to an entity of that kind. The most obvious way to spell this out is as endurance theory. The temporal parts of a natural region are occupied successively by an enduring

---

[14] See Sider (1995) for further discussion of this issue.
[15] In this section I switch back and forth between talk of natural regions and talk of natural series of stages. I hope that this is not too irresponsible.

object, whilst an unnatural region is not completely occupied by any enduring object.

A perdurance theorist could also be an ontological inegalitarian. It is customary for perdurance theorists to be unrestricted mereologists, to believe that any two objects make up a third. The joint consequence of perdurance theory and unrestricted mereology is that every collection of temporal parts composes an object, and thus that there are very many persisting objects, only a small fraction of which are 'recognized' by us. However, a perdurance theorist could reject unrestricted mereology, and suppose that only certain collections of temporal parts have sums, that only certain, natural, regions of space–time are exactly occupied by objects, whilst others are not.

But, like ontological inegalitarianism about properties, both perdurance-based and endurance-based ontological inegalitarianism about individuals face problems arising from the fact that naturalness seems to come in degrees. Most objects seem to have some vagueness about their boundaries; there are regions of space–time about which it seems unclear whether they exactly contain a natural object. As we will see in the next chapter, an attractive way of accounting for this phenomenon is to say that it is unclear, or indeterminate, how natural a region has to be in order to count as containing an ordinary object. But this presupposes a sliding scale of naturalness for regions, which is difficult to understand if the naturalness of a region is supposed to consist in its being associated with an object.

In contrast to ontological inegalitarians, egalitarians about individuals claim that there is no objective difference between natural and unnatural regions, that any perceived difference simply reflects our priorities and interests. Quine may be an egalitarian of this sort, and it is a common conception that temporal parts theorists *must* be egalitarians. Goldman, drawing on evidence from cognitive science and arguing that unnatural objects exist, argues for a kind of projectivism about naturalness, combined with an error theory about our judgements that naturalness is an objective feature of some collections of stages (Goldman 1987).

But the rotating disc case causes problems for egalitarianism, as we have seen. Not all four-dimensional regions are created equal, for some contain series of stages bound together by the non-supervenient relations which determine the transmission of immanent causation, whilst others do not, and the former correspond to ordinary objects. More promising is some kind of elitist inegalitarianism, which acknowledges an objective difference between natural and unnatural regions, without claiming that natural regions are associated with objects whilst unnatural regions are not. Elitists about properties may take naturalness as primitive, or else attempt to analyse naturalness, perhaps in terms of similarity. What about naturalness for stage series?

I, of course, have argued that non-supervenient relations best account for what I am now calling 'naturalness' for series of stages. A natural series of stages is one whose members stand in non-supervenient relations to one another. But to claim this is not simply to take naturalness of series of stages as a primitive. Admittedly, there is something slightly mysterious in the notion of non-supervenient relations, but the notion is not empty—it is characterized by its theoretical role. I have claimed that there is no supervenient relation, no spatio-temporal and no Humean causal relation which can do the job, that non-supervenient relations are a breed apart from these. And I have offered the analogy with Teller's non-supervenient relations in quantum mechanics.

Dean Zimmerman argues that perdurance theorists are obliged to provide informative criteria of identity for natural persistents. My non-supervenient relations account might, on his view, not count as sufficiently informative. What am I obliged to provide, and why? Zimmerman says:

Since the properties of and relations among parts determine the intrinsic properties of wholes, and since being a persisting mass of K is intrinsic to things that have it, then—on a temporal parts account—being a persisting mass of K must supervene on the properties of and relations among the momentary temporal parts of any given mass of K. And the supervenience of *being some persisting K* implies that there is a necessary and sufficient condition of some sort that can be given in terms of intrinsic properties of momentary stages and relations among them. (Zimmerman 1997: 440.)[16]

Zimmerman cannot be asking under which circumstances some stages form an object since it is open to the stage or perdurance theorist to say that every series of stages forms some natural or unnatural object. Instead he is asking the stage or perdurance theorist to say something about which series of (K-)stages are natural. And of course I have done this: the answer is couched in terms of

---

[16] Note that Zimmerman assumes that being a persisting mass of K is neither a temporally nor a spatially maximal affair.

non-supervenient relations. Being a natural series supervenes upon properties of and relations between the stages in the series, so long as non-supervenient relations are allowed into the supervenience base. There are no grounds for demanding that the relations in question must reduce to intrinsic properties of the stages; after all, it is commonly thought that persistence is partly a matter of (non-supervenient) spatio-temporal relations between stages.[17] My analysis of naturalness is not overly mysterious, although nor is it reductive.

Is there, perhaps, an epistemic worry about non-supervenient relations? We cannot tell the velocity of a single stage simply by examining that stage alone. But that seems to be the right result: as I have already argued, an isolated stage would not have a velocity, not even a velocity of zero. What a thing is like depends in part upon its relations to other things. Non-supervenient relations provide a way of spelling out elitist inegalitarianism with respect to series of stages (or four-dimensional objects, in the context of perdurance theory). It is worth holding on to this middle ground between egalitarianism on the one hand, which flies in the face of the rotating disc argument, and ontological inegalitarianism on the other, which has problems if there are degrees of naturalness. In the remainder of this chapter I will spell out some useful consequences of recognizing an objective difference between natural and unnatural series of stages, advantages that accrue equally to stage theorists and to perdurance theorists who are willing to recognize an objective difference between natural and unnatural perduring things.

3.7 Change

Non-supervenient relations, by marking out objectively natural series of stages, allow us to quell any remaining worries about the stage theory account of change. Mellor, for example, argues that perdurance theory, and by extension, stage theory, is unsatisfactory, since it does not allow for genuine change (Mellor 1998: ch. 8). Genuine change, according to Mellor, is the possession of incompatible properties at different times by *one and the same object*, whereas both perdurance

---

[17] Indeed, Zimmerman motivates his requirement by arguing that the intrinsic properties of spatial wholes supervene upon the intrinsic properties of their spatial parts, with the (crucial) exception of emergent properties, if there are any.

theory and stage theory see change as the possession of different properties by different things (different temporal parts or different stages, respectively). When I grow taller, it is because one of my parts or stages is one metre tall, whilst a *different* part or stage is two metres tall.

As I argued in Chapter 1, we need not allow endurance theorists to write their theory into the very definition of change; from alternative points of view, genuine change is the possession of different properties by different stages of a single object, or by different temporal parts of a single object. These alternative accounts of change are satisfactory, however, only if they can accommodate a distinction between change in a single object, and differences between successive objects. To take Mellor's example, my having a different blood group from a long-dead ancestor does not constitute a change in the world, for in this case no single object has the two different blood groups. How does this variation in blood groups between me and my ancestor differ from the variation in heights between my earlier and my later parts or stages?

Endurance theory marks a clear distinction between a difference between my ancestor and me on the one hand, and a change in me on the other: the former but not the latter involves two distinct objects. Stage theory and perdurance theory must distinguish certain series of stages or temporal parts from others, marking a distinction between stages/parts of the same object, and stages/parts of different objects. A few might see this as a purely conventional distinction, claiming that there is no deep difference between a change in me and a difference between my ancestor and me. But the rotating disc shows that in some cases at least, non-supervenient relations mark an objective difference between natural and unnatural series of stages. Just as individuals which share natural properties are genuinely similar, a natural series of stages displays genuine continuity, as opposed to disruption.

Non-supervenient relations can ground the distinction between genuine change and mere difference over time between different objects. Genuine change is the possession of incompatible properties by stages which are linked by non-supervenient relations. My present stage is not so linked to any stage of my ancestor, which is why the difference in our blood groups is not a change in anything. But I am so linked to my earlier stages, which is why my being taller than those earlier stages is a genuine change. Indeed, we can usefully recall that stage theory comes closer to meeting endurance theory intuitions about change than perdurance theory does. After all, according to stage theory, I am not an extended four-dimensional thing, I am just my present stage, and I used to be each of my earlier stages. The things which satisfy the predicate 'is a person' are the very things that possess the incompatible height properties. This contrasts with the perdurance theory account according to which I am the sum of all those momentary things.

Moreover, stage theory marks a clear distinction between changes in persisting objects and temporal variation in events. An event, a concert for example, is a four-dimensional temporally extended thing. If it is first quiet and then loud, it has an early temporal part which is quiet and an later temporal part which is loud. This differs from the stage theory account of what it takes for *me* to be first quiet and then loud. Such an account talks of persons and not their temporal parts. First there is a stage which is me, and which is quiet. Then there is a stage which is me, and which is loud. Of course, the difference between stage theory and perdurance theory may be only a matter of semantics, but stage theory seems better to satisfy certain intuitions.[18] Those who wish to distinguish between changes in objects and temporal variation in events can thus find satisfaction in stage theory where perdurance theory disappoints.

3.8 Reference

In order to account for the rotating disc, and to provide an objective grounding for change, I have invoked a difference between natural and unnatural series of stages, and underpinned this with the notion of non-supervenient relations. This distinction between natural and unnatural series also helps explain how it is possible for us to refer to things as we do. For stage theory to be viable it must be the case that, in general, when we refer to a stage we thereby privilege a certain collection of stages which provide truth conditions for historical and lingering predications, and which are eligible to be the referent of the same term as it is used to talk about different times. Recall that in Chapter 2 I briefly discussed assigning the name 'Billy' to a banana. The namer is confronted by a banana, a stage, but somehow attaches

---

[18] See Chapter 2 for further discussion of the differences between stage and perdurance theories, and Chapter 1 for the endurance theory distinction between processes and persisting things.

the name in a way which allows us to use the name to talk about different stages.

Perdurance theory must provide for something similar. When a name is attached to a persisting object, there must be something which makes it determinate *which* persisting object is being named, how to trace the object backwards and forwards from the present temporal part. When a dubbing event takes place, the present stage or part is a stage or part of an enormous number of different series and four-dimensional objects, yet somehow we seem able to name a single one of these. My account of this can be anticipated. It seems that series of suitably related stages attract reference, are eligible targets of dubbing. An analogous point is perhaps more familiar from Putnam's account of natural kind terms. According to Putnam, natural kind terms are attached to kinds via dubbing of a sample, or exemplar of the kind. But any sample belongs to very many different groups of objects. It is important for the viability of Putnam's account that some groups are more eligible for reference than others, that the world itself cuts down the number of kinds we might be intending to dub (Putnam 1975).

The role I am suggesting for naturalness in making reference determinate can be seen as an externalist version of the Fregean dictum that part of the sense of a proper name is a criterion of identity for the thing in question. Here is Dummett:

Merely to know that a name has as its referent an object with which we are confronted, or which is presented to us in some way, at a particular time is not yet to know what object the name stands for: we do not know this until we know, in Frege's terminology 'how to recognize the object as the same again', that is, how to determine, when we are later confronted with an object or one is presented to us, whether or not it should be taken to be the same object. (Dummett 1981*b*: 545.)

It is notoriously difficult to make this 'recognize' plausible when it is read epistemologically (Lowe 1989*a*: ch. 2). And it is also remarkably difficult to come up with adequate and explicit criteria of identity through time for objects of various kinds (persons are a notable case in point, as, of course, are disc segments). But the externalist version of this principle seems entirely plausible. If we are to refer to a persisting thing, there must be something that determines when we are confronted with the same thing again (however 'same' is spelt out), even if we cannot tell when that has happened. Non-supervenient relations, by marking out suitable referents, can play this role.

For David Lewis, one reason that natural *properties* are important is that they have a role in making language and thought determinate: principles of charity or humanity tell us to attribute natural properties to predicates wherever possible, and this breaks any under-determination as to what our predicates pick out (Lewis 1983*c*; 1984). An analogous role can be played by naturalness in series of stages, by the objective distinction between natural and unnatural persistents. If Lewis is correct about predicates, then the same will be true of individual names: we should charitably assume that natural, not unnatural objects are the referents of names and other referring devices.

3.9 Personal Persistence

The message of this chapter has been that both perdurance and stage theories can and ought to recognize close connections between parts/stages of the same object, and that they can do so without taking that close connection to be the relation of identity, as the endurance theorist does. Neither perdurance theorists nor stage theorists are compelled to believe that the relationship between me at present (or my current part) and me in the future is simply on a par with the relationship between me at present and my children in the future, or indeed anyone else in the future or in the past. Indeed, this egalitarian position is inadvisable, given the rotating disc argument.

Derek Parfit offers a 'reductive' account of personal identity in terms of psychological continuity between person-stages. He thinks this view of personal identity breaks down the boundaries between the self and others, that there is little reason for me to care more about myself in the far future (were I to live long enough and change in enough ways) than about you right now (Parfit 1984: 304). This is because such psychological continuity is non-transitive, and seems to be a matter of degree. It may be (although I doubt it) that special considerations about the persistence of persons compel us to adopt Parfit's position. But not all stage or perdurance accounts of persistence can be labelled 'reductionist' or egalitarian. To deny endurance theory is not to believe that all series of stages are on a par, nor that facts about persistence reduce to or supervene upon intrinsic features of stages.

It may be that non-supervenient relations can form the basis of rational concern for one's own future, if anything can. It is, after all, rather difficult to say why one should care about one's future self even on an endurance theory account of the self—why should identity do the job more effectively than non-supervenient relations? One concern, however, may be that, although non-supervenient relations mark out a difference between natural and less natural series of stages, there is still an alarming degree of vagueness in questions of personal persistence. The next chapter tackles questions about vagueness.

4

Vagueness

There are cases, real and imaginary, in which we do not know how to answer questions about persistence through time. Sometimes this is a result of ignorance: is this the person I met two years ago? Is that the bag I checked in at the beginning of the flight? In such cases, we contemplate an object and do not know whether it is the same as some 'other' object we are contemplating. But we think that with more information we could find out whether these are the same thing: there is a fact of the matter about whether I have seen this person or bag before, a fact which I might discover through empirical investigation.

In other cases, it is not so obvious that there is some unknown fact of the matter. Is this restaurant the same as the one that used to be here, before the refit and the change of management? Is this much-repaired bicycle the bicycle I bought many years ago? Is this post-brain-surgery patient the person who signed the pre-operation consent form? Was I once a foetus? In such cases it is not obvious that further information about the history and properties of the relevant objects would settle all questions. Perhaps I could find out every empirical detail of the transformation of the restaurant, of the repair history of the bicycle, of the neuroscience of the operation, and of my early development, without knowing how to answer the questions.

Such cases exhibit vagueness, with which we are all familiar. Are those curtains red or orange? Is Fred, whose hair is thinning, bald yet? Is this molecule a part of me right now? We do not know how to answer these questions, and it does not seem that further information about the curtains, Fred, or this molecule would help us answer the questions. This situation arises because our concepts seem to have borderline cases: we do not know where to draw the line between the red things and the orange things, between the bald men and the non-bald men, or between those things which are my parts and those which are not. There are cases which we are not happy to place on one side of the line or the other.

Borderline cases also infect questions about persistence. Take the bicycle, for example. We seem unable to draw a sharp line between the changes which merely constitute repair of a single bicycle, and those which involve destroying one bicycle and creating another using some of the same parts. This apparent lack of sharp boundaries, whatever its source, is characteristic of vagueness. Thinking about vagueness may help resolve some of the problems I have already raised about personal identity—for example, was there an exact first moment at which I existed? It is definite that I exist right now, that I existed yesterday, and that I didn't exist one hundred years ago. But we seem unable to draw a sharp line between the moments at which I existed and those at which I did not—there are plenty of times during my gestation at which it seems entirely unclear whether I existed.

Where does vagueness come from? Is the world vague in its own right, or is vagueness always a matter of our loose talk or ignorance, a mismatch between the world and our representations of the world? Some believe that it makes no sense to claim that the world is vague in its own right, but I will try to make good sense of this very claim in the sections which follow. After exploring various approaches to vagueness, I will compare the three main theories of persistence—endurance, perdurance, and stage theories—to see what accounts they can offer of apparent vagueness in persistence. One requirement of a theory of persistence is that it make sense of apparent vagueness in persistence, in a way which is consonant with explanations of vagueness elsewhere.

4.1 Sources of Vagueness

It seems indeterminate whether the Welsh mountain Snowdon has a surface area of exactly 1,500 acres, it seems indeterminate whether Fred is bald, and it seems indeterminate whether that molecule on Fred's fingertip is a part of Fred. What is the source of all this vagueness?[1] There are three main views of the matter. The first is that we talk precisely, but that we do not know exactly which things or which properties we are talking precisely about. The way in which we use the predicate 'is bald' determines an exact cut-off point between the bald men and the non-bald men—either Fred is bald or he is not—but we

[1] There is a large literature on vagueness; a good starting point is Keefe and Smith (1997).

simply do not (perhaps cannot) know where that cut-off point is. According to this epistemic view of vagueness, our claims about persistence through time, or about Fred's baldness, are either determinately true or determinately false, even when we cannot know which (Williamson 1994). I shall return to this view below.

The second and third views both admit indeterminacy, claiming that vague statements have some intermediate status—perhaps they have a new kind of truth value, or perhaps they have both the traditional truth values, true and false, or perhaps they have no truth value at all. I will not investigate the different possibilities here: as a shorthand, I will call statements 'indeterminate' when I want to encompass all these different kinds of intermediate status. The second view is that vagueness is a matter of indeterminacy which results from loose talk—we haven't made it clear exactly which thing is Snowdon, exactly how few hairs a man must have in order to be bald, nor exactly how well attached a molecule must be in order to be part of an organism. This is the semantic, or linguistic view of vagueness (Lewis 1993). The third view is that at least some indeterminacy is due to the way the world is—for example, perhaps Snowdon just doesn't have sharp boundaries. This is the ontic view of vagueness (van Inwagen 1988, 1990*b*; Parsons and Woodruff 1995).

If there is indeterminacy of some kind, if not all vagueness is due to our ignorance, might some of it be due to the world, as opposed to our loose talk? For some, the notion of worldly vagueness seems almost incomprehensible; part of this incomprehension, I think, is a result of a inadequate grasp of exactly what it would be for the world to be vague. My first task in this chapter, then, is to establish what it would be for the world to be vague, and to clarify the distinction between ontic and semantic indeterminacy. We will then have three accounts of vagueness—ontic, semantic, and epistemic—with which to address vagueness in persistence.

Here is an argument against the very possibility of worldly vagueness: if something is vague, this is either because of our ignorance or because of indeterminacy. Suppose that vagueness is a matter of ignorance: then its source is partly in us. Suppose instead that vagueness is a matter of indeterminacy. If something is indeterminate then it has some kind of intermediate truth status. So if something is indeterminate, it is at least potentially a truth-bearer. Non-linguistic objects, properties, and states of affairs cannot be indeterminate, because they cannot have determinate truth-values either. No cloud is indeterminate, just as no cloud is either determinately true or determinately false.

This seems to be a compelling argument: the non-linguistic world could not be indeterminate in this sense. But there is a different sense in which the world might be vague. Let us take utterances to be truth-bearers—the kinds of thing which can be true or false—and assume that some utterances are indeterminate.[2] That is, there are utterances that are neither determinately true nor determinately false. Now we can ask, of any such utterance, whether its indeterminacy is due to the extra-linguistic world or whether it is due to language. We can distinguish two different *sources* of indeterminacy in utterances, instead of two different kinds of indeterminate thing.

But any indeterminate utterance owes its indeterminacy both to the way the extra-linguistic world is, and to the way language is. I say 'Fred is bald', and my utterance lacks a determinate truth value. It is uncontroversial that the indeterminacy is in part due to the way Fred's worldly head is. If Fred had been much more or much less hairy, then there would have been no indeterminacy in whether Fred was bald. Similarly, it is uncontroversial that the indeterminacy is in part due to language: if 'bald' had meant what 'human' in fact means, then the utterance would have had a determinate truth value. All indeterminacy has a dual source.

Nevertheless, we can make a useful distinction amongst sources of indeterminacy. All indeterminacy is in part due to the meanings of words, but some indeterminacy is due to semantic *indecision*, whilst some, perhaps, is not. Semantic indecision occurs when a word has no unique referent or semantic value. By the 'semantic value' of a word, I mean the element of the world which corresponds to the word, at the level of reference, rather than sense: in most cases this is a non-linguistic item. For example, if the indeterminacy in 'Fred is bald' is due to semantic indecision, this may be because no unique property is the semantic value of the predicate 'is bald'. Another example: I say 'Snowdon has a surface area of exactly 1,500 acres', and my utterance is indeterminate. If the indeterminacy is due to semantic indecision, this may be because no unique large lump of Welsh rock is the referent—the semantic value—of the name 'Snowdon'.

The metaphor of semantic indecision is not to be taken literally. It is rare that semantic values are explicitly decided upon, even in

---

[2] Other views about truth-bearers are compatible with this argument, so the choice of utterances is not crucial.

determinate cases. And in indeterminate cases the lack of decisiveness may be inevitable. Our physiological limitations as human beings may mean that we could not eliminate semantic indecision from our language, even if we tried really hard. To say that a term suffers from semantic indecision is not to be committed to the practical elim- inability of that indecision, or to the existence of explicit decisions in other cases. Instead, it is to be committed to the existence of a range of candidate semantic values, none of which determinately is the unique value of the term, and none of which determinately is not.[3]

When I say that the indeterminacy of some utterance is semantic I will mean that it is a consequence of semantic indecision, that the utterance would have been determinate if there had been no semantic indecision in its component terms. When I say that the indeterminacy of some utterance is ontic I will mean that the indeterminacy is not a consequence of semantic indecision in the component terms of the utterance. Roughly speaking, semantic indeterminacy can be put down to loose talk; ontic indeterminacy cannot.

I have defined semantic indeterminacy to be that indeterminacy which arises from semantic indecision. To attribute indeterminacy to semantic indecision is to locate the source of indeterminacy, but it is not to say how arguments involving the utterance should be assessed. In particular, this definition does not commit me to a supervalua- tionist approach to the logic of semantic indeterminacy (Fine 1975). A supervaluationist approach involves consideration of what the truth value of the utterance would have been if semantic indecision had been resolved in this or that way—such an approach is clearly compatible with attributing indeterminacy to semantic indecision. But a degree-theoretic approach to indeterminate utterances, which assigns degrees of truth between zero and one, is also compatible with talk of semantic indecision. For example, an object's properties may qualify it as red to degree 0.79, because there is no unique property the instantiation of which qualifies an object as red. To define semantic indeterminacy as indeterminacy due to semantic indecision is not to be committed to a supervaluationist logic.

My treating utterances as truth-bearers, and thus treating indeter- minacy as a feature of utterances, complicates the question of whether there might be worldly vagueness. If there is ontic indeterminacy then there is an indeterminate utterance which does not owe its

---

[3] Lewis (1993) writes of 'semantic indecision'. On the inevitability of such indecision, see Wright (1976).

indeterminacy to semantic indecision. So there is no ontic or semantic indeterminacy in a possible world without utterances. (Similarly, if utterances are truth-bearers then there is no truth or falsity without utterances.) Moreover there is no ontic indeterminacy unless there are utterances free from semantic indecision.

Thus the interesting question about a possible world is not whether it in fact contains a certain kind of indeterminate utterance. The more interesting question is whether the possible world contains the conditions for ontic indeterminacy, whether there could have been indeterminate utterances concerning that world which did not owe their indeterminacy to semantic indecision—I will address this question below. In particular, we will see that different accounts of persistence may give different answers to the question of whether vagueness in persistence could be an ontic rather than a semantic matter.

4.2 Against Vague Objects (and Vague Properties and Vague Relations)

I have tried to clarify the distinction between ontic and semantic indeterminacy, and in doing so I have avoided a more standard way of talking, in terms of 'vague objects' or 'vague properties'. This is because I believe that there is no important distinction to be drawn between cases where indeterminacy is due to the object involved and cases where indeterminacy is due to the property involved, and so talk of vague objects and properties can only be misleading.[4] In this section, I will explain why this is. To do so, I will suppose that the world can indeed be vague, and then ask whether we can make sense of worldly vagueness due to objects and that due to properties (or relations).

Suppose then that the indeterminacy of 'Snowdon has a surface area of exactly 1,500 acres' and that of 'Fred is bald' both have an ontic source. It is usual to suppose that Snowdon is a vague object whilst Fred is not, and that *being bald* is a vague property whilst *having a surface area of exactly 1,500 acres* is not.[5] This distinction between vague

---

[4] Parsons and Woodruff (1995) also focus upon states of affairs, not objects or properties. But they do so because they think there are epistemic difficulties in attributing blame to either object or property, whereas I think that no attribution of blame could be correct: the difficulty is not merely epistemic.

[5] Sainsbury (1989), Hughes (1985), Tye (1990: 536–7), and Burgess (1990: section 1).

objects and vague properties is superficially plausible. After all, what could be more precise than the property *having a surface area of exactly 1,500 acres*? And surely the ontic indeterminacy in whether Fred is bald is not enough to make him a vague object?

In one sense, a 'vague object' is one which features in an ontically indeterminate identity claim, but this is not the sense used here. Snowdon—and not Fred—is supposed to be a vague object because Snowdon has fuzzy or indeterminate boundaries, whilst Fred is indeterminate in respect of baldness.[6] Ontic indeterminacy in respect of boundaries is to be attributed to the object, whilst ontic indeterminacy in other respects, such as baldness, or colour, is to be attributed to the property. R. M. Sainsbury, for example, says that an object, O, is a vague object if and only if there is some second object such that it is indeterminate whether the second object is a part of O (Sainsbury 1989). Similarly, Michael Tye (1990: 536) says that an object is vague iff '(a) [it] has borderline spatio-temporal parts and (b) there is no determinate fact of the matter about whether there are objects that are neither parts, borderline parts, nor non-parts of [it].' Both authors attribute ontic indeterminacy in boundaries to the object in question.

Of course, we could use the phrase 'vague object' in this way. But there is no deep difference between ontic indeterminacy in boundaries (or in parthood), and ontic indeterminacy in other respects, and thus there is no deep difference between ontic indeterminacy which is due to vague objects and that which is not due to vague objects. Suppose that there is ontic indeterminacy in whether Rock is a part of Snowdon: 'Rock is a part of Snowdon' involves only Rock, Snowdon, and the relation *parthood* in its truth conditions, but it is indeterminate whether it is true. Why should we connect this indeterminacy more closely with Snowdon than with Rock? After all, if Rock had been differently located, the utterance would have been determinate. And why should we connect the indeterminacy more closely with either Snowdon or Rock than with the worldly relation *parthood*? If *parthood* had had a more definite extension, then the utterance would have been determinate.

What is supposed to distinguish indeterminacy in boundaries or parthood from indeterminacy in other respects? Perhaps if an object is indeterminate in respect of its boundaries, then sharp versions of the object also exist, whereas if an object is indeterminate in respect of

---

[6] Fred may have indeterminate boundaries too, but his indeterminate baldness alone is not supposed to make him a vague object.

colour or baldness there are no corresponding precise objects: it is indeterminate whether Fred is bald, but determinately bald versions and determinately non-bald versions of Fred do not also exist. This proposal collapses, however, because it is perfectly consistent, even well motivated, to believe that Snowdon has indeterminate boundaries and yet believe that no sharp versions of Snowdon exist. Moreover, whether or not an object is vague should not depend upon the existence of other 'non-vague' objects.

Perhaps we should blame Snowdon for the ontic indeterminacy in 'Rock is a part of Snowdon', because Snowdon is the subject of many ontically indeterminate utterances. Perhaps objects count as vague if they are vague in *many* respects, if they feature in *many* vague states of affairs. The vagueness of a state of affairs should be attributed to that element—object, property, or relation—which features in the greatest number of other vague states of affairs. Even supposing that we can count states of affairs, and that weight of numbers is important, this suggestion has two flaws. First, it is not obvious that if an object is indeterminate in respect of its boundaries then it is vague in more respects than if it is indeterminate in respect of its colour, say. Second, the relation *parthood* almost certainly features in more vague states of affairs than does Snowdon. Even the property *having a surface area of exactly 1,500 acres* features in many vague states of affairs if there are many things of about Snowdon's size which have ontically indeterminate boundaries. The 'counting' proposal fails.

The standard distinction between ontic indeterminacy due to a vague object, and that due to a vague property coincides with the distinction between ontic indeterminacy in boundaries (or, correlatively, in parthood), and that in other respects, but we have seen no reason to think that this is an important distinction. A last-ditch suggestion might be that properties like *having a boundary B* are not real properties at all, that *parthood* is not a real relation, and thus that objects with vague boundaries are vague by default, there being no property to take the blame. Even if there really is no such relation as *parthood*, this does not explain why we should blame Snowdon rather than Rock for the indeterminacy in whether Rock is a part of Snowdon. Moreover, the non-existence of *parthood* does not explain why *being bald* is a vague property, for Fred most definitely exists.

In his 'Why the World Cannot be Vague' (1994) Sainsbury drops his earlier claim that an object, *O*, is vague iff it is indeterminate which things are parts of *O*, seemingly because he sees that such indeterminacy

cannot be blamed on *O* rather than parthood. But instead of conclud-
ing that worldly vagueness should not be attributed either to objects or
to properties, he concludes that indeterminacy in parthood cannot be
genuinely ontic. The thought is that because the indeterminacy cannot
be blamed upon objects, it cannot arise from vagueness in the world. Of
course, indeterminacy in parthood need not be ontic: there might be
semantic indecision in 'is a part of'. But Sainsbury gives no reason to
think that all indeterminacy in parthood must be like this, a result of our
failure to decide which relation is the parthood relation. He ignores the
possibility that indeterminacy in parthood may be ontic, even though it
cannot be blamed on the object. There may be worldly vagueness without vague objects, vague properties, or vague relations.

The earlier Sainsbury and Tye both define vague objects in terms of
vagueness in parthood. And they both take vague properties to be
those which can have non-vague objects as borderline instances. Here
is Tye:

Suppose that P is a property of concrete objects. Then we may hold that P is
vague if and only if (a) P could have as a borderline instance a concrete object
that does not have borderline spatio-temporal parts, and (b) there is no
determinate fact of the matter about whether there could be an object of this
sort which is neither an instance, a borderline instance nor a non-instance of
P. (Tye 1990: 537.)[7]

Here is a problem with Tye's definition. If *having only a few parts* is a
vague property, then so, presumably, is *having only a few borderline
spatio-temporal parts*. Yet the latter property fails condition (a) of Tye's
definition: the property could not have a sharply bounded concrete
object as a borderline instance. Anything without borderline parts
would determinately not be an instance of the property. Tye considers
an analogous objection (due to Timothy Williamson) to an analogous
definition of a vague *predicate*: vague predicates are supposedly those
which could have precise objects as borderline cases, but 'has many
borderline parts' is intuitively a vague predicate although it could not
have precise objects as borderline cases. In response, Tye loosens his
definition, allowing that any predicate which has a vague predicate or a
vague modifier (like 'many' or 'few') as a component is itself a vague
predicate (Tye 1994*b*: 3–4). But an analogous loosening of the definition of a vague *property* is unappealing, because *having only a few
spatio-temporal parts* is not a component of *having only a few borderline*

---

[7] Tye extends the definition to properties of properties, and so on.

spatio-temporal parts (an object could have the latter property without having the former). Moreover this 'borderline cases' approach to vague predicates is inherently flawed, as I shall explain below.

This problem is partly an artefact of Tye's definition but it illustrates my broader point. The standard approach, which Tye makes rigorous, distinguishes between ontic indeterminacy in boundaries and ontic indeterminacy in other respects. But ontic indeterminacy in whether something has only a few borderline spatio-temporal parts cannot neatly be classified on one side or the other of this distinction. Once we appreciate that ontic indeterminacy is simply indeterminacy without semantic indecision, we can give up trying to distinguish between boundary indeterminacy and other indeterminacy, between vague objects and vague properties.

If there can be ontic indeterminacy, then some objects are indeterminate with respect to what parts they have, other objects are indeterminate with respect to what they are parts of, and others are indeterminate in other respects, in colour or baldness, say. There is no deep distinction between objects of these three kinds, and, indeed, we should never have expected there to be. For what else could it be for an object to be vague except that it be indeterminate whether it has a certain property, or indeterminate whether it bears a certain relation to a certain other object? And what else could it be for a property or relation to be vague except that it be indeterminate whether that property or relation is instantiated by certain objects?

4.3 Vague Words

The term 'vague' is not properly applied to either objects or properties, but to states of affairs; a vague state of affairs provides the conditions for ontic indeterminacy. What of the distinction between semantic indeterminacy due to vague subject terms and semantic indeterminacy due to vague predicates? Is the term 'vague' properly applied to sub-sentential units? Should we ask only whether whole utterances are determinate or indeterminate? Unlike objects and properties, words can indeed be properly called 'vague', but only if we think in terms of semantic indecision. A word is vague iff it suffers from semantic indecision, iff there is a range of things no one of which either determinately is or determinately is not its semantic value. In turn we can distinguish between utterances where indeterminacy is due to semantic indecision in subject terms, and utterances where indeterminacy is due to semantic indecision in predicates (although the indeterminacy of some utterances may be due to both).[8] Whether we can in practice make this distinction is a different question.

This way of thinking about vague and precise words differs from the standard view, according to which a word is vague even if it has a unique semantic value, if that value is a vague object or a vague property. I have, of course, dispensed with the notions of vague object and vague property, and thus cannot adopt this standard view. But I have sacrificed nothing, for the standard view encourages confusion, by obscuring the distinction between ontic and semantic indeterminacy, especially regarding predicates.[9]

The standard view of vague predicates is that they are those which are susceptible to borderline cases, or those whose extensions are boundaryless. 'Is bald', for example, has borderline cases: sometimes it is indeterminate whether or not the predicate applies. Indeed, I introduced the notion of vagueness at the beginning of this chapter by talking about borderline cases. The existence of borderline cases is a good indicator of vagueness, but talk of borderline cases can lead to confusion between ontic and semantic indeterminacy. First, borderline cases must be objects, not words. The mere fact that a predicate features in an indeterminate utterance should not make the predicate vague: the subject term might be vague. For a predicate to be vague there must at least be an object to which it is indeterminate whether the predicate applies.

But the possibility of ontic indeterminacy creates more problems. Consider 'has a surface area of exactly 1,500 acres'—there is an object, Snowdon, to which it is indeterminate whether this predicate applies. Yet this hardly seems to make the predicate vague. If ontic indeterminacy is possible, then a predicate can determinately have a semantic value (can correspond to a unique property) without having a determinate extension. The standard view obscures the important distinction between a predicate which has an indeterminate extension because it stands for a property with an indeterminate extension (ontic indeterminacy), and a predicate which has an indeterminate

[8] Semantic indecision in a subject term may often be traced to indecision in some predicate—perhaps this is the relationship between 'Snowdon' and 'is a mountain'. Nevertheless, within an individual utterance we can in principle distinguish between indecision in the subject term (whatever its source) and indecision in the predicate.

[9] Adopting this standard view may be a cause of Sainsbury's self-proclaimed inability to find a deep distinction between semantic and ontic indeterminacy (Sainsbury 1994).

extension because it is indeterminate which property it stands for (semantic indeterminacy).[10] We should characterize vague predicates as those which do not have unique semantic values.[11]

4.4 Might the World be Vague?

I have established that we should think about ontic and semantic indeterminacy in terms of the absence or presence of semantic indecision. If the world is vague, then it contains the conditions for ontic indeterminacy—there could have been an utterance which was indeterminate even though it was determinate which elements of the world it was about. But is this a genuine possibility? Think first about determinate utterances. These are made determinately true or determinately false by the arrangement of particulars, properties, and relations in the world. In the simplest case, a predicative utterance picks out a unique particular and a unique property; the utterance is determinately true if the particular instantiates the property, and it is determinately false if the particular does not instantiate the property (whatever particulars and properties may be, and however particulars persist).

How many elements are involved in the truth conditions of such simple utterances? Perhaps there are just two: particular and property. Or perhaps there are at least three: particular, property, and something corresponding to the notion of instantiation. Now, recall that ontic indeterminacy is indeterminacy which arises when it is

---

[10] This distinction may be respected even if properties are just sets of concrete particulars: there is a difference between a predicate which determinately corresponds to a unique set with fuzzy membership, and a situation where it is indeterminate which sharply bounded set the predicate corresponds to. It may be, however, that so-called 'ostrich nominalism' cannot respect this distinction, and thus cannot distinguish ontic from semantic indeterminacy. This seems to me to count against ostrich nominalism.

[11] Peacocke (1981: 132) says that '[I]t is natural to construe the suggestion that the world itself is vague as the suggestion that the world has to be described by (*inter alia*) vague expressions, where this need is not in some way a result of limitations on our capacities.' According to me, the world is vague iff there could be indeterminate utterances whose indeterminacy is not due to semantic indecision. The sentiment of my suggestion matches that of the 'natural' construal, but avoids a problem which arises from Peacocke's adoption of the standard view of vague expressions. On my account we distinguish between those expressions which do and those which do not suffer semantic indecision. Using the standard view, Peacocke must invoke the rather hazier distinction between those expressions which do and those which do not owe their vagueness (their appearance in indeterminate utterances?) to our limitations.

determinate which elements of the world feature in the truth conditions of an utterance. If the simplest determinate utterances have just two elements to their truth conditions, then ontic indeterminacy in the simplest utterances will be that indeterminacy (if any) which arises when it is determinate which particular and which property the utterance is about. If, on the other hand, the simplest determinate utterances have three elements to their truth conditions, then ontic indeterminacy in the simplest utterances will be that indeterminacy (if any) which arises when it is determinate which particular, which property, and which instantiation-like tie feature in the truth condition of an utterance.[12] In general, indeterminacy is ontic if and only if it arises in the absence of semantic indecision: what scope there is for attributing the indeterminacy of an utterance to semantic indecision depends upon what sorts of things make determinate utterances true or false.

So is ontic indeterminacy possible? Could my utterance be indeterminate even if it were determinate which elements of the world I was talking about? Some might argue that no indeterminacy is possible, whatever its source—these arguments may be based upon the desirability of retaining classical logic, or upon considerations about higher-order vagueness (Williamson 1994). But if there are genuinely indeterminate utterances, is there any reason to suppose that such indeterminacy is always due to semantic indecision, that an utterance free of semantic indecision would have to be determinate?

No. Determinately true (or false) utterances are true (or false) because of what they are about, and because of how what they are about is arranged. A simple predication is determinately true (or false) because of how particulars and properties (and perhaps instantiation) are arranged in the world. Given a particular and a property (and perhaps instantiation), they may be arranged in such a way that the corresponding utterance is true. They may be arranged in such a way that the corresponding utterance is false. May they not be arranged in such a way that the corresponding utterance is indeterminate? If there are things arranged in this way, such that utterances concerning those very things would be indeterminate, then there is vagueness in the world.

Isn't this entirely mysterious? How can a particular and a property be 'arranged in such a way' that an utterance concerning them is indeterminate? This is undoubtedly mysterious, but it is no greater mystery

---

[12] I do not claim to make sense of the notion of a range of instantiation-like ties, merely to indicate what is available to those who can make sense of this notion.

than that concerning how a particular and a property can be 'arranged in such a way' that an utterance concerning them is determinately true or determinately false. If we concede the possibility of indeterminate utterances, then ontic indeterminacy is in principle no more objectionable than semantic indeterminacy. There are simply two possible sources for indeterminacy in utterances: one is semantic indecision, and the other is vagueness in the world.

Moreover, if there can be higher-order indeterminacy—indeterminacy in whether something is indeterminate—there is no reason to suppose that this must be semantic. There is no barrier to supposing that it can be indeterminate whether an utterance is indeterminate, even in the absence of semantic indecision. In the simplest such case, a particular and a property (and perhaps instantiation) are arranged in such a way that it is indeterminate whether the corresponding utterance is indeterminate. And so on up the hierarchy: as far as we can make sense of higher-order indeterminacy in utterances, we can make sense of this indeterminacy being ontic.

Indeed, we can see semantic indecision itself as an example of vagueness in the world. Semantic indecision arises when it is indeterminate whether a given word refers to a given object, for example. An uttered claim that that word refers to that object would be neither determinately true nor determinately false. It makes sense to see this indeterminacy as ontic, arising even though it is determinate which word, object, and referring relation are in question. The alternative is to suppose that there is no unique *refers to* relation, no unique semantic value of the relational predicate 'is the semantic value of'. Further exploration of this issue, and of whether there is a vicious regress here, requires investigation of the nature of reference. But there seems no special reason why indeterminacy in utterances about reference should always be traceable to semantic indecision instead of being due to worldly vagueness. In other words, semantic indecision, inexact fit between words and objects, may itself be an example of vagueness in the world.

4.5 Is the World Vague?

It is one thing to concede the possibility of ontic indeterminacy, but it is quite another to decide whether the source of indeterminacy in some particular utterance is ontic. To claim some indeterminacy as ontic is to rule out any relevant semantic indecision, making a commitment to the determinacy of the truth conditions of the utterance. Conversely, to claim some indeterminacy as semantic is to be committed to the existence of a range of possible semantic values for words concerned.

Recall the indeterminate utterance 'Fred is bald'. There seems to be no relevant indecision about what 'Fred' refers to.[13] So to claim this indeterminacy as semantic is to suppose that there is semantic indecision either in the predicate, or in the notion of instantiation. Perhaps there is a range of properties, none of which determinately is or is not the semantic value of 'is bald'. This is plausible if we think that properties are relatively abundant. If properties are sets, then perhaps there is a range of sets, none of which determinately is or is not the set to which Fred must belong if 'Fred is bald' is to be true. Or perhaps there is a range of universals, none of which determinately is or is not the universal which Fred must instantiate if 'Fred is bald' is to be true.[14] Alternatively, we might accept that 'Fred' has a unique referent, and that a unique property corresponds to 'is bald', yet suppose that there are several ways in which particulars and properties might be connected, none of which is the unique instantiation tie. Of course, this approach can work only if the notion of instantiation is apt to have a worldly correlate at all.

What if the indeterminacy of 'Fred is bald' is ontic, *not* due to mere semantic indecision? Then 'is bald' has a unique semantic value, and there is no semantic indecision in the notion of instantiation. Perhaps 'is bald' has a unique semantic value because the properties are not abundant enough to permit semantic indecision. Or perhaps the properties are abundant, but nevertheless there is a clear winner, a single best candidate for being the semantic value of 'is bald'. Even if there are very many levels-of-hairiness properties, there may be a further property, distinct from all these, which is the unique semantic value of 'is bald'.

For example, there are many determinately membered sets of men, but perhaps there is also a further set, the set of bald men, not to be identified with any of these sets, to which it is indeterminate whether

---

[13] Perhaps there is indecision in which sum of particles (if any) is the referent of 'Fred', but this indecision is not the source of the indeterminacy in 'Fred is bald'.

[14] Or perhaps there is a range of clusters of universals, and no single cluster either is or is not the cluster of universals which Fred must instantiate. I will ignore this kind of option; I think the simplification is not a distortion. For properties as sets, see Lewis (1986*a*: section 1.5); for abundant universals see Jubien (1993).

Fred belongs (Tye 1990; 1994*a*). If properties are sets, then that set is the semantic value of 'is bald', there is no semantic indecision and the indeterminacy is ontic. Parsimony might discourage us from believing in such a set, when we have the resources to offer a semantic account of the indeterminacy in 'Fred is bald'—this kind of consideration may help us resolve questions about ontic and semantic indeterminacy. But we should be clear that, although belief in ontic indeterminacy is an unparsimonious position for those who believe that properties are sets, this does not show that it is an incoherent position.

A different example: I say 'Snowdon has a surface area of exactly 1,500 acres', and my utterance is indeterminate. If this indeterminacy is semantic, it is presumably due to indecision in 'Snowdon', rather than in the predicate, and there is a range of concrete things, none of which determinately either is or is not the referent of 'Snowdon'.[15] This is plausible only if, in the relevant area, there are very many large, mostly overlapping lumps of rock and soil: I will investigate this type of view in Chapter 5. A claim of semantic indecision here is available only to those who are liberal about composition (Lewis 1993). Such liberality is a necessary but not a sufficient condition for semantic indecision. If the indeterminacy is not ontic, there must be no better candidate than those in the range. Even if one believed in all the rocky lumps, one might think that no such lump is the referent of 'Snowdon', on the grounds that such lumps cannot change their parts, whilst any mountain can survive some such change.[16] Then there are all the precisely bounded rocky lumps, and there is in addition the referent of 'Snowdon'.

To posit semantic indecision is to posit a range of entities—universals, sets or lumps of rock, for example—but also to suppose that, outside this range, there is no better candidate for being the semantic value of the predicate or name in question. Conversely, to posit ontic indeterminacy is to suppose that there are unique things the arrangement of which is relevant to the truth of the utterance in question. If there is indeterminacy, then there seems to be no reason why its source must always be semantic indecision. But establishing the source of indeterminacy of any particular utterance requires much confidence in both ontology and semantic theory, since it amounts to

---

[15] Indecision in 'Snowdon' may be due to indecision in 'is a mountain' or 'is a part of'.

[16] As we will see in Chapter 5, E. J. Lowe adopts a position like this regarding lumps of feline flesh and cats (Lowe 1995*a*).

establishing the existence or otherwise of a range of potential semantic values. Moreover, we must begin from premisses about ontology
and semantic theory, and end with a conclusion as to whether a given
indeterminacy is ontic or semantic. It is illegitimate to argue from
prior prejudice about the source of an indeterminacy to conclusions
about ontology or semantic theory, because such a view about indeterminacy could have no grounds other than ontology and semantic
theory.

These issues bear upon the question of whether there must be
vagueness 'all the way down' in order for the world to be vague. One
view is that if there is a base level of precisely describable facts, upon
which all others supervene, then the world is not really vague. Of
course, we could thus define what it would be for the world to be
'really' vague, but such a definition is unmotivated unless the base
level properties and particulars are all the properties and particulars
there are.[17]

For example, it seems likely that that whether it is true, false, or
indeterminate that Fred is bald supervenes upon precisely describable
facts about the number and arrangement of hairs on his head.
Nevertheless, the indeterminacy in 'Fred is bald' may be ontic, so long
as there is a property *being bald* and a particular Fred. The existence
of subvening precise facts is compatible with ontic indeterminacy in
descriptions of the supervening level: if there really are properties and
particulars at the higher level, then there may be ontic indeterminacy
in utterances concerning them. It might in general be puzzling how
the instantiation of some properties could supervene upon that of
other, distinct properties, but the possibility of ontic indeterminacy at
the supervening level creates no further puzzle.[18] There is no reason
to consider ontic indeterminacy at supervening levels less 'real' than
that at the subvening level.[19]

4.6 Ontic Indeterminacy and Endurance Theory

We have seen, then, that there are three possible sources of vagueness:
ignorance, semantic indecision, and vagueness in the world. We

---

[17] Here I am in sympathy with Burgess (1990).
[18] Thus I disagree with Tye's formulation of his 'Problem of Generation' (1994*b*: 8).
[19] This conflicts with an account of worldly vagueness considered by Peacocke (1981: part III).

began by considering apparent vagueness in persistence—how long have I existed? Is this my original bicycle? Is this post-surgery person the person who went into the operating theatre? An important constraint on any account of persistence is that it somehow explain the appearance of vagueness in persistence. To explore the possibilities, I will consider in turn ontic, semantic, and epistemic accounts of vagueness, as they apply to issues about persistence.

I have already touched upon various examples of apparent vagueness in persistence, but I will take my central example from van Inwagen, who is an endurance theorist (van Inwagen 1988; 1990*b*: ch. 18). A person, Alpha, steps into the fiendish Cabinet, which then disrupts those features, whatever they are, which are relevant to personal persistence. The example can be adapted to suit different views about personal persistence, since the Cabinet can disrupt physical or biological continuity, brain function, psychological continuity, or whatever else might seem important. Because of these disruptions, it is vague whether Alpha survives to step out of the Cabinet. But somebody, Omega, steps out of the Cabinet at the end of the experiment, and it is a vague matter whether Alpha has survived as Omega.

Let us try the option of treating this vagueness as ontic. For endurance theorists, this amounts to the claim that there can be ontic indeterminacy in identity. What is indeterminate is the question of whether Alpha, who is wholly present as she steps into the Cabinet, is identical with Omega, who is wholly present as she steps out. If the Cabinet were just an ordinary room, then Alpha would be identical to Omega, according to endurance theory, so if there is ontic indeterminacy here, then according to endurance theory there is ontic indeterminacy in whether 'two' things—Alpha and Omega—are identical. I will argue that this interpretation of the case is untenable, but the argument is rather involved. Those who are already willing to accept that there cannot be ontic indeterminacy in identity might skip forward to section 4.11.

4.7 The Evans–Salmon Argument

Arguments against ontic indeterminacy in identity are usually of a very strong form; they attempt to show that claims of ontic indeterminacy in identity are incoherent (Evans 1978; N. Salmon 1981: 243–6). I will not make such a strong claim. I will argue that there are good reasons to suppose that there is no ontic indeterminacy in identity over time, but I will not argue that the very idea is incoherent. But let's begin with the standard argument, due to Gareth Evans, to the effect that ontic indeterminacy in identity is impossible. It runs as follows.

Suppose that 'a' and 'b' determinately refer to objects, and that we assume that it is indeterminate whether a is identical to b. Then Evans argues:

(1*) It is indeterminate whether a is   (Assumption)
      identical to b
(2*) a is such that it is   (from 1*)
      indeterminate whether it is
      identical to b
(3*) It is not indeterminate whether   (since every object is
      b is identical to b determinately self-identical)
(4*) b is not such that it is   (from 3*)
      indeterminate whether it is
      identical to b
(5*) a is not identical to b (from 2*, 4*, and Leibniz's
                                                     Law)

Evans assumes that it is indeterminate whether a is identical to b, and that every object is determinately self-identical, and he concludes that a is not identical to b. If the argument is a good one and if every object is determinately self-identical then any claim of ontic indeterminacy in identity between two objects entails that those objects are not identical—bad news for believers in ontic indeterminacy in identity. But the argument is confusing, and has proved difficult to assess. One source of controversy is the use made of identity-involving properties, like the property of *being an object such that it is indeterminate whether that object is identical to b*. The argument purports to show that a and b differ in their identity-involving properties, and thus that they are not identical.

We can, however, run similar arguments based on more mundane identity-free properties, and these arguments are easier to assess. Recall Alpha and Omega; Alpha steps into the Cabinet, and it is vague whether she survives to step out of the Cabinet. But somebody, Omega, steps out of the Cabinet at the end of the experiment, and so it is vague whether Alpha is identical to Omega, according to endurance theorists. Let us assume for the sake of argument that endurance theory is true, and, moreover, that this vagueness in persistence is ontic, a matter of ontic indeterminacy in identity between Alpha and Omega.

It is indeterminate whether Alpha and Omega differ with respect to the property *steps out of the Cabinet*: it is determinate that Omega has this property (I will consider an objection to this claim below), and it is not determinate whether Alpha has the property. Moreover the indeterminacy in whether Alpha has this property is the basis of the claim that it is indeterminate whether Alpha and Omega are identical. If it were determinate that Alpha steps out, then it would be determinate that Alpha survives, that Alpha and Omega are identical. And if it were determinate that Alpha does not step out, then it would be determinate that Alpha perishes in the Cabinet, that Alpha and Omega are not identical.

Alpha and Omega are not determinately indiscernible; it is not determinate that they both step out of the Cabinet, and nor is it determinate that neither steps out of the Cabinet. In most cases of alleged ontic indeterminacy in identity, the objects concerned are not determinately indiscernible. This vast majority includes the standard puzzles about personal identity over time, and, in particular, the Cabinet case. Indeed, Parsons and Woodruff, staunch defenders of ontic indeterminacy in identity, claim that all cases of indeterminacy in identity have this feature: '[I]t is indeterminate whether *a* is identical to *b* iff there is no property such that *a* has it and *b* lacks it (or vice versa), and there is some property that one of them has or lacks and such that the other is indeterminate with respect to having it' (Parsons and Woodruff 1995: 181).

But it is this very feature, the lack of determinate indiscernibility, which seems to undermine the claim that it is indeterminate whether Alpha and Omega are identical. Here is an Evans-type argument about Alpha and Omega.

(1) It is indeterminate whether Alpha steps   (premise)
    out of the Cabinet
(2) Alpha is such that it is indeterminate   (from 1)
    whether she steps out of the Cabinet
(3) It is not indeterminate whether Omega   (premise)
    steps out of the Cabinet
(4) Omega is not such that it is indeterminate   (from 3)
    whether she steps out of the Cabinet
(5) Alpha is not identical to Omega   (from 2, 4,
                                                     and Leibniz's Law)

This argument differs from the standard version of the Evans argument given above ((1*)–(5*)), the argument which depended upon identity-involving properties. The present argument uses the substantial premises that it is indeterminate whether Alpha steps out of the Cabinet, and that it is not indeterminate whether Omega steps out of the Cabinet. That is, it relies upon the very indeterminacy which underpinned the claim of indeterminate identity in the first place (Noonan 1995).

The argument does not take the form of a *reductio*: I nowhere assumed that it is indeterminate whether Alpha is identical to Omega. Rather, I used the substantial premises (1) and (3) to deduce that Alpha and Omega are not identical. The argument attempts to show that whenever there is a respect in which it is indeterminate whether two objects differ, then there is a respect in which they differ, and it is therefore determinate that the two objects are not identical. I will argue that in potential cases of indeterminacy in persistence, the premisses of the argument are true, and the argument is valid. So such cases do not provide examples of ontic indeterminacy in identity. Endurance theorists, who take persistence to be a matter of identity, cannot take vagueness in persistence to be ontic.

4.8 Leibniz's Law and its Contrapositive

As Parsons and Woodruff point out (1995: 178), it is misleading to display the argument as I have just done. The inference from lines (2) and (4) to line (5) depends upon the contrapositive of Leibniz's Law, rather than the Law itself. Leibniz's Law says that if objects are identical then there are no properties in which they differ. But the inference in question moves from a difference between Alpha and Omega, as specified in (2) and (4), to the non-identity of Alpha and Omega. This is an application of the contrapositive of Leibniz's Law, the principle that if two objects differ in some property, then they are not identical.

In determinate situations, the contrapositive is true: if it is determinate that two objects differ in some property, then it is determinate that they are not identical.[20] But we cannot suppose that, if it is merely indeterminate whether two objects differ in some property (like *stepping out of the Cabinet*) then they must be determinately

---

[20] That is, if they determinately differ in some property which is not merely a matter of our attitudes towards those objects—I will return to this point below.

non-identical, for this would beg the question against indeterminacy in identity. Alpha and Omega are determinately non-identical if and only if it is *determinate* that they differ in some property.[21] The argument must demonstrate that if it is indeterminate whether Alpha and Omega differ in some respect—in whether they step out of the Cabinet—then it is also determinate that they differ in some respect, and thus determinate that they are not identical.

Recall the argument in question:

(1) It is indeterminate whether Alpha steps out   (premise)
    of the Cabinet
(2) Alpha is such that it is indeterminate   (from 1)
    whether she steps out of the Cabinet
(3) It is not indeterminate whether Omega   (premise)
    steps out of the Cabinet
(4) Omega is not such that it is indeterminate   (from 3)
    whether she steps out of the Cabinet
(5) Alpha is not identical to Omega   (from 2, 4, and the
    contrapositive of
    Leibniz's Law)

Let us read (2) and (4) as 'ontologically loaded'. That is, if both (2) and (4) are determinately true, then Alpha and Omega determinately differ and thus (5) is determinately true. If (2) and (4) are to be read in this strong way, then we must examine the property-abstraction inferences from (1) to (2) and from (3) to (4). Not every predicate corresponds to a property (Mellor 1991; Hirsch 1993: ch. 3). Perhaps satisfying 'it is indeterminate whether x steps out of the Cabinet' does not amount to possessing a property of *being an object such that it is indeterminate whether that object steps out of the Cabinet*. Notice, however, that for the argument to succeed, there need not be a unique property of *being an object such that it is indeterminate whether that object steps out of the Cabinet*. All we need assume is that if two objects differ with respect to satisfying 'it is indeterminate whether x steps out of the Cabinet', then they must differ in some property or other, even if there is no direct predicate–property correspondence.

Is there reason to suppose that Alpha and Omega could differ with respect to predicate-satisfaction without differing in some property

---

[21] Broome (1984), however, argues that two objects may be indeterminately identical even if it is determinate that they differ in some respect, at least when that respect is a peculiar and indeterminacy-involving respect.

or other? In other words, is there reason to doubt the inferences from (1) to (2) and from (3) to (4), where (2) and (4) are ontologically loaded? In this section I will consider various general doubts about these inferences. I will argue that these doubts are unfounded, and, moreover, that the believer in ontic indeterminacy has very good reason to endorse the inferences. In the following section, however, I will consider a more specific objection which applies only to the inference from (3) to (4).

Doubts are raised about phrases like 'it is indeterminate whether x steps out of the Cabinet' by comparing them to phrases like 'John believes x to be a spy', or to predicates like 'x is non-self-instantiating' (Parsons 1987: 14; van Inwagen 1990*b*: 245–6). If we suppose that the latter predicate corresponds to a property of *being non-self-instantiating*, then we encounter paradox: the property would be both self-instantiating and non-self-instantiating. So there is no property of *being non-self-instantiating*. But this is an unhelpful analogy in the present context: if one object satisfies 'x is non-self-instantiating', and another object does not, then we infer that these objects differ in some property or other, and thus that they are not identical, even though the predicate corresponds to no property. Similarly, if one object satisfies 'it is indeterminate whether x steps out of the Cabinet' and another object does not, we are licensed to infer that they differ in some property or other, even if the phrase does not correspond directly to any property.

In contrast, if John believes that Beta is a spy, and John does not believe that Gamma is a spy, this does not show that Beta and Gamma differ in some property. Why not? This, of course, is a difficult question. But what's crucial is that involved in the truth conditions of these claims are propositions, modes of presentation, meanings, or the like: which 'belief predicates' the object satisfies depends upon how it is represented, and so apparent differences in such predicates need not reflect differences in the objects concerned. There is no analogous reason to suppose that objects may differ in whether they satisfy 'it is indeterminate whether x is P' without differing in their properties. Ontic indeterminacy is not a matter of how an object is represented. It is the way the object is, the way in which it instantiates various properties, which determines which indeterminacy predicates it satisfies, and a difference in such predicates reflects some difference or other in the objects concerned.

It is *prima facie* extremely peculiar for believers in ontic indeterminacy to claim that objects can differ in whether they satisfy indeterminacy predicates without differing in the ways they are. Believers in ontic indeterminacy say that it is indeterminate whether Alpha steps out of the Cabinet because of the way the world is, not because of how we represent or encounter Alpha. Similarly, if it is not indeterminate whether Omega steps out of the Cabinet, this is because of the way the world is. We may not wish to call this difference between Alpha and Omega a difference in *properties*. But if we attribute such dignity to the title of 'property', then we need a weaker, less dignified notion of attribute, respect, or way in which Alpha and Omega certainly seem to differ.

Are the inferences to (2) and (4) legitimate? Cases in which we standardly deny abstraction are not analogous to these ontic indeterminacy contexts. Believers in semantic or epistemic indeterminacy have good reason to think that a difference in satisfaction of indeterminacy predicates does not reflect a difference in the objects, for they believe that indeterminacy contexts are in some ways similar to propositional attitude contexts (Williamson 1994: ch. 9). But believers in ontic indeterminacy should at least have the default assumption that differences with respect to indeterminacy predicates reflect differences in objects, even if they do not wish to talk about 'properties' in this context.[22]

4.9 Transference

If indeterminacy is supposed to be ontic, then there are no good general reasons to deny that differences in predicate satisfaction reflect differences in objects. But there may be other, more specific reasons to question the move from (3) to (4), reasons which do not apply to the corresponding inference from (1) to (2). Recall the argument.

(1) It is indeterminate whether Alpha steps out   (premise)
     of the Cabinet
(2) Alpha is such that it is indeterminate   (from 1)
     whether she steps out of the Cabinet

---

[22] The fact that believers in ontic indeterminacy locate these differences in the objects is obscured when we focus upon the original Evans argument, which depends upon identity properties and predicates. The property *being identical to Omega* already sounds more dubious than the property *steps out of the Cabinet*, which may encourage the thought that related predicates should not be abstracted.

(3) It is not indeterminate whether Omega   (premise)
    steps out of the Cabinet
(4) Omega is not such that it is indeterminate   (from 3)
    whether she steps out of the Cabinet
(5) Alpha is not identical to Omega   (from 2, 4, and the
                                                  contrapositive of
                                                  Leibniz's Law)

To succeed, the argument must show that Alpha and Omega determinately differ in some respect. Let us accept (2). Then supporters of
ontic indeterminacy in identity might question (4). They need not
claim outright that (4) is false, that Omega *is* such that it is indeterminate whether she steps out of the Cabinet. They need only claim
that it is *indeterminate* whether Omega is such that it is indeterminate
whether she steps out of the Cabinet. They need only claim that it is
indeterminate whether (4) is true.

What could support this claim? The basic idea is this: if we take
seriously the assumption that it is indeterminate whether Alpha is
identical to Omega, then we must take seriously the consequent claim
that Alpha and Omega cannot determinately differ, and thus that (2)
and (4) cannot both be determinately true. Now, we have accepted
that (2) is determinately true, that Alpha is such that it is indeterminate whether she steps out of the Cabinet. So (4) *cannot* be determinately true. It must (at least) be indeterminate whether Omega is such
that it is indeterminate whether she steps out of the Cabinet.[23]

Supporters of ontic indeterminacy thereby invert the argument
against ontic indeterminacy. If we suppose that (4) is determinately
true, that it is determinate that Omega is not such that it is indeterminate whether she steps out of the Cabinet, then it cannot be indeterminate whether Alpha and Omega are identical. So if we are not to
beg the question against indeterminacy of identity, we cannot suppose that (4) is determinately true. Given that it is indeterminate
whether Alpha and Omega are identical, nothing true of Alpha can be
determinately false of Omega. This is an application of what we can
call the 'transference principle': if it is indeterminate whether two
objects are identical, then nothing determinately true of one can be
determinately false of the other.

---

[23] This is the strategy both of van Inwagen (1988, 1990*b*) and of Parsons and Woodruff
(1995), though their formal apparatus differs.

The claim is that (2) is determinately true whilst (4) is merely indeterminate. This asymmetry might look suspicious, but in fact there is no asymmetry in the treatment of Alpha and Omega. Consider the following pair:

(2#) Alpha is not such that it is not indeterminate whether she steps out of the Cabinet.

(4#) Omega is such that it is not indeterminate whether she steps out of the Cabinet.

(4#) is determinately true, a consequence of (3). Given that it is indeterminate whether Alpha is identical to Omega, by transference we infer that (2#) must be merely indeterminate. Both (2) and (4#) are determinately true. But to demonstrate a determinate difference between Alpha and Omega, we need to show that either both (2) and (4) or else both (2#) and (4#) are determinately true.

4.10 Is Alpha Identical to Omega?

The transference principle is true: if it is indeterminate whether Alpha is identical to Omega, then nothing determinately true of Alpha can be determinately false of Omega. So if it is indeterminate whether Alpha is identical to Omega, then it is indeterminate whether Omega is such that it is indeterminate whether she steps out of the Cabinet. In this section, however, I will argue that the consequent of this conditional is false, and thus that it is not indeterminate whether Alpha is identical to Omega. Believers in ontic indeterminacy must claim that it is indeterminate whether Omega is such that it is indeterminate whether she steps out of the Cabinet, that it is indeterminate whether (4) is true. But how plausible is this? Is it really indeterminate whether (4) is true?

We must now think not about the logic or semantics of abstraction, nor of the demands of ontic indeterminacy in identity, but of what appears to be going on in the Cabinet case. According to endurance theorists, we are confronted by a wholly present person, Omega, who steps out of the Cabinet: that much is determinate, whatever may be indeterminate about her historical properties or her relation to Alpha. Now, believers in ontic indeterminacy in identity must maintain that it is indeterminate whether that very person has the properties which would make it indeterminate whether she steps out of the Cabinet. But, I claim, this is *not* an indeterminate matter.

Let us change the scenario slightly: imagine that nobody enters the Cabinet, but that Omega is created *ex nihilo* just before leaving the Cabinet. Then, on stepping out, she would have been perfectly determinate.[24] In particular it would have been determinate whether she was such that it was indeterminate whether she steps out, for it would have been determinately false that she was such that it was indeterminate whether she steps out. Now, what difference does it make that, in the original story, Omega is the result of disrupting Alpha?

It makes a difference to what we can say about the history of Omega. But can it really affect what we can say about Omega with respect to whether she steps out of the Cabinet? The evidence of our senses gives us no reason to suppose that there is any vagueness as to whether Omega is such that it is indeterminate whether she steps out of the Cabinet. The only reason to suppose this, to claim that it is indeterminate whether Omega is such that she is indeterminate whether she steps out, is that this is the only way to save the claim that it is ontically indeterminate whether Alpha is identical to Omega.

We are at the very crux of the issue, where the reader must weigh up the arguments. Why did anyone suppose that Cabinet-like scenarios were cases of ontic indeterminacy in identity? When we consider such scenarios, we simply do not know what to say about the relation between Alpha and Omega, and some find it implausible to suppose either that there is an unknown fact of the matter or that our hesitation is purely a consequence of the term 'person' being ill-defined for such bizarre cases. We are not *compelled* to see these scenarios as cases of ontic indeterminacy in identity, even if we accept endurance theory. It's just that this view has seemed to some to be the most plausible option, more plausible than either semantic or epistemic accounts of the vagueness here.

But I have shown that if we insist on viewing the Cabinet as a case of ontic indeterminacy in identity then we are committed to the claim that it is indeterminate whether Omega has the properties which would make it indeterminate whether she steps out of the Cabinet. The only reason for making this incredible claim is to preserve the ontic indeterminacy claim which was itself established only on grounds of relative plausibility, as being a sensible description of the

---

[24] That is, she would have been determinate in all respects relevant to this discussion, although presumably she would have been slightly indeterminate with respect to spatial boundaries.

scenario. It is time to give up the idea that it is ontically indeterminate whether Alpha is identical to Omega.

Supporters of ontic indeterminacy in identity might object as follows. It is perfectly determinate that Omega is such that it is determinate whether she steps out of the Cabinet. But we cannot infer that it is determinate that Omega is not also such that it is indeterminate whether she steps out of the Cabinet. The considerations to which I have just alluded help establish the first, uncontentious point, but they do not establish the second. But the second must be established if I am to object to the claim of ontic indeterminacy in identity.

There is no logical fallacy in this objection, so again I must turn to considerations of plausibility. Let us examine the case closely. We are sure that it is determinate that Omega has properties which make it determinate whether she steps out of the Cabinet. Are we *also* sure that it is determinate that she does *not* have properties which make it indeterminate whether she steps out of the Cabinet? I think we are. It is as determinate as could be that Omega does *not* have the properties which would render it indeterminate whether she steps out of the Cabinet. It is not indeterminate whether Alpha is identical to Omega: we know this because we know that Omega does not have the properties which would render it indeterminate whether she steps out of the Cabinet.

Unlike Evans, I have not tried to show that ontic indeterminacy in identity is incoherent. Instead, I have argued that there is very good reason to suppose that a case like the Cabinet does not exemplify ontic indeterminacy in identity. My claim is that, in such a case, we would have very good reasons, supplied by perception, to think that it is determinate that Omega steps out of the Cabinet, and, further, to think that there is no higher-order vagueness about this matter.

Choosing to work with more mundane, identity-free properties like *stepping out of the Cabinet* has helped matters a great deal. Against the original Evans argument, based upon identity-involving properties, believers in ontic indeterminacy in identity must maintain that it is indeterminate whether Omega is such that it is indeterminate whether she is identical to Omega. This claim is just more difficult to understand, and thus more difficult to test for plausibility against the Cabinet case. But with identity-free properties, matters are at least a little clearer. Applying the transference principle is legitimate for cases of ontic indeterminacy in identity, but the results of this application are just not plausible in the Cabinet case, and so ontic indeterminacy in identity is ruled out.

4.11 Perdurance, Stages, and Ontic Indeterminacy

So can there be ontic indeterminacy in persistence? If endurance theory is true, there cannot be ontic indeterminacy in persistence, for the consequences of ontic indeterminacy in *identity* are incredible, and endurance theorists claim, of course, that persistence is a matter of identity. Endurance theorists must turn to another, non-ontic account of vagueness in persistence, and I will consider the options below. In the meantime, however, can either stage theorists or perdurance theorists maintain that there is ontic indeterminacy in persistence?

Stage theorists claim that when we talk about ordinary objects we talk about instantaneous stages. Each stage is wholly present at some moment, and does not exist at more than one time. We use the same name or description to refer to each of a series of stages, stages linked by causal, qualitative, and non-supervenient relations, of the kind I discussed in Chapter 3. But the thing which is me now is not identical to the thing which was me five minutes ago. For stage theorists, then, if it is ontically indeterminate whether Alpha is Omega, then it is ontically indeterminate whether the appropriate relations hold between earlier and later stages. Is Omega related to Alpha as I am related to my past self, or is Omega related to Alpha in some less intimate way? Ontic indeterminacy in persistence would be indeterminacy in whether this peculiarly intimate relation holds between certain stages.

Is this a genuine possibility? For stage theorists, ontic indeterminacy in persistence stands and falls with ontic indeterminacy in general. If there can be ontic indeterminacy in whether Fred is bald, or in whether Snowdon has a surface area of exactly 1,500 acres, then there is no barrier to ontic indeterminacy in whether Alpha and Omega stand in appropriate relations to one another, relations which would guarantee that they are the same person. Earlier in this chapter, I argued that ontic vagueness arises where there is indeterminacy which is not due to semantic indecision. So according to stage theory, there is ontic vagueness in persistence if and only if there is a unique relation, or cluster of relations, which must hold between stages in order for those stages to be stages 'of' the same natural object, and yet it is sometimes indeterminate whether two given stages stand in those very relations.

Consider the question of when I began to exist, for example. There is an early stage such that it is indeterminate whether that stage is me, whether it stands in the appropriate relations to the stage which is now me. If this vagueness is ontic, then there is genuine worldly vagueness in whether the two stages in question stand in the appropriate relations, and this is the source of the vagueness in my temporal 'extent'. Similarly, there may be genuine worldly vagueness as to whether the Alpha-stage which entered the Cabinet stands in the appropriate relations to the Omega-stage which left the Cabinet, as a consequence of the mysterious goings-on therein. If there can be ontic indeterminacy at all, then stage theorists can claim that there may be ontic indeterminacy in persistence.

Can perdurance theory permit ontic indeterminacy in persistence? According to stage theorists, we talk about stages existing at different moments, and it may be indeterminate whether those stages are 'the same', whether they stand in the right relations to one another. But according to perdurance theorists we do not, as a matter of course, talk about stages or temporal parts of things. We talk about long-lived persisting four-dimensional things. It is those things which satisfy sortal predicates like 'is a tennis ball', 'is a banana', and 'is a person'. According to perdurance theorists, when I say that I am the same person as the one who sat down at this desk this morning, I am expressing an identity claim, a claim about long-lived four-dimensional things. 'I' and 'the person who sat down at this desk this morning' refer to one and the same four-dimensional object.

But the Cabinet is disruptive. Let us take it that the Cabinet introduces ontic indeterminacy in the relations which hold between the personal temporal parts which stood outside the Cabinet before the experiment, and those personal temporal parts which stand outside the Cabinet after the experiment. Stage theorists would describe this as ontic indeterminacy in whether Alpha is the same person as Omega, picking out two temporally separated stages and talking about the relations between them.

For perdurance theorists, matters are less clear cut. To what do 'Alpha' and 'Omega' refer? It can't be that 'Alpha' refers to an extended four-dimensional thing which ceases to exist somewhere inside the Cabinet, and that 'Omega' refers to an extended four-dimensional thing which begins to exist somewhere in the Cabinet, for then it would be just plain false that Alpha was identical to Omega. Nor can it be that both 'Alpha' and 'Omega' refer to the long-lived four-dimensional thing which started many years before the experiment, and continues for many years afterwards. For then it would be just plain true that Alpha was identical to Omega. It is tempting to say that it is indeterminate what 'Alpha' and 'Omega' refer to, but this is to suppose that the indeterminacy here is semantic, not ontic, an option I will consider below.

Can perdurance theorists see the case of Alpha and Omega as one of ontic indeterminacy? The only possibility would be to claim that 'Alpha' refers to some four-dimensional thing which definitely includes the pre-Cabinet parts, but which suffers massive ontic indeterminacy in its temporal boundaries. Alpha is a thing such that it is ontically indeterminate whether it contains any post-Cabinet parts. Similarly, Omega is a thing such that it is ontically indeterminate whether it contains any pre-Cabinet parts. So it is ontically indeterminate whether Alpha is identical to Omega, because their boundaries are ontically indeterminate. The most powerful argument against this perdurance theory claim that vagueness in persistence may be ontic is that any such claim would be a claim of ontic indeterminacy in *identity*, just as it is for endurance theorists. It is indeterminate whether Alpha is identical to Omega, because of their indeterminate boundaries. This claim is vulnerable to the arguments from Leibniz's Law which I have already examined at length.

If they insist that vagueness in persistence is ontic vagueness, endurance theorists must maintain that it is indeterminate whether Omega is such that it is indeterminate whether she steps out of the Cabinet. I argued that this position is untenable. Similarly, if they insist that vagueness in persistence is ontic indeterminacy, perdurance theorists must maintain that it is indeterminate whether Omega is such that it is indeterminate whether she has any post-Cabinet temporal parts. Similarly, this is untenable: it is perfectly determinate whether Omega is such that it is indeterminate whether she has any post-Cabinet temporal parts. For it is determinately false that Omega is such that it is indeterminate whether she has any post-Cabinet parts.

If there can be ontic indeterminacy at all, then stage theory can permit ontic indeterminacy in persistence. In this respect, stage theory is unique. Both endurance and perdurance theories see persistence as a matter of identity, between either enduring or perduring objects. For this reason, as I have argued, neither can maintain that there is ontic indeterminacy in persistence. Is this an advantage of stage theory? It is certainly an advantage for those who believe that there can be ontic vagueness in persistence, that sometimes the world itself makes no 'decision' as to whether an object still exists. Stage theory is uniquely flexible, a direct consequence of the fact that stage theory does not analyse persistence in terms of identity, between three-dimensional objects existing at different times, or between four-dimensional objects. I turn now to other, non-ontic accounts of vagueness in persistence, to ask whether either perdurance or endurance theorists can find solace there.

4.12 Semantic Indeterminacy and Persistence

Perhaps vagueness has its source in language, in our use of words whose meanings are unspecific. It is indeterminate whether Fred is bald because we have (perhaps inevitably) failed to decide exactly how few hairs someone must have before they qualify as bald. We have failed to select a unique semantic value for 'is bald'. Similarly, perhaps it is indeterminate whether Snowdon has a surface area of exactly 1,500 acres because we have failed to decide exactly which lump of rock is the referent of 'Snowdon'. There are many candidates, but we have not discriminated between them.

Even if we agree that the source of vagueness is semantic indecision, there are various different possible approaches to the logic of vagueness. I will not, however, explore these different logics, but will confine myself to discussing how and whether endurance, perdurance, and stage theories can trace vagueness in persistence to semantic factors. It is vague whether Alpha is the same person as Omega. According to endurance theorists, for two things to be the same person is for them to be identical, so this is to say that it is indeterminate whether Alpha is identical to Omega. Can endurance theorists trace this indeterminacy to semantic indecision? There seem to be two options: either 'is identical to' has an underspecified meaning, or else the names in question do not have definite referents, like 'Snowdon' in the example above.

The first option is unattractive: have we really failed to decide which relation is the semantic value of 'identity'? What could the candidate relations possibly be, and how could this idea fit with the endurance theory claim that persistence is a matter of identity? Endurance theorists are better advised to locate semantic indecision in the names 'Alpha' and 'Omega'. The suggestion must be that there is a range of candidate referents for each name, and that indeterminacy arises because we have failed to decide exactly which of the candidates we are talking about. Some Alpha candidates are identical to some Omega candidates, but some are not. We haven't decided which things we are talking about, so our claims remain indeterminate.

We saw how semantic indecision can be used to explain the indeterminacy in Snowdon's surface area. Some Snowdon candidates have a surface area of exactly 1,500 acres, and some do not, but we haven't decided which candidate we are talking about, so our claims remain indeterminate. This picture requires that there be a multiplicity of Snowdon candidates, many lumps of rock which have exact but slightly different boundaries, containing other candidates as proper parts. Although some object to this multiplicity of objects—van Inwagen for example—others will find it acceptable. The picture is rather like that of the nested spheres inside an onion, each of which has a slightly different boundary.

But the picture is less appealing for Alpha and Omega. Endurance theorists must claim that there are various Alpha-candidates and various Omega-candidates, amongst which (or amongst whom?) we have failed to select referents for the names 'Alpha' and 'Omega'. But where are those candidates? According to endurance theory, Alpha is wholly present at every moment before she enters the Cabinet. So all the Alpha candidates, including those which are identical to some Omega candidates and those which are not, must all walk around together before entering the Cabinet, wholly present at every moment and sharing their spatial boundaries. Several exactly coinciding objects walk into the Cabinet; some of these walk out, others meet their demise within the Cabinet. And we must tell a similar story about the Omega candidates (Stalnaker 1988: 352).

How many candidates must there be? One answer is that there must be two coincident Alpha candidates, and two coincident Omega candidates. One Alpha candidate perishes in the Cabinet, and the other lives for many years after the experiment. One Omega candidate was created in the Cabinet, and the other was created thirty years previously. The second Alpha candidate is identical to the second Omega candidate. This is a rather modest account: endurance theorists need not posit more than two wholly coincident entities walking around together in the same skin (although we will encounter problems for even this idea in Chapter 5).

Unfortunately, the rather modest account is problematic. Consider the situation before the Cabinet experiment. According to the modest account, there are two coincident things walking around together, one of which will perish in the Cabinet and the other of which will not. But there could have been two consecutive Cabinet experiments lined up, instead of just one. In that case, there would have been three coincident Alpha candidates walking around together, one to perish in the first experiment, a second to perish in the second experiment, and a third to die a natural death in the distant future. And of course, there could have been more than two Cabinet episodes.

The modest account must have it that the number of exactly coincident objects in a place at a time is determined by what events happen in the future, despite the fact that all the objects are wholly present right then and there. The alternative is to give up the modest account, and to claim that there are as many exactly coincident objects as there are possible disruptive future events. Neither option is attractive. Recall that endurance theory is supposed to be the 'common-sense' approach to persistence, the account which fits best with our intuitions about everyday material objects. Vagueness about personal persistence is a dramatic feature of the Cabinet case, but it is also a feature of everyday life. It seems to be a vague matter when I began to exist: the endurance theorist who offers a semantic indecision account of this vagueness must suppose that when I (?) say 'I', I fail to discriminate between a range of candidates, all of whom are wholly present sitting in this chair right now, and which came into existence at slightly different times. It is an especially serious matter for endurance theorists to be forced so far from commonsense.

What of perdurance theory? I have already argued that perdurance theorists should not account for vagueness in persistence by positing ontic indeterminacy, for this amounts to claiming that there is ontic indeterminacy in identity. But can perdurance theorists offer a semantic account of vagueness in persistence? On the face of it, perdurance theory is more successful here than is endurance theory (Forbes 1987). Again, the best option is to claim that there is indeterminacy in the names 'Alpha' and 'Omega', not that there is indeterminacy in the relational predicate 'is identical to'. And this is a rather natural position for perdurance theorists to adopt.

Perdurance theorists think that persisting objects, like Alpha and Omega, are four-dimensional sums of temporal parts. Those who believe in arbitrary sums of the things they believe in will believe that any temporal part is a temporal part of a vast number of persisting objects, just as any spatial part is a spatial part of a vast number of spatially extended objects. The temporal parts picture, when combined with this liberalness about composition, can supply the vast number of candidate referents required for a semantic indecision account of vagueness in persistence. Moreover, these candidate referents all have slightly different boundaries from one another, and need not be thought of as wholly coincident objects.

Perdurance theorists may claim that, when we attempt to assign the name 'Alpha' to a persisting object, by picking out various pre-Cabinet temporal parts, we have not done enough work to achieve determinate reference to a particular persisting thing. For example, those pre-Cabinet parts are parts of a four-dimensional thing which ceases to exist during the experiment, and the very same parts are parts of a four-dimensional thing which lasts for many years beyond the experiment. And the same goes, of course, for 'Omega'. This explains the indeterminacy in whether Alpha is the same person as Omega: there is indeterminacy in which four-dimensional objects we are referring to, and so there is indeterminacy in whether we are referring to a single object twice, or to two distinct objects. The perdurance account is more attractive than the endurance account, since perdurance theorists do not need to posit wholly coincident things. The various Alpha candidates share temporal parts, but their boundaries are distinct; they do not completely coincide, despite overlapping at certain times.

What of stage theory? Unlike perdurance and endurance theorists, stage theorists do not see persistence as a matter of identity, between either four- or three-dimensional objects. If it is indeterminate whether Alpha is the same person as Omega, then it is indeterminate whether the distinct stages Alpha and Omega stand in appropriate 'same person' relations. I have already gestured at an ontic account of this indeterminacy, but it is also possible to give a semantic account. Perhaps it is ontically determinate which relations hold between Alpha and Omega, between pre- and post-Cabinet stages, but we have failed to decide exactly which relations are the ones that matter for 'is the same person as'. This is, of course, similar to the perdurance theory account, according to which we have not decided which relations between temporal parts make them count as parts of the same person.

Stage theory, I think, locates the indeterminacy in the right place. According to perdurance theorists, our terms 'Alpha' and 'Omega' fail to refer to anything definite. In contrast, stage theory claims that our terms 'Alpha' and 'Omega' may have perfectly determinate reference, but that we have failed to decide what makes two things count as the same person. And this seems to be the right picture: it is perfectly determinate what we refer to when we talk about Omega, for there is just one person standing there outside the Cabinet. The indeterminacy arises when we wonder what to say about Omega's past, about which past things she is the same person as.

This is, admittedly, just to reassert the intuition, shared by stage theorists and endurance theorists, that it is whole people (and tennis balls and bananas) that we encounter in everyday life, that it is possible to see a whole person all at once, without finding out about their past and future states. In the present context, this becomes the claim that we can refer determinately to a person, tennis ball, or banana, even if there is uncertainty about the future or past of the object we are referring to. Perdurance theorists, presumably, will reject this intuition. But it is an attractive feature of stage theory that it locates semantic indeterminacy in 'sameness over time', instead of in reference to people at times—stage theory allows that the indeterminacy in when a person began to exist does not produce any indecision or indeterminacy in our talk about that person as an adult. Stage theory is the only account of persistence which can accept that vagueness in persistence may be ontic—and now we have seen that stage theory gives the most satisfactory account of how vagueness in persistence may be a matter of semantic indecision.

4.13 Epistemic Accounts of Vagueness

According to an epistemic account of the vagueness in whether Alpha is the same person as Omega, either Alpha is the same person as Omega, or she is not, but we don't know which. Similarly, at any moment between conception and birth, either I existed or I did not, but we don't know which, for many of those moments. Vagueness here is a matter of ignorance, not a lack of determinate fact. How could we be ignorant of whether Alpha is the same person as Omega, given that we have extensive knowledge of goings on in the Cabinet?[25] According to endurance theorists, the claim would be that we simply

---

[25] It is hard to specify what this extensive knowledge amounts to; of course it cannot include knowledge of whether Alpha is the same person as Omega.

do not know whether Alpha is identical to Omega. As we look at Alpha, before she enters the Cabinet, there is a fact of the matter as to whether she will emerge, but we just don't know what that fact is, and nor do we know, on seeing Omega, whether she is Alpha.

According to perdurance theorists, the claim would also be that we do not know whether Alpha is identical to Omega. We do not know whether Alpha has temporal parts existing after the Cabinet episode, nor whether Omega has temporal parts existing before the Cabinet episode. We could express this by saying that we do not know which objects are the referents of our terms 'Alpha' and 'Omega'. The pre-experiment temporal parts are parts both of something which perishes in the Cabinet, and something which does not. Recall that according to the semantic account of vagueness, we have failed to decide which of these things to label 'Alpha'. In contrast, according to the epistemic account we have labelled one thing rather than the other, but we do not know which.

This fits rather well with the account of natural objects I gave at the end of Chapter 3. If reference is in part determined by relations between temporal parts of things, then there is no reason to think that we have privileged knowledge about what, exactly, we are referring to. We can compare this to a similar account of natural kinds. I dub a natural kind via a sample of the kind, but the sample is a member of many sets of things. It is the relations in the world between the sample and other kind members which determine which set of things I have dubbed, but I have no privileged knowledge about what it is I have dubbed. Similarly, it might be that default referents are the natural objects, those whose temporal parts stand in certain relations to one another, whilst it is not transparent to us which are the natural objects. Stage theorists, of course, can take a similar approach. I determinately refer to each of Alpha and Omega, and, indeed, I know what I'm referring to when I do so. But I don't know whether they are linked by the relations required for them to be the same person. Again, given the considerations of Chapter 3, this is rather a plausible position.

What, then, is the source of vagueness in persistence? We have seen that stage theory is fully compatible with ontic, semantic, and epistemic accounts of vagueness; that perdurance and endurance theories are incompatible with an ontic account of vagueness, compatible with an epistemic account, and in rather uncomfortable positions regarding a semantic account. But these conclusions can only help us to decide between the different views of persistence if we have some independent guidance as to the nature and source of apparent vagueness in persistence. If such vagueness turns out to have an ontic source, then this is a substantial advantage for stage theory, whereas if vagueness in persistence is epistemic, then all three accounts of persistence would seem to be on a par.

So far as stage and perdurance theories go, much depends, I think, upon the role of natural objects and the 'suitable relations' I discussed in the preceding chapter. If there is a single relation or cluster of relations which binds together the stages of natural objects, then we must offer either an ontic or an epistemic account of apparent vagueness in persistence. If that relation can enter into vague states of affairs, then vagueness in persistence may be ontic. If, on the other hand, such ontic indeterminacy is impossible, then vagueness in persistence must be epistemic—either two stages are stages (or temporal parts) of the same object, or they are not, even if we cannot know this. Alternatively, there may be degrees of naturalness, more and less natural objects, and perhaps there is an element of decision in the question of how natural an object must be in order to count as a natural object, or suitable referent—this would allow for semantic indecision as an explanation of indeterminacy in persistence.

Finally, what of endurance theory? In a sense, endurance theorists suppose that the only 'suitable relation' which binds stages together to make objects is the relation of identity, a relation which, as Evans has shown, must be all-or-nothing. The endurance theorist is compelled to adopt epistemicism about apparent vagueness in persistence—a position which many have found unappealing.

4.14 Vagueness, Persistence, and People

What of personal identity? Throughout my discussion of vagueness in persistence, I have been discussing people, using van Inwagen's example of Alpha and Omega. But little I have said so far has turned upon this feature of the example. Indeed, both van Inwagen and I are deliberately unspecific about the exact workings of the Cabinet: it is supposed to be a machine which disrupts those factors, whatever they are, which are relevant to personal persistence. We can imagine an analogous machine designed to operate on rabbits or bicycles, disrupting those factors, whatever they are, which are relevant to rabbit or bicycle persistence.

Are there any special considerations about people? A few. First, semantic accounts of vagueness are unattractive when applied to people. The thought was that we have failed to decide whether 'Alpha' refers to something which perishes in the Cabinet, or to something which survives the Cabinet, although both things are available for reference. This semantic indecision may be supposed to be the root of the indeterminacy in whether Alpha is the same person as Omega. Thinking of this as semantic indecision makes it seem that we could simply have decided to be more precise about 'Alpha', and thus decided whether or not Alpha survives the Cabinet. Then it sounds as if we can just decide for ourselves what sorts of events we could survive, and which we could not survive, simply by tightening up our language. And unfortunately human life doesn't seem to be like that.

This objection to the semantic account of vagueness in personal persistence is misformulated, however. On confronting the Cabinet, I cannot affect my survival chances just by affecting linguistic convention. Certain things will perish and certain things will survive, regardless of how we speak. But nevertheless there seems to be a certain amount of leeway in our usage of 'person'; in one sense of the word, people can survive the Cabinet, whilst in another sense of the word, people cannot survive the Cabinet. This does not combine very happily with the idea that people form a morally significant category of things. If it is wrong to kill people, is it wrong to put me in the Cabinet? In one sense of 'person' I will survive, in another I will not, but it seems that one of these ought to be the morally significant sense of 'person'. Such special considerations against the semantic account of vagueness do not seem to apply to predicates like 'is a banana'.

The second, related, special point about personal persistence is this. It is easier to believe that there are unknown facts about personal persistence than it is to believe that there are unknown facts about bicycle persistence. That is, the epistemic account is particularly attractive where persons are concerned. If I contemplate entering the Cabinet, I may feel strongly that the person who emerges either will be me, or will not be me. If, on the other hand, I contemplate a major renovation of my bicycle, I find it harder to believe that there is some fact of the matter as to whether I am about to replace or merely repair the machine. Facts about personal survival seem deeper and more robust than facts about bicycle survival, and if we cannot decide whether Alpha is Omega, we may nevertheless wish to claim that there is some unknown fact of the matter.

Third, there is a special worry about coinciding person-like things which does not arise in the same way for other objects. Recall that if endurance theorists wish to offer a semantic account of vagueness in persistence, they are committed to the claim that two Alpha candidates completely coincide and walk around together before the experiment. One, but not the other, survives the Cabinet experience. I objected to this multiplicity, but it seems worse if we focus on the fact that Alpha is conscious. Are both candidates conscious, or is only one? If the latter, can we decide which is conscious by tightening up our language one way rather than another? Similar questions arise for perdurance theory, and we have already encountered this problem, towards the end of Chapter 2. Problems about coinciding entities are the focus of the next chapter.

5

Sheer Coincidence?

Will I survive the night? It depends partly upon what events will take place tonight, and partly upon whether I am the sort of thing that can survive those sorts of events. For example, suppose that tonight I will receive a bump on the head, and lose my memory entirely. Then whether I will survive the night depends upon whether I can survive such a complete memory loss. And this in turn seems to depend upon my relationship with this human organism. Wherever I go, there too goes a large, squishy, highly-organized system of organs, flesh, and bones, which takes up space, maintains itself, reacts to internal and external stimuli, and both constrains and supports me in pursuing my projects and plans. If I am identical to this human organism, then I will survive exactly those events which this organism will survive. But if we are two different things, then there might be events in which I would perish whilst this organism survives—complete memory loss might be such an event. And there might be events in which this organism would perish whilst I survived—perhaps this would happen if part of my brain were transplanted into another organism, whilst this organism were destroyed.

If I am identical to this organism, then we have the same persistence conditions—we would survive under the same circumstances—and if we are not identical then we may have different persistence conditions. If I am identical to this organism, there is a constraint on theorizing about persistence conditions, although not a tight constraint. For example, suppose I have a strong intuition that I could not survive complete memory loss, and also have a strong intuition that this organism could survive such a complete memory loss. If I am identical with this organism, then I ought to give up one of these intuitions—but which one? As usual, we have no infallible method of arriving at the truth. All we can do is examine the consequences of making different choices, attempting to discover how these would fit in with other fallible beliefs we have about the world.[1]

---

[1] Bernard Williams (1970) illustrates some of the perils of this approach.

Suppose I sacrifice the intuition that I could not survive complete memory loss, and instead accept that I go wherever this organism goes, even if what seem to be 'my' memories are removed and instantiated in a different organism (Olson 1997). It seems that, if I knew that 'my' memories would be 'transferred' in this way, I would have an intimate kind of concern about the future welfare of the organism which would have 'my' memories, even if that organism were not me. This leads us (although not by Parfit's route) to Derek Parfit's remarkable conclusion that our most intimate concern for the future need not be based on considerations of identity (Parfit 1984).

Suppose that instead I sacrifice the intuition that this organism could survive complete memory loss, and accept that it would be destroyed by my amnesia. This has strange consequences of its own: if I underwent complete memory loss tonight, then tomorrow morning's largish mass of flesh, bones, and organs could not be this very organism, despite its continuity with, similarity to, and causal dependence upon this very organism. Moreover, if we think that human organisms are destroyed by memory loss, we are committed to thinking that human organisms have persistence conditions very different from those of many other types of organism. I take it that goldfish can survive complete memory loss.

None of these lines of argument is irresistible; as we have already seen, and will see, philosophers are skilled at resisting even the most inviting thoughts. But if we accept the initial claim that I am identical to this very organism, and if we have conflicting intuitions about my persistence conditions and those of this organism, then accommodation and adjustment must be made somewhere along the line. Identity places constraints upon persistence conditions, and means that I can use what I believe about this organism to help me decide what to believe about myself and my chances of making it through the night. In contrast, if I am not identical to this organism, then there may be events which I could survive and in which this organism would perish, or events which this organism would survive and in which I would perish. My beliefs about my own persistence conditions would not be constrained by the requirement that these be the same as my beliefs about the persistence conditions of this organism. Discovering, then, whether I am identical to this organism is a valuable part of an investigation into whether I will make it through the night.

How can we investigate whether human persons are identical to human organisms? First, we might think about whether human organisms can instantiate the properties necessary for the existence of our rich mental lives. Could a mere organic system really have the sensations and feelings I am experiencing right now? Second, we might argue that human organisms form a natural kind, that persons form a natural kind, and that there are or might be non-human persons (Lowe 1996). If nothing can be a member of two natural kinds (unless one is a sub-kind of the other) then this suggests that nothing can be both a human organism and a person.

I will set both of these intriguing arguments to one side, and consider a third. Let's take it that human persons have spatial locations. Now, if human persons are not identical to human organisms, then a person and an organism can be in the same place at the same time without being identical. Assuming that two distinct things cannot simultaneously each be a part of the other, this leaves us four options: either I have this organism as a part, or it has me as a part, or I am located in space without being extended in space, or there can be two spatially extended objects in the same place at the same time, without either being a part of the other. If we take the first option, saying that this organism is merely one of my parts, we must explain the nature of my other part. What is it made of, if anything? What would happen if these two parts of me became separated? If we take the second option, we should explain which part of this organism I am—perhaps some important part of my brain? If we take the third option, we might wonder how an extensionless thing—me—is managing to transform thoughts into the motion of fingers on a keyboard.

None of the first three options is an appealing account of how I might be distinct from this organism. If we take the fourth option, we are committed to the idea that there can be two objects in the same place at the same time without either being a part of the other. If, in addition, we suppose that I am a material object, then this commits us to the claim that there can be two material objects in the same place at the same time, a person and an organism. Is this a genuine possibility? Can material objects completely coincide, completely occupying the same spatial region at the same time? If they cannot, then I cannot be both material and life-sized and yet distinct from this organism. If I am a human-shaped material object then I am this organism, and we have the same persistence conditions.

If we are interested in our chances of survival, and, more broadly, in what kinds of thing we are, then we will turn eventually to such questions about co-location, coincidence, and identity—could I coincide with this organism without being identical to it, for example? An answer to these questions will not entail any particular claim about what we are, but it will place interesting, powerful constraints upon what we might consistently be. In this chapter I will examine questions about the coincidence of material objects. Such questions are ancient, but have been the focus of renewed interest in recent years.[2] Thinking about the relationship between human persons and organisms presents special problems. If we are interested in answering questions about the possibility of two objects being in the same place at once partly because we are interested in whether a person and an organism can be in the same place at once, we should begin by considering more general, perhaps more straightforward examples.[3]

Imagine that I knit a long thread of wool into a seamless sweater (Sidelle 1998). The sweater weighs 1kg, let's say, and it hangs from a peg on my office door. How many things are hanging from the peg? Well, the sweater is certainly hanging from the peg. Where is the thread? I didn't destroy the thread by knitting it into a sweater; indeed I was careful not to damage the thread at all. I wouldn't have destroyed the thread if I had tangled it into a knotty mess, so there seems no reason to suppose that I destroyed it by knitting it into a neat sweater. In short, it looks as if the thread and the sweater are co-located, that they occupy the same region of space at the same time. Wherever the thread is right now, there is the sweater, and vice versa.

A natural thought is that the thread just is the sweater, that they are identical. The thread used not to be a sweater, but now it is a sweater. This may indeed be a viable claim, but *prima facie* it is problematic. The thread is rather old, it has existed for a few years—indeed, I unravelled an old cardigan in order to make the sweater. But the sweater is brand-new—it came into existence only as I knitted. So the thread used to be a cardigan, whereas the sweater was never a cardigan, for it began to exist only after the cardigan ceased to exist. The sweater and the thread have different persistence conditions: if I unravel the sweater, it will cease to exist, but the thread will survive. Conversely, if the sweater begins to wear out, and I replace worn parts of the thread with new wool, then the sweater will survive such repairs, but the thread may not.

---

[2] The selections in Rea (1997) are representative, and Burke (1992) has a particularly helpful bibliography.

[3] Rea (1995) provides a useful survey of a variety of related puzzles.

So we have a tension here: on the one hand, it makes sense to say that the sweater and the thread are identical, that there is only one 1kg object hanging on my office door. But on the other hand, the sweater and the thread seem to have different histories, and different persistence conditions. They cannot be identical and yet have different properties, for if they were truly one and the same, they would share all of their properties. How should we resolve this apparent tension? Some favour giving up the assumption that there is just one thing hanging from the peg—they argue that the sweater and the thread are distinct, despite the fact they occupy the same spatial region at the same time. What are the consequences of making this move? As we will see, the consequences depend in part upon which theory of persistence we adopt—endurance theorists must pay a high price for distinguishing coincident objects, higher than either perdurance or stage theorists must pay. So if we must distinguish between coincident objects, then endurance theorists face extra costs, which is a point in favour of non-endurance accounts of persistence.

Must we distinguish between coincident objects? Can't endurance theorists retain the identity assumption—take it that the sweater and the thread are one and the same object—and thus avoid incurring extra costs? To do this, they must show that the apparent differences—in history and in persistence conditions—are merely apparent, that the sweater and the thread are in fact identical in every respect. Below we will consider some attempts to make good this move, to explain how it is that, contrary to first impressions, the sweater and the thread share all their features. If such attempts are successful, then we cannot use cases like that of the sweater and the thread to cause problems for endurance theory.

Above, I asked whether I am identical to this organism—an answer to this question will have implications for my chances of surviving various different sorts of events, and for questions about when my existence began. Either I am identical to the organism, in which case we have the same persistence conditions, or else I am distinct from the organism, in which case we may have different persistence conditions, different chances of survival in various circumstances. Rather than directly addressing difficult questions about personal persistence, I will address questions of coincidence and identity, asking whether a sweater is identical to the woollen thread of which it is made. If they are identical, then the apparent differences between them must be merely apparent. If the differences are genuine, then the sweater and

the thread are not identical. What can we learn about personal survival from thinking about knitting? We cannot settle every issue—
there are bound to be special considerations concerning people and
organisms that do not apply to sweaters and woollen threads. But in
attempting to resolve the tension between thinking of two things as
co-located and thinking of them as differing in their features, we can
work out the options for persons and organisms. Is the cost of accepting co-located distinct objects too high? If it is, then we cannot think
both that persons are physical objects and that they are distinct from
organisms.

The problem, then, is this: on the one hand, it looks as if there's
only one 1kg sweater-shaped object on the peg in my office. But on the
other hand, it seems as if the sweater and the thread have different histories—the thread used to be a cardigan, the sweater did not—and
different persistence conditions—unravelling would destroy the
sweater but not the thread. First, then, let's try giving up the identity
assumption, taking it that the sweater and the thread are distinct but
coinciding objects.

5.1 Constitution Theories

Suppose that the thread and the sweater are distinct material objects
which occupy the same place at the same time—what follows from
that supposition? In a later section I will discuss perdurance and stage
theory accounts of coincidence, but in the present section I will confine myself to endurance theory. So we have a thread, and a sweater,
occupying the same region of space: in standard terminology, the
thread is said to 'constitute' the sweater. The thread is the sweater, but
this doesn't entail that the thread is *identical* to the sweater: the thread
merely *constitutes* the sweater.[4]

What is this relation of constitution that supposedly holds between
the thread and the sweater and which may also hold between an
organism and a person? Perhaps constitution is reflexive, and thus
every object constitutes itself. Perhaps it is symmetric: the sweater
constitutes the thread, as well as vice versa. Some think that constitution is not symmetric. Despite these differences of opinion, I will call

---

[4] This approach, in one form or another, for one problem or another, is adopted by
Wiggins (1980), Lowe (1989*a*), Chisholm (1976), Thomson (1983), Levey (1997), and
Johnston (1992), amongst others.

all these various accounts 'constitution theories'. Constitution theorists are endurance theorists who believe that there can be more than one object exactly occupying a spatial region at a certain moment, that there can be objects that have the same boundaries at the same time and yet are distinct. In the case of the sweater and thread, at least, the coinciding objects seem to be made of the same microphysical parts.

According to constitution theorists, the thread and the sweater are made of the same basic parts, arranged in the same way at the same time, and both the thread and the sweater are wholly present right now, hanging from the peg in my office. Yet the thread and the sweater apparently have different features: different histories and different persistence conditions. Indeed, it is to explain these differences that constitution theory is introduced, on the grounds that if two things differ in these ways, then they must be distinct objects.

In Chapter 3 I argued that four-dimensional objects have properties that do not supervene upon the intrinsic properties of and spatio-temporal relations between their temporal parts. Constitution theorists make the stronger claim that two objects could differ in their properties even though their parts were indiscernible in every respect, *including* the non-supervenient relations which hold between those parts. The thread and the sweater are not just made of indiscernible parts arranged in the same way; they are made of the very same parts. They cannot differ in the relations which hold between their parts, not even in some holistic, non-supervenient way, for they have the same parts, and thus the parts of the sweater are related exactly as are the parts of the thread. The parts stand in the relation *jointly composing a sweater*, and they also stand in the relation *jointly composing a woollen thread*.

How can the thread and the sweater differ, despite being made of the same parts at the same time? It is, presumably, because they belong to different kinds that the thread and the sweater have different persistence conditions, that one can survive unravelling whilst the other cannot. There is a reason that the thread survives unravelling, whilst the sweater does not, even if that reason is just that the sweater is a sweater, and sweaters can't survive unravelling. It is not mere chance that the thread survives unravelling whilst the sweater does not. If kind-membership is to do this sort of explanatory work, then it must correspond to property-instantiation: constitution theorists need to posit sortal properties of *being a thread* and *being a sweater*, as grounds for the differences between the thread and the sweater.

The constitution theorist is committed to the existence of sortal properties, and to those properties being non-supervenient in a certain peculiar sense. The fact that something is a sweater is not determined by anything about the way its parts are arranged and related (for the parts of the thread are arranged and related in just the same way); it is an extra feature of the object over and above anything which is determined by the nature of its parts. Those who suspect that the properties are few and far between, that there are only properties like charge, mass, spin, and so on, will thus not be friendly to the present position, which requires commitment to a large number of high-level sortal properties, like the property *being a sweater.*

These sortal properties are instantiated in strange ways. Although no object is a sweater merely in virtue of having parts arranged in a sweater-composing way, it is nevertheless the case that wherever there are objects arranged in a sweater-composing way, there is an object which has just those things as parts, and which is a sweater. Somehow, the existence of suitably arranged things compels the instantiation of the property *being a sweater,* although not everything made up of those suitably arranged things instantiates the property *being a sweater.* If we are reluctant to posit sortal properties which behave like this, we might think of distinguishing the sweater and the woollen thread via their relational properties. We might be tempted to say that they differ in the relations they bear to past states, that the thread used to be a cardigan whereas the sweater was never a cardigan. But the problem just reiterates: how can two things, made of the same parts at the same time, stand in different relations to past objects?

This might suggest that the difference between the sweater and the thread is a difference in their relations to our concepts. Perhaps persistence conditions are a matter of convention, and it is because we think of sweaters and woollen threads differently that the sweater is destroyed by unravelling, and the thread is not. This is not a plain fact about the mind-independent world, which is why we cannot distinguish the sweater from the thread in respect of their intrinsic properties, nor in respect of their ordinary relations to other non-minded things.

It is certainly a matter of convention that the string of letters 'sweater' applies to objects which are destroyed when unravelled. This is a contingent fact about the English language. It may even be part of what we mean by 'sweater' and 'thread' that sweaters and threads have different persistence conditions. Perhaps if we know what 'sweater' means, then we know that a sweater cannot survive unravelling. But it cannot merely be a matter of convention that there are things which can survive unravelling, and things which cannot. The conventionalist suggestion is that the same physical processes of unravelling, with the same qualitative results, can result either in the persistence of a single object, or in the destruction of an object, depending upon what our conventions are: it is because we have the concept 'sweater' that there is something which does not survive unravelling. But this to say that we can, simply by agreement, and from a distance, make it the case that the material object I see before me today either will or will not exist tomorrow. This would be a remarkable metaphysical party trick, if only we could arrange it. But unless we are idealists, we cannot suppose that objects exist only courtesy of our conventions.

Could there be a more modest position, according to which the existence of things is not a matter of convention, but that which objects we opt to think about and privilege is a matter of convention?[5] Such a position is indeed possible, but it will not help endurance theorists here. The claim would be that there are very, very many persisting objects in the world, and that it is merely a matter of convention which of those we find natural. In other words, there are very many objects coincident with the thread and the sweater, hanging from the peg, and it is a matter of convention which of these we distinguish and, sometimes, give names to.

This simply aggravates the initial problem. We were trying to explain how there can be two otherwise indiscernible things with different persistence conditions. The present 'explanation' is that there is a whole multitude of otherwise indiscernible things with different persistence conditions. But this is no explanation at all. Unless they are willing to take the idealist stance, and to accept creation and destruction by power of thought, then endurance theorists must acknowledge that objects do not have their different persistence conditions in virtue of our different attitudes towards them. Endurance theorists who also wish to be constitution theorists should claim that there are sortal properties like *being a thread* and *being a sweater*, and that whether or not a given object instantiates one of those properties is not fully determined by other properties of that object or its parts.

---

[5] I briefly discussed such a position in the introduction to this book.

5.2 Perdurance Theory

There seems to be a tension in our ordinary beliefs about material objects like sweaters and woollen threads. On the one hand, we suppose that when I put on my sweater, I am handling just one sweater-shaped object, that the thread and the sweater are one and the same object. On the other hand, we take it that sweater and the thread might have different histories and different fates, that they differ in what it would take for them to survive. Are the sweater and the thread identical or distinct? Constitution theorists try to make good the idea that the sweater and the thread are distinct, whilst holding on to the endurance theory claim that ordinary objects are wholly present whenever they exist. This amounts to the claim that two objects can be made of exactly the same parts arranged in the same way at the same time, and yet differ in certain respects, and thus be distinct objects.

Perdurance theorists have a different way of spelling out the idea that the sweater and the thread are distinct objects. Remember the story: the thread existed before the sweater, and will exist after the sweater's demise if I unravel the thread tomorrow. According to perdurance theory, things like the sweater and the thread are four-dimensional objects, which are extended in time and have different temporal parts at different moments. Early temporal parts of the thread are not temporal parts of the sweater; middle temporal parts of the thread, between knitting and unravelling, are temporal parts of both the sweater and the thread; later temporal parts of the thread, after unravelling, are not temporal parts of the sweater, which no longer exists. Indeed, the sweater itself is a long-ish temporal part of the woollen thread.

A useful and well-worn analogy is with a road. The A1 road stretches for many miles, through several different counties. As it passes through a certain town, it is known as High Street. What is the relationship between the A1 and High Street? More northerly parts of the A1 are not parts of High Street, and more southerly parts of the A1 are not parts of High Street, but those parts of the A1 which lie within the town are also parts of High Street. High Street itself is a spatial part of the A1. Both High Street and the A1 pass through the town centre, you can stand on one of these roads by standing on the other, damage one by damaging the other, and so on. Analogously, both the thread and the sweater are hanging from the peg right now, I can pick up one by picking up the other, wash one by washing the other, and so on. The A1 and High Street differ in their properties: the A1 is hundreds of miles long, whereas High Street is not. Analogously, the thread and the sweater differ in their properties: the thread used to be a cardigan—it has earlier temporal parts which are temporal parts of a cardigan; the sweater was never a cardigan—it does not have earlier temporal parts which are temporal parts of a cardigan.

Both constitution theorists and perdurance theorists argue that the thread and the sweater are distinct objects, and that this is why they have different properties (only the thread used to be a cardigan) and different persistence conditions (only the sweater can be destroyed by unravelling). Constitution theorists at least have the advantage of retaining the apparently commonsensical endurance account of persistence. Does perdurance theory have any compensating advantage over constitution theory?

Perdurance theory is preferable for those who reject the type of sortal properties which constitution theorists are forced to posit. According to constitution theorists, both the sweater and the thread are wholly present as they hang from the peg, and they are made from exactly the same parts, standing in the same relations. In contrast, perdurance theorists take a four-dimensional perspective and argue that the thread and the sweater are not (atemporally) made of the same parts. There are many temporal parts of the thread which are not parts of the sweater, and it is this difference which explains why the thread and the sweater are not the same kind of thing.[6]

Perdurance theory is congenial to a certain kind of conventionalism about sortals and kinds. The present temporal part is a part of both the sweater and the woollen thread, but, if we accept unrestricted mereology, that temporal part is also part of very many different persisting objects. For example, it is a part of that short-lived thing made up exactly of the temporal parts of the sweater/thread which exist during the present hour. It is also a temporal part of a peculiar object which is made up of all the temporal parts of the Eiffel Tower at times up until half an hour ago, the temporal parts of the sweater/thread during the present hour, and the temporal parts of the Taj Mahal in the further future. If we accept all this, then the sweater and the thread are just two of the enormously many persistents which share the

---

[6] In the following chapter I will discuss the perdurance theory response to cases in which two objects seem to be *permanently* coincident.

temporal part presently hanging from the peg. Then it may well be a matter of convention, and most likely a rather indeterminate matter, which of these discernible persistents we distinguish from the others and refer to as 'the sweater' and which we refer to as 'the thread'. The non-supervenient relations I discussed in Chapter 3 may put some constraints upon exactly what we can and cannot name, but nevertheless some flexibility remains.

I argued that endurance theorists should not be conventionalists about persistence conditions, on pain of becoming idealists. A conventionalist about persistence conditions believes that it is a matter of convention whether an object O survives until tomorrow, where O confronts me now. Perdurance conventionalists can spell this out as the claim that there are very many overlapping objects which confront me now, all of which share a present temporal part. It is at least partly a matter of convention whether the name 'O' is applied to an object which also has temporal parts tomorrow, or to an object which does not have temporal parts tomorrow, for objects of both sorts confront me now and are available for naming. Perdurance conventionalism about persistence conditions can be spelt out as a metaphysically harmless claim about the relationship between language and the world.

We have seen two versions of the idea that the sweater and the woollen thread are distinct objects. According to endurance theorists the objects are distinct, sharing all of their microphysical parts, yet differing in which sortal properties they instantiate. According to perdurance theorists the objects are distinct, though they share all of their present microphysical parts, because they differ in their temporal parts, in the past and, perhaps, in the future. We will see later that this perdurance theory account is incomplete without some story about the modal differences between sweaters and threads, but at least the broad shape of the account is clear. In the final section of this chapter, I will discuss how these competing views could apply to the case of a person and 'her' organism. If we accept either constitution theory or perdurance theory, then it is open to us to distinguish between a person and an organism, even whilst claiming that a person is a physical object.

5.3 Dominant Sortals

Both constitution theory and perdurance theory take it that the sweater and the thread are different objects, and have different histories and different persistence conditions. Michael Burke has a different approach.[7] He argues that the sweater is identical to the thread, that both were created at the moment when they began to coincide, and that the *original* thread was destroyed in the process. So the thread never was a cardigan, since it was created when I knitted the sweater, and the thread will be destroyed when I destroy the sweater by unravelling it. The original tension was between the temptation to claim that the sweater and the thread are one and the same object, and the temptation to suppose that they have different properties. Burke takes the first option, identifying the sweater and the thread, and so he owes us an account of why we 'mistakenly' tend to suppose that the sweater and the thread have different histories and different persistence conditions.

The problem is that the terms 'sweater' and 'thread' seem to be associated with different and incompatible persistence conditions. A sweater, we suppose, cannot survive unravelling, whereas a woollen thread is flexible with regard to its shape, and cannot be destroyed simply by knitting or unravelling. Burke agrees that different sortals are associated with different persistence conditions, but argues that an object can fall under a sortal without satisfying the persistence conditions associated with that sortal. In this case, the thing on the peg can be correctly described by (at least) two sortal terms—'sweater' and 'thread'—but it does not and cannot satisfy the conflicting persistence conditions associated with these two sortals. A single object cannot have incompatible persistence conditions, for this would entail that there are events in which the object would both survive and perish. Instead, the thing on the peg, which is both a thread and a sweater, satisfies the persistence conditions associated with 'sweater' and not those associated with 'thread'. In Burke's terminology, the sortal 'sweater' *dominates* the sortal 'thread'.

Burke maintains that a thing can be a thread without having the persistence conditions associated with that sortal. As E. J. Lowe points out, he must also claim that the persistence conditions associated with being a thread are not what we might have expected (Lowe 1995*b*: section 2). Burke must maintain that if something has the persistence conditions of a thread, then it cannot survive certain changes, if those changes result in the existence of a sweater. The original woollen thread pre-dated the existence of the thing, hanging on the peg, which is both the present thread and the sweater. That original thread was

---

[7] Burke (1992) argues against constitution theories. The main source for the arguments I discuss in this section is Burke (1994*b*). Burke replies to critics in his 1997.

governed by the persistence conditions associated with 'thread', for it fell under no more dominant sortal. But, according to Burke, it perishes in the creation of the sweater and the new thread. He points out that the particles which make up the thread survive the creation of the sweater, and that they compose first the original thread and then the present thread. In his view, this is what leads us mistakenly to suppose that the original thread is identical to the one which is now identical with the sweater.

There are problems here. Woollen threads which are not sweaters (or cardigans) can survive *some* tangling, some changes of shape. If I tie a knot in a woollen thread, I do not thereby destroy the thread. Threads can survive some deformations, at least those which do not result in the existence of a sweater or other garment. But these destructive changes which produce garments cannot be picked out from non-destructive changes as the most drastic, or the fastest: the difference between the destructive and the non-destructive changes is only that one produces a woollen thing in a useful shape, and the other does not.

The implausibility of Burke's position is in fact more obvious if we consider the example he himself describes. Instead of a thread knitted into a sweater, we are to consider a piece of copper shaped into a statue. Burke's claim is that the resulting object is both a piece of copper and a statue, but that it satisfies the persistence conditions associated with being a statue, and not those associated with being a piece of copper. That's to say, the statue cannot survive a radical change in shape. Now, the piece of copper that existed before the statue existed is no longer in existence; it was destroyed by the process of making the statue, and a new piece of copper was created in its place, just as a new thread is created as the sweater is knitted into existence.

The original piece of copper was destroyed because the result of its deformation was a statue, a kind of thing which has persistence conditions different from those associated with being a piece of copper. If the original piece of copper had merely been deformed by the elements, without the intentional creation of a statue, it would not have been destroyed by the process. On Burke's view, there is a crucial difference between a statue, intentionally created by an artist's manipulation of the copper, and a qualitatively identical piece of copper, created by exactly the same qualitative changes. In the creation of the statue, one piece of copper is destroyed and another created. In the other case, there is neither destruction nor creation, and the present piece of copper is identical with the original.

This is not simply the rather plausible suggestion that whether an object is a statue partly depends upon our attitudes towards it. It is not just the suggestion that the same physical processes with the same qualitative results can differ in whether they result in the creation of a statue. The claim is that the same physical processes with the same qualitative results can result either in the destruction of a piece of copper or the persistence of a piece of copper. The fate of the original piece of copper hangs on whether the physical process in question is the intentional creation of a statue. Like the conventionalism I discussed earlier, this gives intentions a remarkable power of creation and destruction at a distance and through sheer will.

According to Burke, then, a piece of copper is destroyed in the making of a statue, and a woollen thread is destroyed in the knitting of a sweater. Pieces of copper cannot survive statue-creating deformations, although they can survive qualitatively identical deformations which are non-intentional and thus not statue-creating. This position involves us in a kind of psycho-destruction, enabling us to destroy pieces of copper by sheer mind-power and intention: this is an unacceptable consequence of Burke's attempt to identify coinciding objects. If the thread and the sweater are identical, this cannot be because a thread was destroyed in the making of the sweater.

5.4 Temporary Identities

Burke claimed that the thread in my office was created when the sweater was created, in order to sustain his claim that the thread and the sweater are identical. After all, if the sweater and thread are identical, they must have all their properties in common, which seems impossible if the thread used to be a cardigan, whilst the sweater never was. André Gallois challenges this line of thought, with his Occasional Identity Thesis, the thesis that objects can be identical at one time without being identical at all times (Gallois 1998). He claims that the sweater and the thread may now be identical despite their having different pasts. How can this be?

Gallois offers a new account of temporal predication. It seems true that the thread was a cardigan last year, but it seems false that the sweater was a cardigan last year. This looks problematic if we wish to claim that the sweater and the thread are identical: if there is just one large object hanging from the peg, then surely it is either true or false (but not both) that that single object was a cardigan last year. Ordinarily we think that it is true that the sweater was a cardigan last year if and only if it was true, last year, of *the* thing now identical with the sweater, that it was then a cardigan. This is what makes us think that it is false that the sweater was a cardigan last year.

According to Gallois, however, it is now true of the sweater that it was a cardigan last year if and only if it was true, last year, of *at least one* thing now identical with the sweater, that it was then a cardigan. And, according to Gallois, the thread is a thing now identical with the sweater, and it was true last year that the thread was then a cardigan. So it is, after all, now true of the sweater that it was a cardigan last year. Gallois distinguishes between talk about *some* and talk about *all* of the things now identical to the sweater. It is true now of the sweater that it was a cardigan last year, since it was true then of something now identical to the sweater that it was a cardigan. But it is also true now of the sweater that it was *not* a cardigan last year, since it was true then of something now identical to the sweater that it was not a cardigan (for it did not exist). The thread and the sweater are now one and the same object, of which it is both true that it was a cardigan last year, and true that it was not a cardigan last year.

Why should we accept such an account? Part of Gallois's motivation for accepting temporary identity is his dissatisfaction with perdurance theory, which of course denies that things wholly existing at different times can be identical. But in Gallois's system, claims about identity between things existing at different times have a peculiar status, being subordinate to claims of identity at a time (Gallois 1998: ch. 5). The relation of 'transtemporal identity' is not identity, and it is not even an equivalence relation. A thing existing at one time is transtemporally identical to a thing existing at another time if and only if everything identical to the first thing at the first time is identical to the second thing at the second time.

This definition of transtemporal identity sets us off on a regress, by quantifying over things which exist at more than one time. What determines whether everything identical to the first thing at the first time is identical to the second thing at the second time? Presumably, it must be the case that each thing identical to the first thing at the first time is 'transtemporally identical' to something which is identical to the second thing at the second time. And so on. The regress is puzzling.

Moreover, although part of Gallois's motivation is his rejection of perdurance theory, the distinction between perdurance and endurance theory cannot even be formulated in the temporary identity framework. According to Gallois, things wholly present at different times cannot be identical (for transtemporal identity is not a kind of identity), but this is not, presumably, because they are distinct, as perdurance theorists claim.[8] One important attraction of the temporary identity view is that it promises to retain the endurance theory idea that ordinary objects are wholly present wherever they exist, without encountering the problems induced by the endurance theory claim that things wholly present at different times can be identical. This attractive combination is also offered by stage theory, which denies that things existing at different times are identical. But stage theory has the advantage of allowing that claims of identity between things at different times make sense, even though they are false.

5.5 Stage Theory

According to stage theory, 'the sweater', 'the thread', and 'the thing hanging from the peg' all refer to one and the same object. The object is what the perdurance theory would call the present temporal part shared by the sweater and the thread. So the sweater is identical to the thread: in this respect the stage theory account is like that of Burke and Gallois, and unlike perdurance and constitution theories, which claim that the sweater and thread are distinct objects.

How does stage theory account for the apparent differences between the sweater and the thread, in their histories and persistence conditions? Recall the discussion of historical predicates in Chapter 2. An instantaneous stage satisfies a predicate like 'used to be a cardigan' if it stands in appropriate relations to a stage which satisfies the predicate 'is a cardigan' (Sider 1996). In Chapter 3 I began to spell out these 'appropriate relations' in terms of non-supervenient relations between the instantaneous stages, and I suggested that our distinction between natural and unnatural (gerrymandered) objects corresponds to a distinction between series of stages which are and are not linked by these non-supervenient relations, respectively.

---

[8] Compare the discussion of time-indexing in Chapter 1.

Now, however, we can see that matters are more complex. The present stage is both a sweater and a woollen thread, and it is linked by appropriate non-supervenient relations to a past stage which is a cardigan. Yet we ought to deny that the sweater used to be a cardigan—the sweater was created after the cardigan was unravelled and destroyed. The present stage is not the same sweater as the past cardigan, although it is the same thread as that cardigan. For two stages to be the same sweater, it is not enough that they be linked by a natural series of stages—further connections are required. Of course, in this case, the past stage and the present stage are not the same sweater because the past stage is not a sweater at all. But even if I had unravelled an old sweater then knitted up a new one, the present stage would not be the same sweater as the past stage.

A single present object may stand in different relations to different past objects. Earlier, I said that a stage satisfies a predicate like 'used to be a cardigan' if and only if it was suitably related to a past stage which satisfies 'is a cardigan'. But now it is apparent that which relations are in question may partly depend upon how we refer to the present stage. If we ask whether the thread used to be a cardigan, we are asking whether the present stage is the same thread as some past stage which is a cardigan. This differs from asking whether the sweater used to be a cardigan—whether the present stage is the same sweater as some past stage which is a cardigan. The task of discovering what these *same sweater* and *same thread* relations are is the task of discovering persistence conditions or 'criteria of identity through time' for sweaters and threads.

In Chapter 2, I explained how, according to stage theory, a single name picks out different things when used to talk about different times. The same process is at work here. The phrase 'the thread' can be used to refer to the present stage, but also to stages in the past and future if we choose to talk about goings-on at different moments. Certain past stages can be referred to as 'the thread' and they enter into the truth-conditions for historical predications of the present stage when that present stage is referred to as 'the thread'. The mechanism for talking about past stages is intertwined with the mechanism which gives truth conditions to historical predications about present stages.

What are the advantages of a stage theory account of the sweater and the thread? The account has it that the sweater and the thread are identical, without either having to claim that knitting destroys threads (as Burke does) or that identity at a time is more basic than identity over time (as Gallois does). Stage theory has the appeal of Gallois's temporary identities without the complexities and inflexibility of his account of historical predication. Moreover stage theory does not need to posit the existence of free-floating sortal properties, as constitution theory does. Granted, as we saw in Chapter 3, stage theory (and perdurance theory) need to suppose that there are non-supervenient relations between certain stages, but these relations are not as peculiar as the free-floating sortal properties of constitution theory. Finally, we will see in Chapter 6 that stage theory gives a better account than perdurance theory of objects which merely could have differed, but actually do not.

5.6 Scepticism about Objects

So far I have been taking for granted that both the sweater and the thread exist, and focusing on the question of how these objects are related: are they identical or distinct? But for some, cases like that of the sweater and the thread prompt more radical thoughts. Peter van Inwagen denies that either the sweater or the thread exists, because he believes that the world contains neither sweaters nor woollen threads (van Inwagen 1990*b*). He does believe that the world contains mereological atoms (partless things) arranged sweater-wise, and mereological atoms arranged thread-wise. In the case I have been discussing, the very same atoms are arranged both sweater-wise and thread-wise. Van Inwagen denies that those atoms form anything: they make up neither a sweater, nor a thread, nor even a collection, heap, or sum of atoms. He believes only in mereological atoms and in organisms.

Such a theory might seem incredible, but van Inwagen argues that, given certain constraints, his position follows very naturally. For present purposes, the most interesting constraints include an adherence to endurance theory and an insistence that no two objects can be made of exactly the same proper parts at the same time.[9] Van Inwagen believes that, like the rest of us, he himself is an enduring material object, made of different mereological atoms at different times. If his present atoms compose something after they become scattered, then they continue to compose van Inwagen. For if scattering does not stop

---

[9] Preface to van Inwagen (1990*b*). The arguments I summarize in the following paragraph are drawn from Chapter 8 of the same book.

the atoms composing anything, then it does not cause them to compose something different. But they cannot continue to compose van Inwagen when they become scattered, because by that time van Inwagen is composed by different atoms. So the original atoms do not compose anything once they become scattered.

If van Inwagen endures from moment to moment, despite gaining and losing atoms, then atoms compose objects only under certain conditions. But it is remarkably difficult to specify those conditions: it is not simply when the atoms are in contact, or fastened together, for example. In fact, argues van Inwagen, the only circumstances under which atoms compose an object is when their activities constitute a life. Only living organisms can be composed by atoms, and thus only atoms and organisms exist.

Van Inwagen would address the present case by arguing that neither the sweater nor the thread exists. But in a case involving a living organism, he would take a different approach. If, instead of discussing a sweater and a woollen thread, we had been discussing a cat and the matter which makes it up, van Inwagen would have claimed that the only macroscopic object in question is the cat, which is successively composed of different atoms. There is no such macroscopic object as the sum, fusion, or collection of atoms which coincides with the cat at any time.

Van Inwagen's arguments are compelling: he draws out the consequences of adopting certain constraints or premises, most notably the twin assumptions that endurance theory is true, and that distinct objects cannot wholly coincide. Burke and Gallois spell out alternative positions which are also compatible with the rejection of constitution theory and the adoption of endurance theory. But van Inwagen's is perhaps the boldest and the most attractive of this group, for its sheer simplicity, if nothing else.[10]

5.7 A Complication: Two of a Kind?

The sweater and the woollen thread seem to coincide, yet also seem to have different histories; we have seen various attempts to account for this situation. The sweater and the thread belong to different kinds of thing, having different persistence conditions, or so it seems. But

---

[10] Sidelle (1998) provides a very helpful discussion of a range of positions which, like van Inwagen's, involve a sceptical attitude to the status of ordinary objects like sweaters.

there might also be cases of temporary coincidence between objects of
the same kind. For example, consider an amoeba, which reproduces
by binary fission. From one amoeba comes two, or so it seems. There
are various things we could say about the fate of the original amoeba,
Adam. Adam may be identical with his left-hand successor. Adam
may be identical with his right-hand successor. Adam may be identical with each of his successors. Adam may be identical with neither of
his successors. Adam may be identical with both of his successors
(Robinson 1985; Wiggins 1980).

The qualitative symmetry of the situation seems to rule out both
the first and the second options. We can also reject the third option,
since identity is transitive: if Adam is identical with *each* of his successors, they must be identical with each other, yet, by stipulation,
they are not. For a start, they are in disjoint places and have distinct
nuclei. The fourth option, that Adam ceased to exist at the moment of
fission, may be the most straightforward approach to take, and, gen-
eralized, it entails that two things of the same kind cannot coincide.
Then all coincidence would be like that of the sweater and the thread,
between two things of different kinds.

What of the fifth option? *Could* there be coincidence between
objects of the same kind? Denis Robinson suggests that Adam is (or
are) actually two coinciding amoebae, which, at the time of fission, go
their separate ways. How do the various accounts of the sweater and
the thread extend to this case? Constitution theorists, if they accept
Robinson's suggestion, must claim that, before fission, Adam-1 and
Adam-2 are distinct coinciding things, with different future properties, despite the fact that they have just the same persistence conditions. Burke's approach has no application here. His approach to the
sweater and the thread is expressly designed to show how they can be
identical despite belonging to kinds which are characterized by different persistence conditions, but of course the amoebae are of the same
kind. Gallois is better placed to accept coinciding entities of the same
kind; if we accept the principle of temporary identities, we may accept
that Adam-1 and Adam-2 are identical pre-fission, although they are
subsequently distinct. And van Inwagen should say that Adam is
destroyed in fission, when two new organisms are created (van
Inwagen 1990*b*: ch. 16).

Perdurance theorists, like Robinson himself, can accept that there
are two coincident amoebae before the fission, distinguished by their
future properties. They share temporal parts before fission, but not

afterwards. Both perdurance and constitution theorists, then, accept that there is more than one amoeba present before fission, just as they accept that there are two entities on the peg in my office, a sweater and a woollen thread. Unfortunately, of course, Adam's successors will produce yet more successors, and successors of those successors, so endurance and perdurance theorists will have to accept that there are *very* many coincident amoebae before fission.

Stage theorists may either claim or deny that Adam perishes during fission. 'Adam' refers to a single amoeba-stage before fission, a different one at each moment. It is coherent for stage theorists to suppose that none of those stages is the same amoeba as any post-fission stage. On the other hand, it is also coherent for stage theorists to say that any given pre-fission stage is the same amoeba as many post-fission stages, pairs of which are simultaneous and spatially disjoint. That is, a pre-fission stage may be the same amoeba as a left-hand successor stage, and the same amoeba as a right-hand successor stage. *Being the same amoeba as* is not the identity relation, and it may be non-transitive.

In this case, what should stage theorists say about the name 'Adam'? When used to talk about pre-fission stages, it is unambiguous, referring to a unique stage at each moment (subject to the caveats discussed in Chapter 2). But when we discuss Adam's future, we are at risk of speaking ambiguously, for Adam has two futures, and we cannot refer unambiguously by saying 'Adam post-fission'. Again, stage theory has the virtue of flexibility, allowing philosophers to make good sense of whatever biologists choose to say about amoebic persistence. And, as with vagueness, stage theory puts the ambiguity in the right place. Recall that, on a semantic account of vagueness, stage theory has it that we fail to decide which transtemporal relation is the relevant 'sameness' relation, but that this does not give rise to any ambiguity in our referring to Alpha before the Cabinet episode, or to Omega afterwards. Similarly, here, stage theory says that if Adam exists post-fission, then our referring to him post-fission is ambiguous, but that this does not infect our reference to Adam pre-fission.

5.8 How to Decide?

I have been discussing situations in which there seem to be two objects with different properties in the same place at the same time. I have mostly relied upon the example of a sweater and the woollen thread from which it is made. But I might equally well have talked about the relationship between a tree and the large mass of molecules which make it up at a particular moment, or a piece of copper and the statue it forms, or a ship and the collection of planks from which it is made. We have seen that both constitution accounts and perdurance theory argue that the sweater and the thread are distinct objects: according to constitution theorists they are wholly present in the same region at the same time, according to perdurance theory they merely overlap, sharing a present temporal part. In contrast, stage theorists, Burke, and Gallois all suppose that the sweater and the thread are identical, and supply different explanations of why it is that the sweater and the thread at least appear to have different histories and different persistence conditions. Van Inwagen, finally, argues that neither the sweater nor the woollen thread exists, yet provides a way of understanding why I speak truly when I say that a sweater is hanging on a peg in my office.

One reason for investigating coincidence and co-location was in order to gain some insight into special questions about the relationship between human people and human organisms, and about the persistence conditions of persons and organisms. I will return in the final section of this chapter to discuss the particular problems which arise concerning persons. But we might well ask how we can possibly choose between the different accounts of the sweater and the woollen thread—what should we believe? Are they one object or two? And what sorts of objects are they, with what properties? There is, unfortunately, no knowing for certain which theory is true. The best we can do is to compare the different commitments and consequences of the various accounts. In previous chapters we have already seen various commitments and consequences of the different theories of persistence, and the findings of the present chapter can be added into the accounts of costs and benefits of each position. In connection with these issues, the most pressing concerns of philosophers often seem to be related either to questions of economy, or to questions of adhocness.

Take constitution theory, for example. It must be generous in its ontology of properties, for, as we saw, whether or not an object is a sweater, for example, is not determined by the basic properties of and relations between its parts. *Being a sweater* seems to be a property in its own right, on this account, and this multiplies the number of entities in the world. On the other hand, a constitution theorist might respond that both perdurance theorists and stage theorists are committed to vastly more particulars than are any endurance theorists, because of their commitment to momentary stages.

What of Burke, Gallois, and van Inwagen, who combine endurance theory with an identity view of the sweater and the thread? A problem for Gallois was that he leaves us no way to talk about questions of genuine identity through time, and thus undercuts one motivation for his own position. A problem for Burke was that he must attach great ontological significance to the apparently insignificant differences between changes in a thread which create a sweater and changes in a thread which just lead to a knotty mess. A problem for van Inwagen is that he denies that most ordinary macroscopic objects exist. Each of these positions is ontologically economical, but has other drawbacks.

Recall that we began with an apparent tension in our ordinary beliefs, between the thought that the sweater and the thread are one, and the thought that they have different properties. Those who insist that the sweater and the thread are indeed but a single object must offer some explanation of our tendency to attribute different properties to them. On the other hand, perdurance and constitution theorists, who claim that the sweater and the thread are different things, should offer some explanation of why we tend to say that there is just one thing there. Constitution theorists must simply claim that we do not usually 'count by identity'.[11] Perdurance theorists have a rather richer explanation to hand. They may argue that in ordinary contexts we ask how many (momentary yet spatially maximal) temporal parts of persisting objects there are on the peg in my office, in which case the answer at any moment is 'one'. Unfortunately, perdurance theorists believe that momentary temporal parts are neither sweaters nor woollen threads. Perdurance theorists get the 'right' answer only by counting temporal parts, not by actually counting sweaters or woollen threads.

According to stage theory, it is hardly surprising that perdurance theorists must adopt exactly this manoeuvre, claiming that in ordinary contexts we count temporal parts rather than persistents, even when we think we are counting persistents. According to stage theory, of course, these temporal parts or stages just *are* sweaters and woollen threads, the very things we were supposed to be counting. If we ask

---

[11] Although see Noonan (1999) on why this may not be not such a bad thing.

how many sweater-shaped things there are on the peg, the correct answer is 'one': there is exactly one such thing there, which is both the sweater and the woollen thread.[12] Moreover, stage theorists can explain the feeling that there is at least some sense in which it would be correct to answer 'two' when asked how many things there are on the peg. The single thing on the peg is both a sweater and a thread, falling under two different sortals. There are, therefore, two different ways in which we could ask about the history of the thing on the peg, and we could expect different answers to our questions. Nevertheless, there is just one thing there.

Stage theory gets the numbers right at a time, explaining why there is only one sweater-shaped thing on the peg right now. But the theory seems to get the numbers wildly wrong if we ask, for example, how many sweaters there have been on the peg today. For at every moment today there has been something which was a sweater on the peg, and each of those things is distinct from every other. This is one of the heaviest costs of stage theory, one which I discussed in Chapter 2. As we saw, stage theorists need to address this, for example by supposing that we do not, after all, count by identity when we count trans-temporally. The sweater on the peg at midday is, strictly and really, distinct from the sweater on the peg at one o'clock. But they are the same sweater because they are appropriately related.

5.9 The Problems of the Many

Before applying the results of this investigation to our initial questions about persons and organisms, I will discuss a problem which brings together questions about vagueness and about coincidence. This problem is one of several which go under the name 'the problem of the many'. One version of the problem of the many is a diachronic, or over-time problem. Tibbles is the cat on the mat, and she has a hair called 'H'. 'Orlando' is the name of that thing which is all of Tibbles except for H. So Orlando is a proper part of Tibbles. When Orlando becomes separated from H, Tibbles and Orlando come to coincide exactly. How are Orlando and Tibbles now related? They are not identical, because they have different properties: Orlando was once a proper part of a cat, whilst Tibbles never was.

---

[12] Again, this must be subject to some analysis, as in Chapter 2, of our referring to these instantaneous things.

This is an interesting problem, but it is structurally similar to the problem of the sweater and the thread. Constitution theorists say that, after the loss of H, Tibbles is constituted by Orlando, although she used to be constituted by a different lump of cat flesh. Van Inwagen can say that Orlando did not exist before the hair loss, and that, if Orlando exists at all after the hair loss, it is just identical to Tibbles. Burke argues that Orlando no longer exists after the hair loss, that it is destroyed by that minor change in its surroundings. Gallois can claim that Tibbles and Orlando are identical after the hair loss, although they used not to be. Perdurance theorists say that Tibbles and Orlando share some but not all of their temporal parts. Stage theorists say that one and the same object is both Orlando and Tibbles after the hair loss, although that is not the case at every time. And so on.

The problem of Orlando and Tibbles centres on the apparent ability of cats, but not lumps of cat flesh, to gain and lose (spatial) parts, whilst the case of the sweater and the thread centres on the apparent ability of woollen threads, but not sweaters, to become unravelled without ceasing to exist. There seems to be no important difference between the two types of case, except perhaps for the following. Someone impressed by the Orlando/Tibbles problem might be drawn towards mereological essentialism as a possible solution. That is, she might claim that cats cannot, after all, gain or lose spatial parts, and thus that Tibbles does not survive her hair loss. The analogous response to the sweater–thread case would be to claim that threads cannot, after all, survive unravelling. (Burke's solution moves in this direction.) It may be that this sort of essentialism about thread-configuration is more or less plausible than mereological essentialism, and in this respect the problems may differ. But I shall not pursue this diachronic version of the Orlando–Tibbles case any further.

There is also a synchronic problem about cats. If cats have arbitrary undetached parts, then Tibbles has very many large cat-like parts. Before Tibbles loses H, for example, Orlando is very cat-like, despite being a proper part of Tibbles. But there are many things like Orlando, many cat-shaped objects all sitting at once upon the mat. There are two interesting questions: which of these objects is Tibbles the cat? And what should we say about the rest of the objects?

First I will consider a determinate version of this 'problem of the many', in which every hair is firmly attached, and there is a single largest cat-shaped object on the mat. In this case, Tibbles the cat is that largest cat-shaped thing. What about the other cat-shaped objects on the mat, like Orlando? They cannot be cats, for no cat is a proper part of another cat, and each of them is a proper part of Tibbles the cat. If those other cat-like things are not cats, then *being a cat* is a relational property, a matter of being the largest cat-candidate in the vicinity. This makes it sounds as if Tibbles is a cat only because she is lucky enough not to be attached to an extra hair. If she had been attached to an extra hair, then she would not have been the largest cat-shaped thing on the mat, and so would not have been a cat. She would not have miaowed, slept, ate, or been conscious. This may seem like shocking contingency: an extra hair would have made Tibbles unconscious. And Orlando is unconscious just because it is unlucky enough to be attached to H: it misses out by a whisker.

The worry is that the slightest difference would have stopped Tibbles from being a cat. But the worry is unfounded (Hawley 1998*c*). If there had been an extra hair, the lump of flesh which is actually Tibbles the cat would not have been a cat. But Tibbles would not then have been *attached* to an extra hair. Rather, Tibbles would have *incorporated* an extra hair, and would have been a slightly larger cat. The relationship between Tibbles and the lump of flesh which composes her is a contingent one, for Tibbles might have been composed by a larger or a smaller lump of flesh. I shall set this modal problem aside for the moment, since I discuss issues of modality and persistence in Chapter 6. But it seems that the best response to the determinate problem of the many is to claim that the largest cat-shaped candidate on the mat is the cat, and that none of the other candidates is in fact a cat (though perhaps any one of them could have been a cat).

In Chapter 2, I pointed out that perdurance theory must give a temporally maximal account of sortal predicates: no temporal part of a tennis ball is a tennis ball, for example, and no temporal part of a person is a person. We have just seen that many sortal predicates, like 'is a cat', are also spatially maximal. Spatial maximality is, however, less objectionable than temporal maximality. Recall that it is instantaneous stages which instantiate most ordinary, non-sortal properties, and that, according to perdurance theory, persisting things satisfy predicates like 'is spherical' at times in virtue of their having instantaneous spherical parts at those times. So temporal maximality affects not just which things count as tennis balls, but also which things count as being spherical at a time. Qualifying to satisfy predicates in virtue of the properties of parts is a privilege reserved for maximal things.

This is not such an issue for spatial maximality. Take the cat once more. It is true that the cat miaows, and it had better not be true that the spatial parts of the cat are also miaowing. Moreover, this is a maximal matter: the cat miaows because it is the biggest cat-like thing on the mat. But at least the cat miaows in the most direct way in which anything can miaow. The cat does not satisfy 'is miaowing' in virtue of having some spatial part which instantiates *miaows*. Perhaps it cannot satisfy the predicate unless it has spatial parts arranged in the right way, but its spatial parts are not miaowing.

Finally, there is an indeterminate version of the problem of the many, in which there is no clear largest cat-shaped cat-candidate. Suppose that there are some hairs about which it is indeterminate whether they are parts of the cat. Then there are many precisely bounded cat-shaped lumps of feline flesh on the mat, and it would be arbitrary to suppose that any particular one of these is the most cat-like. In particular, it is by no means obvious that the largest candidate is the best candidate for being the cat, since the larger candidates are less cohesive, including hairs which are barely attached to the body of the cat, if at all. This contrasts with the determinate case in which the largest lump is distinguished by its size, and thus overrules the claims of the other lumps to count as cats. So, in the indeterminate case, how many cats are there on the mat?

David Lewis suggests that we take a supervaluationist approach to this situation (Lewis 1993). It is indeterminate which lump of feline flesh on the mat fits the description 'is a cat', because the term 'cat' is imprecise. But on any precisification of the term 'cat', exactly one lump satisfies 'is a cat'. Supervaluationism tells us that if something is true on every legitimate precisification of terms, then it counts as 'super-true'. So it is super-true that there is exactly one cat on the mat, because on any reasonable precisification of 'cat', it is true that there is exactly one cat on the mat. Thus we have a perfectly reasonable sense in which there is exactly one cat on the mat, despite all the cat-shaped lumps of flesh. An epistemic account of this vagueness could also work here. Perhaps there is a precise degree of cohesiveness in which things must engage in order to count as parts of the same cat, and perhaps exactly one candidate satisfies 'is a cat', although we cannot tell which.

E. J. Lowe's approach is also supervaluationist, but according to him *no* lump of flesh fits the description 'is a cat'. Lowe is an endurance theorist and a constitution theorist: he believes that lumps of flesh merely constitute cats, on the grounds that lumps and cats have different persistence conditions. Now, it is indeterminate at any moment which lump of feline flesh on the mat fits the description 'constitutes a cat', and thus which lump constitutes Tibbles. But on any precisification, exactly one lump fits the description. So if we adopt supervaluationism, we can say that exactly one thing constitutes a cat, and thus that there is exactly one cat on the mat.[13]

As Lowe points out, on his view there is exactly one cat-constituter on the mat, despite Lewis's disparaging claim that he is committed to many. There are many lumps of flesh, but on any precisification exactly one lump satisfies 'constitutes a cat'. There is, however, a different, genuine problem for this account, as I shall now explain. Before precisification, it is indeterminate which lump satisfies 'constitutes a cat'; afterwards it is determinate. But which term needs sharpening up? It is not 'lump', for there are very many of these lumps, no matter how we precisify. Nor is it 'constitutes'. For a lump to constitute a cat, it must have exactly the same boundaries as a cat.[14] If it were determinate where there were cat-boundaries, then it would be determinate which lumps constituted cats. But it is not determinate where there are cat-boundaries, because 'cat' needs sharpening. In fact, it is indeterminate which lump constitutes a cat because it is indeterminate what kind of thing a cat is, how loose its hairs may be.[15]

On different precisifications of 'cat', a different lump satisfies 'constitutes a cat'. And on different precisifications of 'cat', a thing with different boundaries satisfies 'is a cat'—a thing which is not a lump. (Recall that, according to Lowe, no mere lump can actually, predicatively be a cat, as opposed to merely constituting a cat.) There are two readings of this. Either a single thing satisfies 'is a cat', and that thing is differently sized on different precisifications of 'cat'. Or things have their sizes irrespective of our concepts, and different things satisfy 'is a cat' on different precisifications.

---

[13] Mark Johnston has a similar-looking account of clouds and clusters of water droplets: 'with respect to various sharpenings, or legitimate ways of drawing the boundaries of the cloud, slightly different such clusters will constitute the cloud.' 'What is important for our purposes is that on no legitimate sharpening is [the cloud] identical with any one of [the clusters].' (Johnston 1992: 100.) If Johnston's approach is supervaluationist (and it may not be), then it is subject to the objection which I raise against Lowe.

[14] This is merely a minimum requirement: for example, it introduces no asymmetry between constituter and constituted.

[15] If you still think that 'constitutes' is imprecise, then try to imagine what the precisifications of 'constitutes' could be.

Consider the former. On this view, there is a single constituted thing on the mat, which has different boundaries according as our concepts differ. If we sharpen up 'cat' one way, then that thing is a certain size, and if we sharpen up 'cat' a different way, then that very same thing is a different size. But that thing is a material object, so on this view we can shrink or expand material objects just by thinking about them. This is reminiscent of the creation and destruction at a distance by thought power which the conventionalist is committed to, and it is incredible.

Those who believe that lumps of flesh merely constitute cats have two options. There may be a single constituted thing on the mat, a vague object with fuzzy boundaries. It is ontically indeterminate which lump constitutes that thing, for it is ontically indeterminate which lump shares its boundaries with that thing. Now, the only precisely bounded objects on the mat are mere lumps. So if we sharpen up 'cat', nothing will satisfy 'is a cat', and thus nothing will satisfy 'constitutes a cat'. This is to abandon the supervaluationist approach and accept that cats are vague objects.

The alternative view is that there are many precisely bounded constituted things on the mat, and that which of these counts as a cat depends upon us. Call the constituted things 'cat-candidates'. Then every suitable lump of flesh constitutes a cat-candidate, and different cat-candidates satisfy 'is a cat' on different precisifications of 'cat'. This doubles the population on the mat. Supervaluation allows us to say that there is exactly one cat, and thus exactly one cat-constituting lump. Nevertheless, there are many lumps of flesh, *and* many cat-candidates, each constituted by a different lump. Lowe doesn't mind that there are many lumps of flesh, for on his account none of these is the sort of thing which purrs, eats, or sleeps. But cat-candidates, in contrast, are exactly the sort of thing which purrs, eats, and sleeps. After all, each cat-candidate is *identical* to a cat on some precisification of 'cat'.

For those who believe that lumps of flesh merely constitute cats, supervaluationism about cat-talk only makes things worse. The natural remaining option is to believe that cats have ontically vague boundaries. So endurance theorists' views about persistence lead naturally to a commitment to ontic vagueness at a time. Belief in endurance often accompanies belief in constitution, which in turn makes the at-a-time supervaluationist approach untenable, and thus commits the endurance theorist to metaphysical vagueness. We saw in

Chapter 4 that it is difficult for the endurance theorist to avoid an untenable commitment to ontic indeterminacy in identity over time, and now we see that it is also difficult for the endurance theorist to avoid commitment to ontic indeterminacy at a time. However, the indeterminacy in question here is an indeterminacy concerning the boundaries of Tibbles the cat; it is not, at least, an ontic indeterminacy in *identity*.

Another connection with the discussions of Chapter 4 is as follows. The indeterminate problem of the many is the problem of saying which of many apparently good cat-candidates is the cat. This is analogous to the perdurance theory treatment of indeterminacy in persistence. Most living organisms do not seem to have either a very precise moment of beginning, or a precise moment of demise; there is some temporal fuzziness at the beginning and at the end of life. (The same is true, of course, of many non-living things.) In such a situation the perdurance theorist can see a plethora of 'nested' four-dimensional objects, many of which are good candidates for being the living organism. In a determinate case, the longest four-dimensional object would take the honours, but in the indeterminate case, the perdurance theorist can adopt a supervaluationist approach (or, indeed, an epistemic approach) to the matter. So, for the perdurance theorist, indeterminacy in temporal boundaries can be treated in the same way as indeterminacy in spatial boundaries. Moreover, as we have seen, ordinary sortals have a temporally maximal feature to them, in the absence of vagueness. This maximality is complicated by vagueness, and vagueness is ubiquitous.

5.10 Personal Persistence

Am I related to this organism somewhat as the sweater is to the thread? What is that relationship, anyway? And how is this organism, a dynamic system, related to the collection of molecules from which it is currently composed? First let's think about the relationship between living organisms and the matter of which they are made, before returning to think more specifically about persons. Issues of this first kind arise for trees and insects as they do for human beings. It is characteristic of living organisms, like trees for example, that they exchange matter with their environment and that, at least during some phases of life, they grow, coming to consist of larger portions of matter. In some respects, then, a tree and its present matter may be compared to the sweater and the thread. The tree coincides with a collection or lump of matter, though it differs from that lump of matter in respect of its history and, if it survives, in respect of its future. An organism and the matter with which it coincides seem to have different persistence conditions.

We have already encountered a whole range of responses to this sort of situation. One suggestion is that organisms are temporarily constituted by lumps of matter, by different lumps or collections at different times. This is constitution theory, exemplified by Lowe's account of cats and their constituters. Van Inwagen's treatment of organisms is different from his account of artefacts and other things. Van Inwagen denies that either the sweater or the thread exists. He does believe in living organisms, but does not believe in collections or lumps of matter. So an organism has different parts at different times, but there is no other macroscopic object in question. Burke expresses some scepticism about the existence of arbitrary fusions. Setting this aside, he argues that, at any rate, such fusions cease to exist when they undergo changes which result in the existence of an organism like a tree. Just as the original thread ceased to exist when it 'became' a sweater, the fusion of a set of atoms ceases to exist when the atoms in the set begin to make up the tree. Gallois, presumably, would have it that the tree and the lump of matter are now identical, although they used not to be. The lump, unlike the tree, used to be scattered, and the tree, unlike the lump, used to be made of different molecules, but nevertheless they are now identical. According to perdurance theory, the lump and the tree share some but not all of their temporal parts. And according to stage theory, the present stage is both the tree and the lump, although it used to be that one stage was the lump and another was the tree.

So far, so good. There seems to be little extra to add to the accounts given of the sweater and the thread, and the criticisms of those accounts, except in van Inwagen's case. The only important difference is perhaps that turnover of matter in a living organism is much more inevitable and frequent than for a sweater, which may affect the plausibility of certain accounts.

But more difficult questions arise when we consider the relationship between human persons and human organisms. A key question in the traditional debate about personal identity is whether human persons and human organisms have the same criteria of identity, the

same persistence conditions. This question is made vivid by considering apparently possible situations in which people survive the demise
of their bodies, or bodies survive the demise of their 'occupants', or
bodies and persons become otherwise distinct. If any of these are
genuine possibilities, then bodies and persons have different persistence conditions. These were the kinds of situations I imagined at the
beginning of this chapter—what if I lose my memory? What if I lose
my memory and 'my' memories are instantiated in a different organism? Could I become separated from this organism?

If people have different persistence conditions from 'their' organisms, what follows? One possibility is that organisms and persons are
distinct, although they often coincide. Persons may then be immaterial, sharing no parts with their organisms, or they may be material
things, made of the same parts as their organisms. If we take the latter
view, and also have a constitution view of the relationship between
organisms and lumps of matter, we will have to suppose that there are
three different human-sized objects sitting at my desk right now—a
person, an organism, and a lump of matter. Another possibility is that
people and organisms may be temporarily identical, if we are willing
to accept Gallois's account of temporary identities.

According to perdurance theory, persons and organisms share temporal parts, though they need not be identical, or permanently coincident. Presumably, in normal cases, a person is a large proper
(temporal) part of her or his organism, whilst in abnormal puzzle
cases, a person can share temporal parts with more than one organism, 'moving' from one to the other. According to stage theory, in
ordinary cases a single stage at any moment is both the person and the
organism, although earlier or later stages may be just the organism.

If none of these positions is acceptable—and as we have seen, they all
have their problems—then the alternative is to deny that people and
organisms have different persistence conditions, despite the puzzle
cases which encourage us to think that people can switch bodies, and
despite the suggestions that organisms pre-date and often outlive the
people with which they are associated. There are, of course, two ways to
identify persistence conditions. The first is to claim that organisms after
all have the persistence conditions we are tempted to associate with persons (perhaps conditions related to psychological continuity). The second is to claim that persons after all have the persistence conditions we
are tempted to associate with organisms (perhaps conditions related to
material, spatio-temporal and/or biological continuity).

Burke offers something like the first option to those who wish to retain a psychological continuity account of personal persistence (Burke 1994*b*: VI D). He argues that where we are tempted to say that a organism is associated with a new person—either in early life or as the result of some bizarre experiment—we should instead say that the old organism has ceased to exist, and a new organism now exists, one which is identical with a person. Presumably the same goes for the end of a person: at my death, my organism will be replaced by a new material thing. This is not exactly to say that organisms have the persistence conditions of persons, but it is to say two things which almost add up to that claim. First, organisms need not have the persistence conditions usually associated with organism, for the sortal *organism* can be dominated by the sortal *person*. Second, organisms cannot survive the sorts of events which lead to the creation of a person, whatever those are.

I outlined some objections to Burke's general account earlier in this chapter, but there is a special problem for this account of persons, one at which Burke himself gestures. Assume that this organism has the persistence conditions that I have, and that people persist through psychological continuity. If we could transfer my mental states into a different body, we would thereby transfer this organism, perhaps at the speed of light, into a different place, where it would instantly come to be composed of entirely new parts. This seems to be an extraordinary suggestion. Moreover, this account suggests that human organisms can have persistence conditions quite different from those of other organisms, since presumably many animals and plants do not 'embody' anything like a person. Of course, any such proposal will have difficulty in drawing a clear line: can a dog change bodies? What about a jellyfish?

Instead of attributing person-like persistence conditions to bodies, we could attribute body-like persistence conditions to persons, as Eric Olson does (Olson 1997). Olson argues that, since the other options are so unattractive, we should believe that human persons are identical with human organisms. A person can, therefore, survive without surviving as a person, just as a kitten can survive as an adult cat without surviving as a kitten. Cases in which a person is apparently transferred from one body to another are not in fact person-transfers. I cannot leave this organism, because I *am* this organism. Olson gives us especially pressing arguments for rejecting a constitution view of the relationship between bodies and people. On such a view, persons and organisms coincide, although they are distinct. But this presents us with an unappealing dilemma. Either organisms are conscious things, in which case there are at least two conscious beings sitting in my chair right now. Or else they are not. But they have the same arrangement of neurones and so on as a person, which makes it utterly mysterious why they are not conscious. This is a special, and perhaps more damaging version of a more general problem for constitution theory which we have already encountered. How can coinciding objects made of the same parts differ in their properties? How can my body fail to be conscious, given that it is made of all the same parts arranged in the same way as a conscious thing, me?

We have already encountered a similar but slightly less serious problem for perdurance theory. As we saw in Chapter 2, instantaneous temporal parts (or stages) are the instantiators of *being conscious*, but nevertheless people satisfy 'is conscious' at times in virtue of this property of their temporal parts. But any person has very many large proper temporal parts which are excellent candidates for being a person, except that they are proper parts of a person. If these large things satisfy 'is conscious', there seem to be far too many conscious things sitting in my chair right now. Perdurance theorists should claim that such things do not satisfy 'is conscious', for they are not maximal. Indeed, 'is a person' is presumably vague, as well as maximal, and thus it is indeterminate which temporally extended thing satisfies 'is conscious'. Stage theory encounters no such difficulties, since it is the instantaneous stage which is both person and organism, and which instantiates *being conscious*.

Finally, there are puzzle cases which encourage us to think that people could divide, that a single person could become two people, as amoebae do.[16] This is most easily accepted by those who believe that personal persistence is a matter of psychological continuity, but it is also possible to devise cases in which two 'fission-products' seem to be physically continuous with the pre-fission person. One option is to claim that fission marks the end of the pre-fission person; perhaps such a demise is nevertheless preferable to ordinary death. We would then need to explain why satisfying the 'standard' criteria for personal persistence (either psychological or physical continuity) is not sufficient to guarantee personal persistence in such cases.

---

[16] See Wiggins (1980: ch. 6), Williams (1973: ch. 5), Lewis (1976a), and Parfit (1984: ch. 12).

The alternative, for perdurance or constitution theorists, is to posit 'multiple occupancy'. Perhaps there were two people all along, even before fission made them spatially separate. We examined such an option for describing amoebic fission. In the present case, of course, there are special costs, for here we are discussing conscious beings, and supposing that there may be more than one such thing in a place at a time, if there is a fission event in the future. As with amoebae, stage theorists have a relatively simple strategy: there is but a single person present before fission, although it may be that she is the same person as two distinct but simultaneous person-stages at some post-fission moment.

Investigation of coincidence and constitution, identity and persistence has not enabled us to arrive at a unique account of the relationship between person and organism, or organism and matter. But we have been able to sort the more viable from the less viable accounts, to see the consequences of adopting this position or that—our decisions can now be informed decisions, even if no single verdict is rationally compelled.

6

Modality

As they hang from the peg in my office, the sweater and the thread seem to coincide temporarily. They occupy the same spatial region at some time, but they have different histories: the thread was created in a factory, whereas the sweater was created on knitting needles at home. Similarly, as they sit on the mat, Tibbles and the lump of stuff which makes her up seem to coincide temporarily. They sit on the mat together, but they have not always been coincident: Tibbles used to be made of a different lump of stuff. At least, that's a tempting way to talk about the sweater and the thread, and about Tibbles and the lump of feline stuff which makes her up.

We can also imagine cases of complete and permanent coincidence. For example, imagine a sculptor, who creates a clay statue of Goliath in a slightly peculiar fashion. The sculptor first creates the two halves of the statue, then sticks them together, simultaneously creating the statue—Goliath—and a large lump of clay—Lump. Eventually, the statue and the lump of clay are simultaneously destroyed when a bomb goes off in the workshop. Now, the statue and the lump of clay are created at the same time, coincide throughout their lifetimes, then are destroyed at the same time. Moreover, they apparently share all their intrinsic properties, being made of the same parts at any given time. But they seem to have different modal properties, which is to say that different possibilities seem to be available to them.

For example, the lump of clay could have been spherical—if the sculptor had had more abstract tastes. But the statue could not have been spherical—if the sculptor had made the lump into a ball, she would have created a different statue, instead of Goliath. And perhaps the statue could have been made of a different lump of clay, if the sculptor had reached over to a different bench. But presumably the lump of clay itself could not have been made of a different lump of clay.

In early sections of this chapter, I will examine rival accounts of the statue and the lump of clay. But what constraints are there on such accounts? As we saw, different accounts of the sweater and the thread must explain why the sweater and thread at least appear to be co-located objects with different features. For example, van Inwagen, who denies that either the sweater or the thread exists, supplies an account of why our ordinary talk about sweaters and threads is perfectly reasonable. And stage theory, which claims that, literally speaking, the thing which is now the sweater and the thread did not exist at all in the past, supplies an account of why our ordinary talk about such things and their histories is reasonable, and why we can truly say different things about the sweater's history and the thread's history.

It is more difficult to establish a consensus about what modal features the statue and the lump of clay even appear to have. Could that very statue really have been made out of a different lump of clay? And couldn't that very statue have been spherical? Of course, if it were spherical, it would no longer be a statue of Goliath (or not a realistic statue of Goliath)—but perhaps it would still have been the same statue. If the statue and the lump do not even appear to have different modal features, then there is no need for a theoretical account of those apparent differences. Nevertheless, even if this particular case is unproblematic, we must provide an account of how apparently permanently coincident objects can appear to differ modally. If there can be temporary coincidence, however that is explained away, then it seems there might be permanent coincidence.

The sweater and the thread differ in their persistence conditions, so, by definition, there are types of possible event in which one would survive whilst the other perished: the sweater but not the thread would be destroyed by unravelling. But a difference in persistence conditions does not guarantee a difference in actual survival, for in general there will be types of event in which both objects would perish. For example, if my office burns down, both the sweater and the thread will be destroyed simultaneously. So if there can be coincident objects with different persistence conditions, then there might be permanently coincident objects with different persistence conditions, and, thus, different modal features.

What about beginnings of existence, as opposed to ends? The spinning processes which brought the thread into existence did not bring the sweater into existence, and thus the thread pre-dates the sweater. Different kinds of thing may be associated with different existence conditions, as well as different persistence conditions, where existence conditions for a kind of thing determine what sorts of events bring into existence objects of that kind. Could coinciding objects of different kinds come into existence in the same event, even though they have different existence conditions? It might be possible to argue that for certain pairs of kinds, there is no type of event which could simultaneously bring into existence objects of both kinds, even where such objects may coincide. But I see no prospects for a general argument along these lines. If we believe in temporary coincidence (or something with the appearance of temporary coincidence) we ought to offer an account of permanent coincidence between objects with different modal features (different existence and/or persistence conditions)—if there are temporarily coinciding things, then there could be permanently coinciding things with different modal features.

Of course, we may eventually settle upon an account which claims that appearances deceive, that permanent coincidence between modally different things is not a genuine possibility. Similarly, we saw various accounts of the sweater and the thread which claimed that appearances deceive, that temporary coincidence between distinct objects is not a genuine possibility. But such accounts owe us an explanation of why temporary and permanent coincidence appear to be genuine possibilities. I will approach the statue and the lump by attempting to apply the various accounts of the sweater and the thread to this new type of case. In general, my discussions will be brief, since I have already considered the merits of the various accounts in Chapter 5. No theory of persistence should be judged on what it says about modality alone, because thinking clearly about the modal features of things is especially difficult. Nevertheless, any account of persistence and of material objects needs to offer some explanation of their modal features, and I will give a stage theory account of the modal features of stages and sums of stages. This will round out the development of stage theory that I have undertaken in this book, and also bring out some attractive features of the theory.

6.1 Constitution Theories

According to constitution theory, the sweater and the thread are distinct objects occupying the same place at the same time; the thread constitutes the sweater without being identical to it. Whatever its problems regarding sortal properties, an attractive feature of this theory is that it can account for the lump of clay and the statue without further modification. Just as the sweater and the thread are coincident but distinct, distinguished by their different historical properties and persistence conditions, the lump of clay and the statue are (always) coincident yet distinct, distinguished by their different modal properties, persistence conditions, and existence conditions. Constitution theory deals with temporary and permanent coincidence in one and the same way.

6.2 Perdurance Theory

As we saw, perdurance theory handles the sweater and the thread rather smoothly. The sweater and the thread share temporal parts, but they do not completely coincide, for they do not share all their temporal parts: the thread existed before the sweater did. But the lump of clay and the statue share all of their temporal parts. They are permanently coincident, coming into existence and going out of existence together. So, unlike constitution theory, the perdurance theory account of the thread and the sweater does not automatically extend to cover the lump of clay and the statue.

It seems that the two four-dimensional persistents—the lump of clay and the statue—have different modal properties, including different persistence conditions, despite the fact that they share all of their microphysical and non-modal properties. Just as constitution theory rather mysteriously claims that the sweater and the thread have different histories and persistence conditions, despite the fact that they share all their microphysical properties, perdurance theory claims that the lump of clay and the statue differ modally whilst being made of the same parts at all times.

To make this claim less mysterious, perdurance theorists must draw upon extra resources. A natural option is to adopt counterpart theory, according to which objects existing in different possible worlds are never identical (Lewis 1986a: ch. 4). Actual objects satisfy modal predicates courtesy of the properties instantiated by their counterparts in other possible worlds. What determines whether a possible object is a counterpart of some actual object? There is no straightforward answer to this question, because different ways of classifying one and the same actual object correspond to different ways of determining its counterparts.

For example, if perdurance theorists adopt counterpart theory, they may argue as follows. The actual lump of clay and the statue are but one and the same thing. But when we talk about what is possible for the lump of clay, we talk about possible things which are lump of clay-counterparts of the single actual lump/statue. And when we talk about what is possible for the statue, we talk about possible things which are statue-counterparts of the single actual lump/statue. We say that the lump could have been spherical, whilst the statue could not: this is just to say that the single actual lump/statue has lump of clay-counterparts that are spherical, but has no spherical statue-counterparts. When asking whether a possible object is a counterpart of the actual lump/statue, we need to specify which sortal we are interested in. Comparably, when asking whether two objects are similar, we need to specify which respect of similarity we are interested in.[1]

Counterpart theory fits well with perdurance theory, but perdurance theorists could adopt either the contingent identity thesis, or the Burkean 'dominant sortals' approach to the lump of clay and the statue instead (or as well)—I will examine these two accounts below. On the first account, the lump of clay and the statue are identical four-dimensional persistents, but they are only contingently identical. On the second account, the lump of clay and the statue are (necessarily) identical four-dimensional persistents, and we are mistaken if we think that they have incompatible modal properties or persistence conditions. They are a single thing, and they both have the modal properties associated with being a statue, since *statue* is the dominant sortal.

6.3 Dominant Sortals

Burke denies that the sweater and the thread have different histories. The thread did not exist before it was made into a sweater, and the thread which did exist, ready for knitting, ceased to exist when the sweater was created. This approach could be extended to the lump of clay and the statue, although Burke himself is not committed to this extension. Perhaps the lump of clay and the statue are identical, could not have been distinct, and do not have different modal properties. The most natural extension of Burke's account would have it that the sortal *statue* dominates the sortal *lump of clay*, and thus a lump of clay, like Lump, which is also a statue, has the modal properties characteristic of a statue, not those characteristic of a lump of clay.

---

[1] There are plenty of similarities between counterpart theory and stage theory.

There is a possible world which we are tempted to describe as one in which the statue is made out of a different lump of clay, and in which the lump of clay is spherical. But perhaps this description is mistaken. Perhaps a better description would be this: in that world, the statue is made out of different molecules than it is in the actual world and thus the lump of clay is also made of different molecules. In that world, the molecules which actually make up Lump and Goliath make up a spherical thing, but a thing which is not the actual lump of clay. The lump of clay has the modal properties of the statue, contrary to our initial intuitions.

I objected to Burke's approach to the sweater and the thread on the grounds that it made the destruction of a thread (or a piece of rock) an easy and arbitrary matter—all we need do is make the thread into a sweater, or the rock into a statue. Analogously, we might complain that the present account gives peculiar identity conditions to lumps of clay (and to other things which can fall under more dominant sortals). For example, the account has it that Lump could have been made out of completely different molecules, because Goliath could have been made out of completely different molecules. But presumably a second lump of clay, one which does not make up a statue, could not have been made out of completely different molecules. Whether or not a lump of clay could have been made out of completely different molecules depends not upon whether it is statue-shaped, but upon whether it is actually a statue, a certain kind of artefact.

These ideas are strange, but it is harder to have secure intuitions about modal facts than it is to have secure intuitions about survival. I am confident in rejecting Burke's account of the sweater and the thread, but less confident in rejecting this modal extension of his position, because I am less confident in my views about the modal features of things. Indeed, we could reject the account of the sweater and the thread whilst accepting the more plausible modal analogue. As we have seen, this combination is open to perdurance theorists, who can explain away the sweater and the thread by invoking temporal parts, and might opt for a 'dominant sortals' approach to the lump of clay and the statue.

6.4 Temporary Identities and Contingent Identities

Gallois argues that things may be identical at some time without being identical at all times. The sweater and the thread are now identical, although they used not to be. But the present problem is not that the lump of clay and the statue are temporarily identical. Instead, the problem is that they seem actually to be indiscernible at all times, yet seem to differ in their modal properties. Although temporary ident-ities cannot account for the lump of clay and the statue, a natural next step is to accept contingent identities, and thereby account for this case. The lump of clay and the statue are actually identical, one and the same thing, but nevertheless they could have been distinct, could have had different properties. Indeed, Gallois champions contingent identity as well as temporary identity (1998: ch. 6).

To believe in contingent identity is not just to believe that there are contingent identity statements. Most people accept that sentences like 'the tallest student is the laziest student' are only contingently true, but the contingent identity thesis goes beyond this. The idea is that a single thing could have been two things. Again, this is a view which, if coherent, could be combined with a disanalogous view of the thread and the sweater, perdurance theory for example. It seems possible to reject temporary identities whilst accepting contingent identities, although considerations both for and against these ideas are broadly similar.

6.5 Scepticism about Objects

Van Inwagen denies that either the sweater or the thread exists, and believes only in their atoms. Similarly, he denies that either the lump of clay or the statue exists, and believes only in the atoms which others would take to be parts of the lump of clay and the statue. So, like con-stitution theory, van Inwagen's view needs no special modification to deal with permanent, as opposed to temporary coincidence. Problems would arise if there were cases of permanently coincident atoms or organisms which could have been distinct, for both atoms and organ-isms do feature in van Inwagen's ontology. But it is hard to come up with plausible cases of this kind. Could I have been identical twins, or become divided in later life? It seems safest to answer 'no' (van Inwagen 1990*b*: 164).[2]

---

[2] See the brief comments on fission at the end of my Chapter 5.

6.6 Stage Theory

According to stage theory, a single stage at present (and each of many stages in the recent past and near future) is both the sweater and the thread, whilst there are past stages which are the thread but which are not the sweater. Some of those past stages—related in a certain way to the present stage—are cardigans, so it is true that the thread used to be a cardigan, whilst it is not true that the sweater used to be a cardigan. However *every* actual stage is either both the lump of clay and the statue, or is neither the lump of clay nor the statue.

To develop a stage theory account of the statue and the lump of clay, we need to recall the stage theory account of reference. A proper name like 'Goliath' or a definite description like 'the statue' refers to different stages when it is used to talk about goings-on at different times. As I said in Chapter 2, the details of this account will depend upon which theory of naming and reference we accept. In brief, stage theory has it that a name is attached (by some mechanism or other) to a certain stage, and to other stages which are suitably related to that stage. What those suitable relations are will depend in part upon the kind of thing we intended to name. The relations which underpin *being the same sweater* are not exactly the same as the relations which underpin *being the same thread*, as we saw in Chapter 5.

Now, the relations which underpin *being the same statue* are not the same as those which underpin *being the same lump of clay*. Nevertheless, any actual stage which bears the *being the same statue* relation to the present stage of Goliath/Lump also bears the *being the same lump of clay* relation to that stage. That's to say, the statue and the lump of clay are permanently coincident. We can construct predicates out of proper names and other referring terms, predicates like 'is Goliath', 'is Lump', 'is the statue', 'is the lump of clay', and so on. Call these predicates *individual predicates*. Stage theory says that instantaneous stages satisfy individual predicates, different stages at different times. In contrast, perdurance theorists believe that extended four-dimensional things satisfy individual predicates, and endurance theorists believe that the things which satisfy individual predicates can exist at more than one moment, and are wholly present whenever they exist. Talk of individual predicates is just a convenient way of representing claims about the reference of terms like 'Goliath' and 'the statue'.

The claims are parallel to those made by the three theories about sortal predicates: according to stage theory instantaneous stages satisfy sortal predicates like 'is a tennis ball' and 'is a statue', according to perdurance theory long-ish four-dimensional things satisfy such predicates, and according to endurance theory, sortal predicates are satisfied by things which can be wholly present at more than one moment. And this is hardly surprising, for Goliath is a statue, the thing which is Goliath is also a statue, the statue is a statue, the thing which is the statue is a statue, and so on.

Stage theory should account for the statue and the lump of clay in the following way: in the actual world 'is Goliath', 'is Lump', 'is the statue', and 'is the lump of clay' all have the same extension, are satisfied by exactly the same stages. But this need not have been the case—'is Goliath' and 'is Lump' are only contingently co-extensional. If the statue had been made of a different lump of clay, then 'is Goliath' and 'is Lump' would have had entirely different extensions from one another. If Goliath and Lump had been created together, after which Goliath was destroyed (by squashing) whilst Lump survived, then some but not all of the stages in the extension of 'is Lump' would have been in the extension of 'is Goliath'. And so on. We are familiar with the idea that predicates may be contingently co-extensional—predicates like 'has a heart' and 'has kidneys'—and stage theory adapts this idea to handle permanent but contingent coincidence.

6.7 Modal Features of Stages

Stage theory accounts for our everyday modal talk about objects in terms of the possible extensions of individual predicates. But to fill out my account of stage theory, I want to explore what modal features stages themselves have, and what modal features sums of stages have. This second question is of particular interest to perdurance theorists, who identify ordinary objects with sums of stages. So what should a stage theorist say about the modal nature of stages? I will be rather restrictive about stages: I claim that a stage necessarily satisfies every individual predicate it in fact satisfies. That's to say, the present stage of Goliath and Lump is essentially a stage of both Goliath and Lump—it is necessary that that very stage satisfies 'is the statue' and 'is the lump of clay', if it exists at all.

One peculiar-sounding consequence of this account is that, although Goliath is a present stage, what is possible for the stage differs from what is possible for Goliath. After all, I claimed that Goliath need not have been Lump, that the statue might have been made from a different lump of clay: this is to say that 'is Goliath' and 'is Lump' might have had different extensions. Yet I also claim that the stage which is Goliath right now is essentially Lump. How can it be true both that Goliath might not have been Lump and that the present stage is essentially Lump, if Goliath just is the present stage?

To explain this, we need the distinction between *de re* and *de dicto* modalities. Assume that every whale is essentially a whale. Could the largest living animal have been a fish? According to the *de re* reading, the question asks, of Moby, who happens to be the largest living animal, whether he could have been a fish. The answer is 'no': Moby is a whale and could not have been a fish. But according to the *de dicto* reading, the question asks whether it could have been true that a single thing satisfied both 'is the largest living animal' and 'is a fish'. Then the answer seems to be 'yes': there could have been fish larger than any whale. Thinking *de dicto*, we do not consider the thing which actually satisfies 'is the largest living animal', then ask whether it is a fish in some possible world. Rather, we should consider each possible world in turn, consider the thing which satisfies 'is the largest living animal' in that world, and ask whether it is a fish in that world.

According to stage theory, we can also distinguish a third reading of the question. According to stage theory, the largest living animal—Moby—is an instantaneous stage. *De dicto*, the largest living animal could have been a fish. *De re*, the largest living animal—Moby—could not have been a fish, but could have been made of different whale-stuff (if it had eaten different plankton). Now, *de strato*, the largest living animal—the present stage of Moby—could not have been a fish, and could not have been made of different whale-stuff. 'Is Moby' could have been satisfied by an object which did not satisfy 'is made of that very portion of whale-stuff', but the stage which satisfies both those predicates satisfies both of them essentially. To speak *de strato* is to speak *de re* of stages, and to speak *de re* of persisting things is to speak *de dicto* of stages. Most modal claims will turn out to be *de dicto* or *de re*, rather than *de strato*: I'm not terribly interested in what would have become of my present stage had I made different decisions in the past; I'm interested in what would have become of *me*. Nevertheless, in practising metaphysics, and especially in discussing stage theory, we will sometimes think *de strato*, asking what is possible for a stage itself.

I have claimed that stages essentially satisfy all the individual predicates they actually satisfy, and in a moment I will provide some support for that claim. But how can we tell what modal properties things have, especially apparently unfamiliar things like instantaneous stages and sums of stages? To answer this, I would have to investigate the nature of modality—Where do facts about possibility come from?—and the epistemology of modality—How can we know these facts?—and this book is already long enough.

But here is a minimal construal of my claims about the modal properties of stages and the like: if we suppose that stage theory is true, then the objects of ordinary reference are instantaneous stages (subject to the qualifications of Chapter 2). Much of our ordinary thought and talk about the world is inherently modal—we talk about how things could have been different, how things have to be, what changes our actions could have effected, and so on. If stage theory is true, then much of this talk concerns instantaneous stages. So, in these pages, I offer an account of the modal properties of stages which makes best sense of the ways in which we ordinarily speak and think. It may be that most of what we ordinarily say is false, in which case my account will be unfounded. Nevertheless, my account shows how stage theory can fit with most of what we say, true or false.

My basic claim is that a stage essentially satisfies every individual predicate it actually satisfies. If a given stage is Goliath, then it could not fail to be Goliath: it could not have existed without being Goliath. There is thus an asymmetry between Goliath and its stages. Goliath could have had different stages, since the statue might have survived for more or less time than it actually did; fewer or more stages could have been Goliath. But no actual Goliath stage could have failed to be a Goliath stage. In this respect, individual predicates are analogous to natural kind terms, and stages are analogous to the members of natural kinds. There could have been more or fewer elephants than there actually are, just as there could have been more or fewer Goliath-stages. But, just as no actual elephant could have failed to be an elephant, no actual Goliath stage could have failed to be Goliath.

First I will argue that a stage must satisfy *some* individual predicate which it actually satisfies, then I will argue that a stage must satisfy *every* individual predicate it actually satisfies. Finally I will discuss sufficient conditions for transworld existence. What essential properties do stages have? There seem to be three plausible options. One is that, as I claim, stages inherit their modal features from the individual predicates they satisfy, that what is possible for the stage depends upon what it is a stage *of*. A second option is to suppose that stages have their spatio-temporal locations essentially. And a third option is to suppose that stages do not have any essential features, that there are no limits on what qualities a stage might have had. These three options are not exhaustive, but I think they are the most plausible. Stages do not have, for example, their colour, shape, or internal structure essentially, unless it is because they are stages of persisting things which have their colour, shape, or internal structure at that time essentially.

I advocate the first option. The second option is problematic: why should we suppose that any material object has its location essentially, that it could not have been elsewhere? We certainly do not think that statues, bananas, or people have their spatio-temporal locations essentially: I could have been on top of Snowdon right now, instead of sitting here at my desk, and I could have taken this banana with me. Do these facts about ordinary objects entail that stages are also modally movable? Mark Heller, who believes only in immovable parts of space–time, takes these 'facts' 'about' ordinary objects as evidence that ordinary objects do not really exist (I will discuss Heller's position later in this chapter). Nevertheless, if we have already accepted stage theory, then there is no reason to think that stages are immovable, having their locations essentially—we can take our ordinary ways of talking as a guide, since we have no compelling reason to do otherwise.

The third option is to suppose that the possibilities for stages are unconstrained, that what is possible for a given stage is independent of any qualitative or spatio-temporal properties of either stage. But, again, although this idea seems coherent, ordinary thought does not suggest that there are any objects like this, for which anything is possible, and we have no compelling reason to reject this ordinary way of thinking. In the absence of any more plausible candidates, I will take it that that it is necessary that a stage satisfy some individual predicate which it in fact satisfies, that the very thing we're looking at when we look at Lump/Goliath couldn't have existed had it been neither the statue nor the lump of clay.

It is also necessary that a stage satisfy *every* individual predicate it actually satisfies, I think. The alternative is to say that the stage must be either the statue or the lump of clay (that it must satisfy at least one of the individual predicates it in fact satisfies) but that it need not be both. It could have been either the statue or the lump of clay without being both. But this recreates the problems about coincident objects which we have been at pains to avoid. Consider a possible world which we would describe as one in which the statue and the lump of clay are distinct objects—perhaps the lump is spherical, and the statue has been made of a different lump. What then are we to say of our present stage in that world?

Either it is a stage both of the lump and the statue, or else it is a stage of only one of these. Then we must say either that the actual stage is really two coincident stages, which are not coincident in the other possible world, or else that the stage has Lump-counterparts and Goliath-counterparts, or that it is merely contingently identical to itself, or else that its statuehood dominates its lumphood. Given stage theory, we can avoid all these complications by supposing that the actual stage is necessarily both Goliath and Lump. Of course, the lump could have existed without being made into the statue (or so it seems). But this does not entail that the present stage could have existed without being made into the statue. We must distinguish between *de re* and *de strato* claims about the lump: *de re*, the lump need not have been the statue, but *de strato* the stage which is actually the lump is necessarily the statue.

Finally, is the joint satisfaction of every relevant individual predicate a sufficient as well as a necessary condition for transworld identity of stages? Unfortunately, it cannot be. Recall the banana. In a nearby possible world, there are very many different stages each of which satisfies, at a different moment, every individual predicate satisfied by the present stage of the banana. But only one of these, presumably, can be the present stage. A first thought is that the actual stage has its time of existence essentially, however we are to identify times across possible worlds. But this seems mistaken: the banana might have existed earlier, and so presumably each of its stages could have existed earlier than it actually does. Satisfaction of each relevant individual predicate is a necessary but insufficient condition for transworld identity of stages, and sameness of spatio-temporal location is not a necessary condition. Must we accept brute facts about transworld identity for stages, or can we accept that such facts can be indeterminate? This depends in part on questions about the source of modal facts, and upon whether we adopt a view of possible worlds according to which there can be transworld *identity*, or one in which there can only be transworld counterpart relations. I will not settle these questions here.

6.8 Vagueness Again

Persistence is often a vague matter. Few things have both a sharp beginning and a sharp end, so most individual predicates have a vague extension. The source of this vagueness, whether it be ontic, semantic, or epistemic, was discussed in Chapter 4. Whatever the source, there are stages concerning which it is a vague matter which individual predicates they satisfy: is this mouldy old thing still the banana? But I have been arguing that a stage essentially satisfies whichever individual predicates it in fact satisfies, so it follows that it is sometimes a vague matter what essential features a stage has.

If the source of vagueness is epistemic, this is unsurprising—some of the modal features of things are hidden from us. And if there can be ontic indeterminacy in what something is, then it seems unsurprising that there can be ontic indeterminacy in what a thing's modal properties are. The consequent seems no more disturbing than the antecedent. What if the indeterminacy is semantic? Imagine a stage at around the time of Descartes's death. It may be indeterminate whether a stage is Descartes, for example, because it is indeterminate whether it stands in the right relations to earlier Descartes stages, perhaps because it is semantically indeterminate which relations underpin the predicate 'is the same person as'. Could the stage have existed without being a person, without being Descartes? In effect, we have not decided, because we have not quite decided what it takes to be a person, or to be Descartes. Again, it is hardly surprising that we have failed to decide whether something *must* satisfy a certain predicate, if we have not decided whether it satisfies that predicate in the actual world.

6.9 Sums of Stages, and Modal Inductility

I have outlined the stage theory account of our ordinary talk about objects and their possibilities, and I have also proposed a stage theory account of the modal features of stages. But what about the modal features of sums of stages? For perdurance theorists, sums of stages are of primary importance. But for stage theorists, sums of stages are not very interesting objects, for they do not feature in our everyday ontology—it is stages themselves which are bananas, tennis balls, or Goliath. It is, however, open to stage theorists to believe in sums of stages, even though they play no important role in everyday ontology. I suggest we take it that a sum of stages is essentially the sum of its actual stages. That is, we should be mereological essentialists about sums of stages. I have already argued that stages essentially satisfy the individual predicates they actually satisfy. The stages of Goliath cannot exist without being Goliath, so if the sum of the Goliath stages cannot exist without having all those stages as parts, then the sum of the stages cannot exist unless Goliath does.

Sums of stages 'inherit' their modal properties from the stages which make them up, which in turn depend upon the individual predicates they in fact satisfy. So sums of stages are modally rather fragile: they cannot exist unless all their actual parts exist, and those parts are also rather fragile, since they cannot exist unless they satisfy all of the individual predicates they actually satisfy. This gives us a pleasing sense in which individual predicates are more basic than either stages or sums of stages—pleasing because individual predicates are at the heart of our talk about the world. The modal features of things in our world are determined by what is possible for this banana or that statue. One consequence of this account is that, if a banana could have existed at a different time or place than it actually does, then the same goes for the stages which are the banana, and thus the same goes for the sum of those stages. And, indeed, bananas don't have either their exact temporal or their exact spatial locations essentially. So sums of stages are flexible in the same way (although perhaps not to the same degree).

I have already drawn an analogy between individual predicates and stages on the one hand, and natural kind terms and kind members on the other. An individual predicate like 'is Goliath' could have had a different extension, could have been satisfied by different stages; Goliath could have lived longer or less long. Similarly, a natural kind term could have had a different extension; there could have been more or fewer elephants. But each Goliath stage is essentially a Goliath stage, just as each elephant is essentially an elephant.

The analogy can now be extended. Just as stage theory takes little notice of sums of stages, we ordinarily take little notice of sums of kind members. But consider that giant, scattered thing which is the sum of all the actual elephants. It seems to have its elephant parts essentially,[3] for it would not have existed had there been fewer elephants, and if there had been more elephants, it would have been part of an even bigger elephant-conglomerate. But the sum does not seem to have its location, or its mass essentially. If all the actual elephants had been a few centimetres to the left, or had been a bit skinnier, the sum of the elephants would have had different properties, for it depends for its properties upon its elephant parts. Similarly, I suggest, a sum of stages has its instantaneous parts essentially, but it does not have its location or its mass essentially. If every Goliath stage had existed a little earlier, and been a little skinnier, then so would the sum of those stages, for the sum depends for its properties upon its instantaneous parts.

6.10 Perdurance Theory and Modal Inductility

Stage theory can give a coherent account of the modal features of sums of stages even though such sums are not an important part of the stage ontology. Perdurance theory, of course, takes it that ordinary objects are sums of stages, and must therefore give some account of the modal features of such sums. Van Inwagen (1990*a*) argues that perdurance theorists cannot give a satisfactory account of the modal features of four-dimensional objects, and his argument is worth exploring.

Assume, for the sake of argument, that perdurance theory is true. Now consider Descartes, say, and consider the sum of Descartes's temporal parts, which I will call 'Sum'. How is Descartes related to the sum of his temporal parts? At first thought, it seems that perdurance theorists should identify Descartes with Sum. Now, says van Inwagen, the sum of Descartes's temporal parts could not have been temporally longer or shorter than it actually is. Sum extends over fifty-four years, and it does so essentially. So if Descartes is identical to Sum, then Descartes essentially lived for fifty-four years.

But this seems absurd: surely Descartes could have lived a few years longer or less long than he in fact did. According to van

---

[3] That's to say, it essentially has as parts all of its actual parts which are whole elephants—it may be that the elephant-sum could have existed with different parts, if one of the elephants had lost a leg.

Inwagen, perdurance theorists must suppose that Descartes is *modally inductile*, that he has his temporal length essentially—this is supposed to be an absurd consequence of perdurance theory. This is a special case of permanent coincidence, one which does not arise for endurance theorists or stage theorists. *Prima facie*, the statue and the lump of clay are indiscernible in all actual respects, yet have different modal properties. Similarly, Descartes and Sum seem indiscernible in all actual respects, but seem to have different modal properties.

How can perdurance theorists respond? There is a host of options, but few are satisfactory. A natural option, as I suggested earlier, is to adopt a counterpart-theoretic account of modality.[4] Descartes and Sum are identical, but the person-counterpart and sum-counterpart of the thing in a given possible world may be distinct. For example, in a world in which Descartes lives longer, the sum-counterpart is a proper part of the person-counterpart. It is far from clear what the sum-counterpart relation is, what essential properties a sum of temporal parts has, but this is a question to which we will return below. Another option is to suppose that Descartes and Sum are contingently identical—this also raises the question of what essential properties are associated with the peculiar sortal 'is a sum of temporal parts'. Or perhaps Descartes is merely constituted by Sum, whilst they are not identical. But this is especially unattractive to perdurance theorists. An important advantage of perdurance theory is that it offers an alternative to constitution accounts of the sweater and the thread.

Alternatively, perdurance theorists might claim that Descartes is identical to Sum, whilst denying that Sum has its temporal length essentially. After all, we do not usually suppose that a sum of spatial parts has its spatial extent essentially, that it is incompressible and unstretchable. Then Sum would have been fifty-five years long, not fifty-four years long, if Descartes had lived to fifty-five—Sum would not in that case have been the first fifty-four-year long temporal part of Descartes. Perhaps the sortal 'is a person' dominates the sortal 'is a sum of temporal parts', although, again, this raises awkward questions about the modal features of sums of temporal parts which do not fall under more dominant sortals. Or perhaps four-dimensional things do not have arbitrary temporal parts, and there are no sums of person-parts which are not persons. If Descartes had lived for fifty-five years,

---

[4] Van Inwagen mentions this option, but sees it as a heavy price to pay for the retention of perdurance theory.

he would have had no fifty-four year long Descartes-part, and Sum would have been fifty-five years long too.

Finally, perdurance theorists might claim that Descartes is identical to Sum, and that Descartes does after all have his temporal length essentially. This is the conclusion which van Inwagen takes to be absurd, but both Mark Heller and Michael Jubien adopt something like this approach. According to Heller, the world is populated by sharply bounded matter-filled regions of space–time, and these things have their spatial and temporal boundaries essentially (Heller 1990). Descartes, bananas, and the other objects of our everyday ontology are what Heller calls 'conventional objects', which do not really exist. Instead, our conventions, together with the real structure of the world, lead us to act as if these conventional objects really exist.

Heller has two main types of argument for his position. First, drawing upon Peter Unger's work, he argues that the vagueness of our concepts and the precision of the world ensures that nothing falls under our everyday object-concepts. Second, citing van Inwagen's argument, he argues that nothing has the modal properties and persistence conditions which we apparently attribute to everyday objects like Descartes. Nothing could have been either temporally longer or shorter than it actually is. Heller accepts the existence of Sum, and he accepts van Inwagen's assumption that Sum has its temporal length essentially. He need not, however, accept that Descartes essentially spans fifty-four years, for he does not accept that Descartes exists.

Jubien's ontology is in some ways similar to Heller's, and his semantics is in some ways similar to the semantics I have developed for stage theory (Jubien 1993). Like Heller, Jubien believes that the world is made up of four-dimensional objects which have their temporal boundaries essentially, but, unlike Heller, he thinks that things have their spatial boundaries accidentally. Moreover, Jubien takes a 'predicative' approach to proper names of ordinary objects, rather than supposing, as Heller does, that names like 'Descartes' fail to refer. According to Jubien, 'that four-dimensional object is Descartes' does not express an identity statement, but instead it attributes the property *being Descartes* to the four-dimensional object in question. The object in question has its temporal boundaries essentially, so it could not have spanned fifty-five instead of fifty-four years. But a different, fifty-five-year-long object could have instantiated the property of *being Descartes*. Thus we may truly say that Descartes could have

lasted for fifty-five years, and we avoid the supposedly absurd conclusion of the modal inductility argument.

Both Heller and Jubien accept van Inwagen's assumption that sums
of temporal parts have their temporal boundaries essentially, but
question the claim that Descartes is necessarily identical to the sum of
his temporal parts. Heller denies that Descartes exists, and Jubien
argues that 'Descartes' does not rigidly designate the sum of temporal
parts which it actually designates. As we have seen, stage theory has a
different approach. In some possible worlds fewer stages satisfy 'is
Descartes' than do in the actual world. In other possible worlds, more
stages satisfy 'is Descartes'. So Descartes could have lived for fifty-five
years: he is 'modally ductile'. But this is unsurprising: we have no special reason to think that the predicate 'is Descartes' essentially has a
certain extension. Indeed, we have good reason to think that
Descartes could have had a different lifespan, and thus that the predicate could have had a different extension.

Stage theory does not identify Descartes with Sum, so there is no
question about whether Descartes must inherit his modal properties
from Sum. At any moment, Descartes is an instantaneous stage, a different stage at each moment, and he is never identical to a sum of
stages. Stage theorists differ from Heller in that they are not committed to conventionalism on a grand scale about ordinary objects.
Unlike Heller, a stage theorist need accept no sense in which it is true
that Descartes does not exist. Any use of 'Descartes' refers to some
stage or other (subject to the caveats of Chapter 2), and those stages
certainly exist.

Jubien is closer to stage theory. Both he and I address the modal
inductility problem by arguing that 'Descartes' could have had a different referent, and that this is why Descartes could have lived for
fifty-five instead of fifty-four years. But nevertheless there are differences in our positions. In particular, of course, Jubien is a perdurance
theorist, who takes it that 'Descartes' actually refers to a fifty-four-
year-long thing. According to stage theory, the name picks out different stages, depending upon the time in question. Moreover, Jubien is
generous about properties, positing a particular property for every
persisting thing. I have avoided commitment to a property for every
individual predicate, and I will explain below how reference can work
without such properties.

6.11 Stage Theory and Sums

Stage theory has significantly different consequences for sums of stages than does either Heller or Jubien's position. Both Heller and Jubien take it that four-dimensional hunks of matter have their temporal boundaries essentially, and Heller thinks they have their spatial boundaries essentially too. But stage theory is not disadvantaged by its failure to recognize things with such modal properties, for we have no pre-theoretical reason to think that there are modally immovable things.

Consider spatial location. For most objects, it seems true to say that the object could have been a millimetre to the left of where it actually is. Are there exceptions? Relationists about space deny that the whole universe could have been a millimetre to the left of where it actually is. But they do not suppose that the universe has its location essentially. Rather, they argue that it makes no sense to talk of the location of the universe as a whole. Heller argues that our intuitions about the accidental locations of ordinary objects must either be rejected, or be taken to show that ordinary objects do not really exist, because he has a prior belief that no objects are really accidentally located. But I have argued that we can handle modal inductility and other problems without adopting Heller's ontology. Essentialism about spatial location is unappealing and unnecessary. We have no reason to think that anything has its spatial location essentially.

What about temporal boundaries? Both Heller and Jubien claim that four-dimensional things have their actual temporal *lengths* essentially. Second, they make the stronger claim that such things have their actual temporal *locations* essentially. Things could not have been longer or shorter, and they could not have existed earlier or later, even with the same length.[5] Why suppose that anything has its temporal location essentially, that there are things that could not have existed a moment earlier or later? One thought may be that this is a last resort, that we have no other means of identifying four-dimensional things across possible worlds. But I have offered an alternative account, which makes the modal features of four-dimensional things a consequence of the modal features of their instantaneous parts. We need not turn to this drastic last resort.

[5] It is the weaker claim about length, not location, which features in the modal inductility argument. It is Descartes's compressibility, not his mobility, which is at issue.

Sums could have existed earlier or later, but could they have been longer or shorter? This is a tricky question for stage theorists. Recall that I am recommending mereological essentialism for sums of stages. A given sum must be made up of all and only its actual parts. But instantaneous things, presumably, are necessarily instantaneous, just as a line could not have been a surface, nor a point a line. Sums of stages are essentially composed of things which have their lengths essentially. What does this tell us about the lengths of such sums? It rather depends upon the questions about the structure of time and stages which I considered in Chapter 2. The key question is this: if the sum had been longer (shorter), would it have been composed of more (fewer) instantaneous parts? If a difference in length would mean a difference in parts, then the sum could not have had a different length. Otherwise, the sum could have had a different length.

If stages have the structure of space–time points, then the sum *could* have been longer or shorter, without thereby having extra parts. If, on the other hand, it turns out that sums do have their temporal lengths essentially, then stage theorists can accept this result with equanimity, for sums are not to be identified with ordinary objects, on this account. Perdurance theorists, on the other hand, should be wary of accepting that four-dimensional things have their lengths essentially, for they identify such things with the apparently flexible things of our ordinary ontology—bananas, tennis balls, and the like. It is exactly this which gives rise to the modal inductility problem.

Sums of stages have their instantaneous parts essentially, which may or may not mean that they have their temporal lengths essentially. But they are neither spatially nor temporally immovable, for the stages themselves are neither spatially nor temporally immovable. This is a welcome result, since we do not usually countenance the existence of metaphysically immovable objects. Finally, recall that the stages essentially satisfy the individual predicates they actually satisfy, and that this has consequences for the modal features of sums of such stages.

6.12 Individual Predicates and Possible Worlds

I have argued that a stage essentially satisfies every individual predicate it actually satisfies, but that individual predicates could have had different extensions. So for example 'is Descartes' and 'is the banana' may apply to different stages in other possible worlds. If I talk about the banana at a certain moment, I refer to a particular stage, but if I talk about how the banana could have been different, that very stage need not enter into the truth conditions of what I say. My claims are made true or false by the stages in the extension of 'is the banana' in other possible worlds, whether or not those are the very stages which are in the extension of 'is the banana' in the actual world. Analogously, if I claim that elephants could have been more numerous, my claim is made true or false by those things in other possible worlds which satisfy 'is an elephant', regardless of whether or not they are the very things which are in the actual extension of 'is an elephant'.

What, then, determines the extension of an individual predicate like 'is the banana' in other possible worlds? This is the stage theory version of a question which also arises for perdurance and endurance theorists: what determines the reference of a singular referring term in other possible worlds? It is apparent that the answer will be complex and disputed, and, moreover, that it is not the job of a theory of persistence to supply a full answer to this question. Here, I aim merely to show that stage theorists face no problems about reference which do not also arise for endurance and perdurance theorists. This section complements those sections of Chapter 2 in which I provide a stage theory account of reference—here I simply extend that account in the light of my discussion of modality.

We can distinguish between rigid and non-rigid designators. A non-rigid designator is one which may refer to different things in different possible worlds. 'The largest living animal' may be used as a non-rigid designator, in which case it picks out, in any given world, the thing which in that world satisfies the description. There are no special problems for stage theorists here. In any particular world, at any particular moment, at most one stage satisfies 'is the largest living animal' (unless there is an equal tie), and is thus the referent of the descriptive term.

But rigid designators might seem more problematic. A rigid designator is one which refers to the same thing in every world in which it refers to anything at all.[6] According to Kripke, proper names like 'Descartes' are rigid designators. 'Descartes' refers to the same thing in every possible world, and thus refers to its actual referent in every possible world. Let us take it that Kripke is right about proper

[6] We could make stipulations about what such a designator refers to in worlds in which its actual referent does not exist, but this is irrelevant to the present discussion.

names—the point here is just to illustrate how stage theory can fit in with such an account of proper names, not to argue in favour of the account itself. Stage theory might seem to have a problem. After all, perdurance theorists and endurance theorists can argue that 'Descartes' refers to any possible object that is identical to the referent of 'Descartes' in the actual world—the name refers to the same thing in any possible world in which it refers at all. But according to stage theory, 'is Descartes' may be satisfied by stages which do not exist at all in the actual world, if, for example, Descartes lives longer in other possible worlds, or if he could have been made of different stuff.

Stage theorists cannot always rely on *identity* to determine reference in other possible worlds, for the things which satisfy individual predicates in other possible worlds are not limited to those things which actually satisfy the predicate. Is this a great loss? If we adopt a counterpart-theoretic account of modality, it is no loss at all, for then objects existing in different possible worlds are never identical. In that case, stage theorists can explain how individual predicates get their extensions in other possible worlds in whatever way perdurance and endurance theorists explain how proper names get their reference in other possible worlds. No special problems arise for stage theorists.

But what if there can be genuine identity between objects existing in different possible worlds? Let us turn again to the analogy between individual predicates and stages on the one hand, and natural kind terms and the members of natural kinds on the other. Like individual predicates, natural kind terms can have different extensions in different worlds. What determines the extension of a natural kind term in another possible world? This, of course, has been the subject of much recent debate, triggered by the work of Hilary Putnam in the 1960s and 1970s.[7] What determines the extension of 'water' or 'elephant' in other possible worlds? The question is not what those strings of letters would refer to in other possible languages. Rather, the question is what determines the extension of terms like 'water' when we use them in actual English to talk about other possible worlds.

According to Putnam, the extension in a possible world of the term 'water' includes all and only those things which are (bits of) the same substance as the stuff in the extension of the term 'water' in the actual world. That is, all and only those things which have the same chemical structure as the stuff in the actual extension.

---

[7] See, in particular, Putnam (1975), and, for discussion, Pessin and Goldberg (1996).

Similarly, the extension in another possible world of the term 'elephant' includes all and only those things which are members of the same species as the extension of the term 'elephant' in the actual world. It is debatable what conspecificity amounts to (Salmon 1981).

By analogy, then, we might expect the extension of an individual predicate like 'is Descartes' in another possible world to be all and only those stages which share some key feature with the stages in the actual extension of the predicate. If, as Jubien argues, there is a property *being Descartes*, then matters are straightforward. The predicate 'is Descartes' is satisfied by exactly those stages which instantiate the property *being Descartes*.[8] If there are such individual properties, then stage theorists can rely upon the transworld identity of properties to do the work which endurance and perdurance theorists demand of the transworld identity of particulars. But we need not be committed to such properties merely by the structure of stage theory.

What determines the transworld extension of individual predicates on the stage-theory picture is whatever determines the transworld identity of particulars on any picture which combines either perdurance or endurance theory with a rejection of counterparts. There are two ways to think about transworld identity of particulars. Either identities between particulars in different worlds are brute, or else there are necessary and sufficient conditions for transworld identity of particulars. Consider the first option. If it is just a matter of brute fact whether two things are identical, and thus are referents of the same name, then it may be a matter of brute fact whether two stages in different possible worlds satisfy the same individual predicate. These two hypotheses about brute fact are equally plausible. On the other hand, if there are necessary and sufficient qualitative conditions for the transworld identity of particulars, according to either perdurance or endurance theories, then the same sorts of condition can determine the transworld extension of individual predicates, according to stage theory.

If there are necessary and sufficient conditions for what perdurance and endurance theorists think of as the identity of persistents existing in different possible worlds, then stage theory can take advantage of these, transforming them into necessary and sufficient conditions for the satisfaction of individual predicates. What sort of conditions might these be? For example, kind membership might be essential:

---

[8] Jubien thinks that such properties are instantiated by four-dimensional things, not by instantaneous stages.

perhaps any water sample is essentially a water sample, and perhaps any elephant is essentially a elephant. In stage theory terms, then, if the actual stages which satisfy an individual predicate also satisfy 'is an elephant' or 'is a sample of water', then so must any possible stage which satisfies that individual predicate. Ernie is essentially an elephant, so any stage which is an Ernie-stage is an elephant. We saw that whether a stage satisfies a sortal predicate is, in general, a relational matter. So stages have some relational properties essentially, as well as some intrinsic properties.

We might also think that certain facts about origins or composition are essential to persisting things. So, for example, perhaps Descartes essentially originated in the gametes he actually originated in, and perhaps this desk is essentially made of the piece of wood it is actually made of. How can stage theorists express these ideas? Perhaps no stage could satisfy 'is Descartes' unless it is appropriately related to stages which are those gametes. This looks circular: the extension of one individual predicate is determined by the extension of other such predicates. But there is no more circularity here than in the more familiar endurance or perdurance accounts of the essentiality of origins: 'Descartes' could not refer to anything which originated in other gametes, however those gametes are to be identified across possible worlds. A similar story can be told about the essentiality of composition, if we agree that composition has this important role. Perhaps no stage could be this desk unless it is also this piece of wood. There is a range of options available to stage theorists, but stage theory does not face problems which perdurance and endurance theorists escape.

6.13 Conclusions

In Chapter 5 I discussed issues about temporary 'coincidence', asking how the sweater and the woollen thread could possibly occupy the same place at the same time, distinguished only by their histories, their persistence conditions, and, perhaps, their futures. How could two objects have different histories yet be made of the same parts arranged in the same way? In this chapter I have addressed the related question of how two objects could differ in their modal properties without differing in their actually manifested features. This led us into questions about the modal status of stages and sums of stages, and about the way in which stage theory can account for our ways of speaking about ordinary things and the possibilities available to them. The goal here has not been to offer a revolutionary new theory of the metaphysics of modality, or of the reference of ordinary terms, but rather to show that stage theory can hold its own, that it is not undermined by considerations about reference and modality. The issues here are murky, but stage theory is not disadvantaged by its treatment of them. In the epilogue, I will draw together the different issues and questions considered throughout this book.

Epilogue

How do things persist? As I argued in Chapter 1, we cannot even raise this question without speaking atemporally about the world. To talk about how things persist, we need to make claims about how things are, rather than just about how things are at one time or another. Granted that atemporal way of talking, we are faced with a choice between endurance theory on the one hand, and perdurance and stage theories on the other. According to endurance theory, we can speak atemporally about persisting objects, but much of what we can say concerns the relations which hold (atemporally) between those objects and various times. In particular, claims about what parts a persisting thing has must be indexed to some time or other, just as claims about whether an object is 'taller than' must be relative to some object or other. Speaking atemporally we can neither claim nor deny that the tooth is a part of the boy, *simpliciter*. The most we can say is that the boy bears the *has-as-a-part-at* relation to the milk tooth and his seventh birthday.

Opponents of endurance theory believe that we can speak atemporally about the parts of material things. I have emphasized that even if we reject endurance theory, we are not thereby committed to perdurance theory—stage theory is also a viable option. Stage theory and perdurance theory share a general metaphysical picture, an agreement about what kinds of things there are in the world. But the theories differ about how our ordinary, non-metaphysical ways of talking latch on to things in the world. According to perdurance theory, when we speak about people, tennis balls, or bananas, we speak about extended four-dimensional objects. According to stage theory, when we speak about such ordinary things, we speak about instantaneous stages, different stages at different times.

Much of this book has been devoted to developing these three rival theories, and investigating which versions of the theories are the most viable. For example, I argued that endurance theorists should adopt a relations-to-times view of temporary features, instead of adopting adverbialism (Chapter 1). And I argued that neither perdurance nor stage theorists should be egalitarians—some series of stages are objectively more natural than others. Moreover, the naturalness or otherwise of a series of stages is not fully determined by the intrinsic properties of the stages concerned (Chapter 3). To oppose endurance theory is not to be 'reductionist' about persistence, and nor is it to believe that all ways of 'tracing out' objects over time are on a par.

Having developed the theories, how then shall we choose between them? The first task is to decide whether to adopt endurance theory— it is only if we reject this account that the differences between perdurance and stage theory are brought into relief. The key feature, of course, of endurance theory is the claim that persistence is a matter of identity between objects wholly present at different times. The theory claims that we can be confronted by a whole object at one moment, then reconfronted with the very same whole object at a different moment. There are two main reasons why we might reject this theory.

First, and simply, we might be tempted by an analogy between space and time. Endurance theory draws a sharp distinction between the way in which things extend through space and the way in which they persist through time. So long as endurance theorists are careful, and are willing to make certain sacrifices (of which more below), then their theory seems coherent—it is possible to believe, for example, that we cannot make atemporal claims about parthood for persisting objects, even though we can make 'aspatial' claims about parthood— right now my nose is a part of me, and we need not specify that it is a part of me in one place rather than another. The role of space–time analogies in the debate about persistence is a curious one—on the one hand, endurance theorists sometimes seem to find it obvious that persistence is entirely different from spatial extension. Indeed, this may be the source of the idea that endurance theory is the 'commonsense' position, not to be given up without a struggle. On the other hand, opponents of endurance theory sometimes seem to think we should not draw such a distinction between persistence and spatial extension unless there is very good reason to do so. After all, isn't it simpler to treat space and time alike? Once we accept that both endurance theory and its rivals are coherent, this issue about space–time analogies looks like a dispute about where the burden of proof lies. Is the onus upon endurance theorists to justify their making an important distinction between space and time, or is the onus upon perdurance theorists to justify their relative neglect of this distinction?[1]

---

[1] A similar disagreement about burdens of proof may underlie disputes between tensed and tenseless theorists of time, once they go beyond disputes about the very coherence of the rival theories.

Although I have not resolved this dispute about the burden of proof, it is worth noting that stage theory offers a middle position—a distinction between persistence and spatial extension which is less drastic than that demanded by endurance theorists and yet bolder than that offered by perdurance theorists. According to stage theory, when we talk about an ordinary persisting object with respect to different moments of its existence, we talk about different objects, different stages. Indeed, we cannot speak atemporally about ordinary objects like bananas and tennis balls, for when we try to do so, we fail to specify what we are talking about. This stands in contrast to the way in which we can speak aspatially about ordinary objects. Nevertheless, according to stage theory, there are also objects—sums of stages— which can be spoken about atemporally, as perdurance theorists claim, but these are not the objects of everyday talk.

Aside from space–time analogies, the other main factor which might sway us against endurance theory is the greater flexibility of perdurance and stage theories. As we saw, endurance theorists cannot claim that vagueness in persistence is ontic. But nor are they well placed to attribute such vagueness to semantic indecision. To suppose that there is semantic indecision in whether Alpha survives as Omega is, on the endurance account, to suppose that there is more than one wholly present 'Alpha-candidate' before the Cabinet episode, and more than one wholly present 'Omega-candidate' after the Cabinet episode. Moreover, there must be as many wholly present objects walking around together as there are dubious episodes in the future and past. Similar considerations arise if we suppose that it is in some way a matter of convention or stipulation how we divide up the world into persisting things. If we are not capable of creation and destruction at a distance, by thought-power alone, then such conventionalism requires a pre-existing range of objects from which we select those we find important or interesting. Again, for endurance theorists, this entails that vast numbers of coincident objects stroll around together.

This massive coincidence might sound very strange, but is it really unacceptable? I think that, whilst coherent, it entirely undercuts any motivation for endurance theory. Endurance theorists reject the perdurance theory (and stage theory) picture of the world, according to which there is a mass of brief objects, existing one after another, together with the sums of those objects (perdurance theory, at least, requires those sums). But if endurance theorists are to leave open the possibility that our division of the world into objects is highly conventional, or that vagueness in persistence may be traced to semantic indecision, then they too need to posit a mass of brief and longer-lived objects. Unlike perdurance theory, endurance theorists will not suppose that these objects are (atemporally) parts of one another—instead, they will coincide for longer and shorter periods, without standing in parthood relations to one another. But this just seems to be an uneconomical version of perdurance theory, and to be entirely unmotivated. Endurance theorists should believe that vagueness in persistence is, on the whole, an epistemic matter, and that the world itself determines how we ought to divide it up into persisting things—those who are happy with such a metaphysical position can remain endurance theorists.

What about the rest of us? If we give up endurance theory, how can we choose between perdurance and stage theories of persistence? These theories are closer to each other than either is to endurance theory, but there is a clear sense in which stage theory permits us the metaphysical flexibility enjoyed by those who reject endurance theory, whilst maintaining the endurance emphasis on differences between spatial extension and persistence. Moreover, there are several independent advantages to adopting stage theory as opposed to perdurance theory.

First, stage theory draws a distinction between processes and persisting objects, as endurance theorists do, but without supposing that the ways in which processes and persisting things have their properties (or have their parts) are fundamentally different. According to endurance theory, parthood is a three-place relation for persisting things whilst it is, presumably, a two-place relation for processes. According to stage theory, parthood is a two-place relation for both things and processes. How, then, can we draw a distinction between processes and persisting things? According to stage theory, when we talk about persisting things with respect to different times, we talk about different brief things, as opposed to a long four-dimensional object. We cannot simply talk about the parts an ordinary persisting thing has atemporally, not because parthood is inherently time-indexed, but because talk about persisting things must be time-indexed. Different things are the banana at different times.

Second, stage theory differs from perdurance theory over what it takes to satisfy a sortal predicate like 'is a cat'. Most obviously, of course, stage theory claims that it is instantaneous stages which satisfy such predicates, whilst perdurance theory claims that it is extended four-dimensional sums of such stages which satisfy sortal predicates. But a further difference is that, according to perdurance theory, satisfaction of such predicates is a temporally maximal matter, which is to say that no perduring thing can satisfy a given sortal if it is a proper temporal part of something which satisfies that sortal. The first year-long temporal part of the cat is not itself a cat. Of course, stage theory also makes the satisfaction of sortal predicates a relational matter, in a rather different way. According to stage theory, whether or not a stage satisfies a predicate like 'is a cat' depends both upon its intrinsic properties, but also upon whether or not it is surrounded by earlier and later stages which are also cats—no isolated cat-like stage could actually be a cat.[2]

But maximality plays a further role in perdurance theory. According to perdurance theory, ordinary things like cats, tennis balls, and bananas satisfy ordinary predicates with respect to times because of the properties and relations instantiated by their temporal parts. Yet this inheritance of predicates by whole from part is not available to all sums of temporal parts—whether or not an extended four-dimensional thing counts as purring at t depends not only upon whether it has a temporal part at t which purrs, but also upon whether the extended thing is itself a temporal part of something larger which counts as purring at t. Stages, in contrast, do not need to compete for the privilege of satisfying certain predicates—I prefer the relationality built into stage theory to that built into perdurance theory, although others may differ.

Third, stage theory is uniquely flexible when it comes to accounting for vagueness in persistence. Stage theory is the only account available to those who accept that vagueness in persistence can sometimes be an ontic matter, since both perdurance and endurance theories base their accounts of persistence in identity. Perdurance theory can, it is true, offer a semantic indecision account of such vagueness—we have simply failed to decide which of many overlapping four-dimensional things is Alpha, and which Omega. But stage theory has the advantage of putting the indecision in the right place. According to stage theory, if there is semantic indecision in the case of Alpha and Omega, it does not infect our reference to the individuals concerned.

---

[2] Considerations of maximality provide another good reason for endurance theorists not to believe in a vast multiplicity of material things—they would presumably be committed to the claim that whether or not an object is a cat depends in part upon whether it permanently coincides with any longer-lived thing which is a cat.

Confronted with Alpha before she enters the Cabinet, we can refer perfectly determinately to her, give or take some fuzziness in her spatial boundaries. The same goes for Omega. Stage theory locates our indecision in the question of what it takes for two temporally separated things to count as 'the same person', rather than supposing, as perdurance theory does, that indecision about persistence conditions leads to indeterminate reference to individuals. Similarly, when we are confronted with coincident objects, like the sweater and the woollen thread, stage theory claims that we are confronted with just a single object. It is when we try to talk about the past or future features of this thing that we risk ambiguity if we do not specify a sortal—no ambiguity infects our present reference.

Fourth, as we saw in Chapter 6, stage theory can satisfy endurance theorists who argue that persisting objects must be more basic in some sense than their temporal parts, if indeed they have temporal parts at all. The modal features of stages depend upon those of persisting things. Fifth, and finally, stage theory is ontologically less demanding than perdurance theory. As we saw in Chapter 2, perdurance theory needs instantaneous parts as stage theory does, to account for the instantiation of three-dimensional shape and the possibility of continuous change. Yet perdurance theory must also posit sums of those instantaneous stages, both to play the role of ordinary persistents, and also to provide the raw material for ideas about our divisions being conventional, or about vagueness being a matter of semantic indecision. Where perdurance theory requires sums of stages, stage theory can make do—if necessary—with the stages themselves, and the relations between them, relations which perdurance theorists must also accept.

The question of whether to reject endurance theory turns on two deep-seated matters—a question about analogies between space and time, and a question about the multiplicity of persisting things. The choice between perdurance and stage theories, on the other hand, must be made on more piecemeal grounds, considering the various advantages and disadvantages of the two theories. One thing is clear—I have not eliminated all contenders but one, or proved beyond a shadow of a doubt that a certain account is the true one. Nevertheless, I think that the evidence favours stage theory.

Despite our fallibility in establishing metaphysical claims about persistence, we might wonder what the status of those claims is. If endurance theory is true, is it necessarily or just contingently true?

And what about stage and perdurance theories? I take it that the debate between stage and perdurance theories does not concern necessary truths—the theories agree on a basic metaphysical picture, and disagree about how our everyday talk fits with that picture. And presumably our everyday talk could have been different. Even if stage theory is true, it need not have been, and the same goes for perdurance theory.

The contrast between endurance theory and its rivals is more marked, especially if we focus upon the question of whether parthood is inherently time-indexed. Suppose that endurance theory is true, and yet that there are processes which have temporal parts.[3] Could there have been only processes? For endurance theorists to establish that their theory is, if true, necessarily true, they would need to establish that there could be no processes unless there were also persisting things which were not the subjects of atemporal parthood. Suppose, on the other hand, that endurance theory is false. As we have seen, arguments against endurance theory are ultimately based upon the ideas that spatial extension and persistence are strongly analogous, and that many of our divisions are conventional and subject to semantic indecision. In a different possible world, one with few, sharply bounded objects, it would be harder to make a case against endurance theory. And even if in actuality there is only a two-place parthood relation, and thus endurance theory is false, is it really impossible that there could have been a three-place parthood relation, one which has a place for times? The suggestion hardly seems to be incoherent. It is a contingent matter how things persist.

---

[3] See Melia (2000) for an attempt to abandon processes altogether in favour of enduring things.

References and Bibliography

Ackerman, Felicia (1994). 'Roots and Consequences of Vagueness', in J. Tomberlin (ed.), *Philosophical Perspectives, 8: Logic and Language*. Atascadero, CA: Ridgeview Press, 129–36.

Armstrong, D. M. (1980). 'Identity Through Time', in Peter van Inwagen (ed.), *Time and Cause*. Dordrecht: D. Reidel, 67–78.

——— (1983). *What Is a Law of Nature?* Cambridge: Cambridge University Press.

——— (1989). *Universals: An Opinionated Introduction*. Boulder, CO: Westview Press.

——— (1993). 'Reply to Lewis', in J. Bacon, K. Campbell, and L. Reinhardt (eds.), *Ontology, Causality and Mind*. Cambridge: Cambridge University Press, 38–42.

——— (1997). *A World of States of Affairs*. Cambridge: Cambridge University Press.

Baker, Lynne Rudder (1997). 'Why Constitution is not Identity'. *Journal of Philosophy*, 94: 599–621.

Bennett, Jonathan (1988). *Events and their Names*. Oxford: Oxford University Press.

Brennan, Andrew (1988). *Conditions of Identity*. Oxford: Clarendon Press.

Brink, David O. (1997). 'Rational Egoism and the Separateness of Persons', in J. Dancy (ed.), *Reading Parfit*. Oxford: Blackwell, 96–134.

Brody, Baruch A. (1980). *Identity and Essence*. Princeton, NJ: Princeton University Press.

Broome, J. (1984). 'Indefiniteness in Identity'. *Analysis*, 44: 6–12.

Burgess, J. A. (1990). 'Vague Objects and Indefinite Identity'. *Philosophical Studies*, 59: 263–87.

Burke, Michael (1992). 'Copper Statues and Pieces of Copper: A Challenge to the Standard Account'. *Analysis*, 52: 12–17.

——— (1994a). 'Dion and Theon: An Essentialist Solution to an Ancient Puzzle'. *Journal of Philosophy*, 91: 129–39.

——— (1994b). 'Preserving the Principle of One Object to a Place: A Novel Account of the Relations among Objects, Sorts, Sortals and Persistence Conditions'. *Philosophy and Phenomenological Research*, 54: 591–624.

——— (1997). 'Coinciding Objects: reply to Lowe and Denkel'. *Analysis*, 57: 11–18.

Butterfield, Jeremy (1984). 'Seeing the Present'. *Mind*, 93: 161–76.

——— (1985). 'Spatial and Temporal Parts'. *The Philosophical Quarterly*, 35: 32–44.

Callender, Craig (2001). 'Humean Supervenience and Homogeneous Matter'. *Mind*, 110: 25–44.

Chisholm, Roderick M. (1967). 'Identity Through Possible Worlds: Some Questions'. *Noûs*, 1: 1–8.

——(1973). 'Parts as Essential to their Wholes'. *Review of Metaphysics*, 26: 581–603.

——(1976). *Person and Object*. London: Allen & Unwin.

——(1996). *A Realistic Theory of Categories*. Cambridge: Cambridge University Press.

Cowles, D. W. (1994). 'On van Inwagen's Defense of Vague Identity'. *Philosophical Perspectives*, 8: 137–58.

Craig, William Lane (1998). 'McTaggart's Paradox and the Problem of Temporary Intrinsics'. *Analysis*, 58: 122–7.

Denkel, Arda (1995). 'Theon's Tale: Does a Cambridge Change result in a Substantial Change?' *Analysis*, 55: 166–70.

Dummett, Michael (1973). *Frege, Philosophy of Language*. London: Duckworth.

——(1981*a*). *The Interpretation of Frege's Philosophy*. London: Duckworth.

——(1981*b*). *Frege: Philosophy of Language* (2nd edn.). London: Duckworth.

Dupré, John (1993). *The Disorder of Things: Metaphysical Foundations of the Disunity of Science*. Cambridge, MA: Harvard University Press.

Ehring, Douglas (1997). *Causation and Persistence*. Oxford: Oxford University Press.

Evans, Gareth (1978). 'Can there be Vague Objects?' *Analysis*, 38: 208.

——(1982). *The Varieties of Reference*. Oxford: Oxford University Press.

Fine, Kit (1975). 'Vagueness, Truth and Logic'. *Synthese*, 30: 265–300.

Forbes, Graham (1987). 'Is there a Problem about Persistence?' *Proceedings of the Aristotelian Society*, supp. vol. 61: 137–55.

Frege, Gottlob (1892). 'On Sense and Meaning', in P. Geach and M. Black (eds.), *Translations from the Philosophical Writings of Gottlob Frege*. Oxford: Blackwell, 56–78.

——(1950). *Foundations of Arithmetic*, trans. J. L. Austin. Oxford: Blackwell.

French, Steven and Krause, Decio (1995). 'Vague Identity and Quantum Non-individuality'. *Analysis*, 55: 20–6.

French, Steven and Redhead, Michael (1988). 'Quantum Physics and the Identity of Indiscernibles'. *British Journal for the Philosophy of Science*, 39: 233–46.

Gallois, André (1998). *Occasions of Identity*. Oxford: Clarendon Press.

Garrett, Brian (1991). 'Vague Identity and Vague Objects'. *Noûs*, 25: 341–51.

Geach, P. T. (1967). 'Identity'. *Review of Metaphysics*, 21: 3–12.

——(1973). 'Ontological Relativity and Relative Identity', in Milton K. Munitz (ed.), *Logic and Ontology*. New York: New York University Press.

—— (1980). *Reference and Generality* (3rd edn.). Ithaca, NY: Cornell University Press.

Goldman, Alvin (1987). 'Cognitive Science and Metaphysics'. *Journal of Philosophy*, 84: 537–44.

Gottlieb, Dale (1979). 'No Entity without Identity', in Robert W. Shahan and Chris Swoyer (eds.), *Essays on the Philosophy of W. V. Quine*. Norman, OK: University of Oklahoma Press, 79–96.

Grunbaum, Adolf (1967). *Modern Science and Zeno's Paradoxes*. Middletown, CT: Wesleyan University Press.

Hale, Bob (1987). *Abstract Objects*. Oxford: Basil Blackwell.

Haslanger, Sally (1989). 'Endurance and Temporary Intrinsics'. *Analysis*, 49: 119–25.

—— (1994). 'Humean Supervenience and Enduring Things'. *Australasian Journal of Philosophy*, 72: 339–59.

Hawley, Katherine (1997). 'Types of Personal Identity'. *Cogito*, 11: 117–22.

—— (1998*a*). 'Indeterminism and Indeterminacy'. *Analysis*, 58: 101–6.

—— (1998*b*). 'Why Temporary Properties are not Relations between Objects and Times'. *Proceedings of the Aristotelian Society*, 98: 211–16.

—— (1998*c*). 'Merricks on whether Being Conscious is Intrinsic'. *Mind*, 107: 841–3.

—— (1999). 'Persistence and Non-Supervenient Relations'. *Mind*, 108: 53–67.

Heller, Mark (1984). 'Temporal Parts of Four-Dimensional Objects'. *Philosophical Studies*, 46: 323–34.

—— (1990). *The Ontology of Physical Objects*. Cambridge: Cambridge University Press.

—— (1996). 'Against Metaphysical Vagueness'. *Philosophical Perspectives*, 10: 177–85.

Hirsch, Eli (1982). *The Concept of Identity*. Oxford: Oxford University Press.

—— (1993). *Dividing Reality*. Oxford: Oxford University Press.

Howard-Snyder, Frances. (1991). 'De Re Modality Entails De Re Vagueness'. *Pacific Philosophical Quarterly*, 72: 101–12.

Hughes, C. (1985). 'Is A Thing Just the Sum of its Parts?' *Proceedings of the Aristotelian Society*, 86: 213–33.

Hume, David (1975): *An Enquiry Concerning Human Understanding*, ed. L. A. Selby-Bigge. Oxford: Oxford University Press.

Johnston, Mark (1987). 'Is there a Problem about Persistence?' *Proceedings of the Aristotelian Society*, suppl. vol. 61: 107–35.

—— (1992) 'Constitution is not Identity'. *Mind*, 101: 89–105.

Jubien, Michael (1993). *Ontology, Modality and the Fallacy of Reference*. Cambridge: Cambridge University Press.

—— (1996). 'The Myth of Identity Conditions'. *Philosophical Perspectives*, 10: 343–56.

212   *References and Bibliography*

Keefe, Rosanna and Smith, Peter (1997). *Vagueness: A Reader.* Cambridge, MA: MIT Press.

Kripke, Saul (1971). 'Identity and Necessity', in Milton K. Munitz (ed.), *Identity and Individuation.* New York: New York University Press, 135–64.

——(1972). *Naming and Necessity*, in D. Davidson and G. Harman (eds.), *Semantics of Natural Language*, Dordrecht: D. Reidl. Reprinted with an additional preface, Oxford: Basil Blackwell (1980).

——(1978). 'Identity and Time'. Unpublished lecture series.

Le Poidevin, Robin (1991). *Change, Cause and Contradiction.* Basingstoke: Macmillan.

——(ed.) (1998). *Questions of Time and Tense.* Oxford: Oxford University Press.

——and MacBeath, Murray (eds.) (1993). *The Philosophy of Time.* Oxford: Oxford University Press.

Leonard, Henry S. and Goodman, Nelson (1940). 'The Calculus of Individuals and Its Uses'. *Journal of Symbolic Logic*, 5: 45–55.

Levey, Samuel (1997). 'Coincidence and Principles of Composition'. *Analysis* 57: 1–10.

Lewis, David (1971). 'Counterparts of Persons and their Bodies'. *Journal of Philosophy*, 68: 203–11.

——(1973a). 'Causation'. *Journal of Philosophy*, 70: 556–67.

——(1973b). *Counterfactuals.* Oxford: Basil Blackwell.

——(1976a). 'Survival and Identity', in Amelie Rorty (ed.), *The Identities of Persons.* Berkeley, CA: University of California Press, 117–40.

——(1976b). 'The Paradoxes of Time Travel'. *American Philosophical Quarterly*, 13: 145–52.

——(1983a). *Philosophical Papers*, vol. 1. Oxford: Oxford University Press.

——(1983b). 'Extrinsic Properties'. *Philosophical Studies*, 44: 197–200.

——(1983c). 'New Work for a Theory of Universals'. *Australasian Journal of Philosophy*, 61: 343–77.

——(1984). 'Putnam's Paradox'. *Australasian Journal of Philosophy*, 62: 221–36.

——(1986a). *On the Plurality of Worlds.* Oxford: Blackwell.

——(1986b). 'Causal Explanation', in Lewis (1986c): 214–40.

——(1986c). *Philosophical Papers*, vol. 2. Oxford: Oxford University Press.

——(1988a). 'Vague Identity: Evans Misunderstood'. *Analysis*, 48: 128–30.

——(1988b). 'Re-arrangement of Particles: Reply to Lowe'. *Analysis*, 48: 65–72.

——(1993). 'Many, but Almost One', in J. Bacon, K. Campbell, and L. Reinhardt (eds.), *Ontology, Causality and Mind.* Cambridge: Cambridge University Press, 23–38.

——(1994). 'Humean Supervenience Debugged'. *Mind*, 103: 473–90.

——(1999*a*). *Papers in Metaphysics and Epistemology*. Cambridge: Cambridge University Press.

——(1999*b*). 'Zimmerman and the Spinning Sphere'. *Australasian Journal of Philosophy*, 77: 209–12.

Loewer, Barry (1996). 'Humean Supervenience'. *Philosophical Topics*, 24: 101–27.

Lombard, Brian (1986). *Events*. London: Routledge & Kegan Paul.

Lowe, E. J. (1982). 'On being a cat'. *Analysis*, 42: 174–7.

——(1987): 'Lewis on Perdurance versus Endurance', *Analysis*, 47: 152–4.

——(1988*a*). 'Substance, Identity and Time'. *Proceedings of the Aristotelian Society*, suppl. vol. 62: 61–78.

——(1988*b*). 'The Problems of Intrinsic Change: Rejoinder to Lewis'. *Analysis*, 48: 72–7.

——(1989*a*). *Kinds of Being*. Oxford: Basil Blackwell.

——(1989*b*). 'What is a Criterion of Identity?' *The Philosophical Quarterly*, 39: 1–21.

——(1994). 'Vague Identity and Quantum Indeterminacy'. *Analysis*, 54: 110–14.

——(1995*a*). 'The Problem of the Many and the Vagueness of Constitution'. *Analysis*, 55: 179–82.

——(1995*b*). 'Coinciding Objects: In Defence of the 'Standard Account'. *Analysis*, 55: 171–8.

——(1996). *Subjects of Experience*. Cambridge: Cambridge University Press.

——(1997*a*). 'Reply to Noonan on vague identity'. *Analysis*, 57: 88–91.

——(1997*b*). 'Objects and Criteria of Identity', in B. Hale and C. Wright (eds.), *A Companion to the Philosophy of Language*. Oxford: Blackwell.

——(1998). *The Possibility of Metaphysics*. Oxford: Oxford University Press.

MacBride, Fraser (1998). 'Where are Particulars and Universals?' *Dialectica*, 52: 203–37.

——(2001). 'Four New Ways to Change Your Shape'. *Australasian Journal of Philosophy*, 79: 81–9.

McCall, Storrs (1994). *A Model of the Universe*. Oxford: Clarendon Press.

Markosian, Ned (1998). 'Simples'. *Australasian Journal of Philosophy*, 76: 213–28.

Mates, Benson (1986). *The Philosophy of Leibniz*. Oxford: Oxford University Press.

Melia, Joseph (2000). 'Continuants and Occurrents'. *Proceedings of the Aristotelian Society*, suppl. vol. 74: 77–92.

Mellor, D. H. (1981). *Real Time*. Cambridge: Cambridge University Press.

——(1991). 'Properties and Predicates', in his *Matters of Metaphysics*. Cambridge: Cambridge University Press, 170–82.

——(1995). *The Facts of Causation*. London: Routledge.

——(1998). *Real Time II*. London: Routledge.

Mellor, D. H. and Oliver, A. (eds.) (1997). *Properties.* Oxford: Oxford University Press.

Merricks, Trenton (1994). 'Endurance and Indiscernibility'. *Journal of Philosophy*, 91: 165–84.

——(1995). 'On the Incompatibility of Enduring and Perduring Entities'. *Mind*, 104: 523–31.

Moravcsik, J. M. E. (1976). 'The Discernibility of Identicals'. *Journal of Philosophy*, 73: 587–98.

Nerlich, Graham (1994). *The Shape of Space* (2nd edn.). Cambridge: Cambridge University Press.

Newton-Smith, W. H. (1980). *The Structure of Time.* London: Routledge.

Noonan, Harold (1976). 'The Four-Dimensional World'. *Analysis*, 37: 32–9.

——(1980). *Objects and Identity.* The Hague: Nijhoff.

——(1982): 'Vague Objects'. *Analysis*, 42: 3–6.

——(1984). 'Indefinite Identity: a Reply to Broome'. *Analysis*, 44: 117–21.

——(1988). 'Substance, Identity and Time'. *Proceedings of the Aristotelian Society*, suppl. vol. 62: 79–100.

——(1989). *Personal Identity.* London: Routledge.

——(1990). 'Vague Identity Yet Again'. *Analysis*, 49: 97–9.

——(1991). 'Indeterminate Identity, Contingent Identity and Abelardian Predicates'. *The Philosophical Quarterly*, 41: 183–93.

——(1993). 'Constitution is Identity'. *Mind*, 102: 133–46.

——(1995). 'E. J. Lowe on Vague Identity and Quantum Indeterminacy'. *Analysis*, 55: 14–19.

——(1996). 'Absolute and Relative Identity', in S. Lovibond and S. G. Williams (eds.), *Essays for David Wiggins: Identity, Truth and Value.* Oxford: Blackwell, 18–32.

——(1999). 'Identity, Constitution and Microphysical Supervenience'. *Proceedings of the Aristotelian Society*, 99: 273–88.

Oaklander, Nathan (1992). 'Temporal Passage and Temporal Parts'. *Noûs*, 26: 79–84.

——and Smith, Quentin (eds.) (1994). *The New Theory of Time.* New Haven, NJ: Yale University Press.

Oderberg, David (1993). *The Metaphysics of Identity over Time.* London: Macmillan.

Oliver, Alex (1996). 'The Metaphysics of Properties'. *Mind*, 105: 1–80.

Olson, Eric (1997). *The Human Animal.* Oxford: Oxford University Press.

Parfit, Derek (1971). 'Personal Identity'. *Philosophical Review*, 80: 3–27.

——(1984). *Reasons and Persons.* Oxford: Clarendon Press.

Parsons, T. (1987). 'Entities Without Identity'. *Philosophical Perspectives*, 1: 1–19.

Parsons, T. and Woodruff, P. (1995). 'Worldly Indeterminacy of Identity'. *Proceedings of the Aristotelian Society*, 95: 171–91.

Peacocke, Christopher (1981). 'Are Vague Predicates Incoherent?' *Synthese*, 46: 121–41.

Pessin, Andrew and Goldberg, Sanford (eds.) (1996). *The Twin Earth Chronicles*. New York, NY: Sharpe.

Plantinga, Alvin (1973). 'Transworld Identity or Worldbound Individuals', in Milton K. Munitz (ed.), *Logic and Ontology*. New York: New York University Press, 193–212.

Prior, Arthur N. (1957). 'Opposite Number'. *Review of Metaphysics*, 11: 196–201.

——(1965). 'Time, Existence and Identity'. *Proceedings of the Aristotelian Society*, 66: 183–92.

——(1968a). *Papers on Time and Tense*. Oxford: Clarendon Press.

——(1968b). 'Changes in Events and Changes in Things', in Prior (1968a).

——(1970). 'The Notion of the Present', in J. T. Fraser, F. C. Haber, and G. H. Müller (eds.), *The Study of Time*. Berlin: Springer, 320–3.

Putnam, Hilary (1967). 'Time and Physical Geometry'. *Journal of Philosophy*, 64: 240–7.

——(1975). 'The Meaning of "Meaning"', in his *Mind, Language and Reality*. Cambridge: Cambridge University Press.

Quine, W. V. O. (1950). 'Identity, Ostension and Hypostasis', in his *From a Logical Point of View*. Cambridge, MA: Harvard University Press, 65–79.

——(1951). 'Two Dogmas of Empiricism'. *Philosophical Review*, 60: 20–43.

——(1960). *Word and Object*. Cambridge, MA: MIT Press.

——(1976). 'Worlds Away'. *Journal of Philosophy*, 73: 859–63.

——(1981a). 'Things and their Place in Theories', in his *Theories and Things*. Cambridge, MA: Harvard University Press, 1–23.

——(1981b). 'Replies to Eleven Essays'. *Philosophical Topics*, 12: 227–43.

Ramsey, F. P. (1925). 'Universals'. *Mind*, 34: 401–17.

Rea, Michael (1995). 'The Problem of Material Constitution'. *Philosophical Review*, 104: 525–52.

——(ed.) (1997). *Material Constitution*. Lanham, MD: Rowan & Littlefield.

Redhead, Michael (1987). *Incompleteness, Nonlocality and Realism*. Oxford: Clarendon Press.

Reichenbach, Hans (1927). *The Philosophy of Space and Time*, trans. Maria Reichenbach (1958). New York: Dover.

——(1956). *The Direction of Time*. Berkeley, CA: University of California Press.

Robinson, Denis (1985). 'Can Amoebae Divide without Multiplying?' *Australasian Journal of Philosophy*, 63: 209–319.

——(1989). 'Matter, Motion and Humean Supervenience'. *Australasian Journal of Philosophy*, 67: 394–409.

Russell, Bertrand (1914). 'The Problem of Infinity Considered Historically', in his *Our Knowledge of the External World*. London: George Allen & Unwin.

Sainsbury, R. M. (1989). 'What is a Vague Object?' *Analysis*, 49: 99–103.
——(1994). 'Why the World Cannot be Vague'. *Southern Journal of Philosophy*, 33 (suppl.): 63–81.
Salmon, Nathan (1981). *Reference and Essence*. Princeton, NJ: Princeton University Press.
——(1998). 'Nonexistence'. *Noûs*, 32: 277–319.
Salmon, Wesley C. (1975): *Space Time and Motion, A Philosophical Introduction*. Encino, CA: Dickenson.
——(ed.) (1970). *Zeno's Paradoxes*. Indianapolis, IN: Bobbs-Merrill.
Schwartz, Stephen P. (ed.) (1977). *Naming, Necessity and Natural Kinds*. Ithaca, NY: Cornell University Press.
Shoemaker, Sydney (1969). 'Time without Change'. *Journal of Philosophy*, 66: 363–81.
——(1971). 'Wiggins on Identity', in Milton K. Munitz (ed.), *Identity and Individuation*. New York: New York University Press, 103–7.
——(1979). 'Identity, Properties and Causality'. *Midwest Studies in Philosophy*, 4: 321–42.
——(1984). 'A Materialist's Account', in S. Shoemaker and R. Swinburne, *Personal Identity*. Oxford: Blackwell.
——(1999). 'Self, Body and Coincidence'. *Proceedings of the Aristotelian Society*, suppl. vol. 73: 287–306.
Sidelle, Alan (1998). 'A Sweater Unraveled: Following One Thread of Thought for Avoiding Coincident Entities'. *Noûs*, 32: 360–77.
Sider, Theodore (1995). 'Sparseness, Immance and Naturalness'. *Noûs* 29: 360–77.
——(1996). 'All the World's a Stage'. *Australasian Journal of Philosophy*, 74: 433–53.
——(1997). 'Four-Dimensionalism'. *Philosophical Review*, 106: 197–231.
Sidgwick, Henry (1907). *Methods of Ethics* (7th edn). Chicago, IL: University of Chicago Press.
Simons, Peter (1987). *Parts: A Study in Ontology*. Oxford: Clarendon Press.
——(2000). 'Continuants and Occurrents'. *Proceedings of the Aristotelian Society*, suppl. vol. 74: 59–75.
Smith, Quentin (1992). 'Personal Identity and Time'. *Philosophia*, 22: 155–67.
——(1994). 'General Introduction', in Nathan Oaklander and Quentin Smith (eds.), *The New Theory of Time*. New Haven, NJ: Yale University Press, 1–14.
Stalnaker, R. (1988). 'Vague Identity', in D. F. Austin (ed.), *Philosophical Analysis: A Defence by Example*. Dordrecht: Kluwer, 349–60.
Strawson, P. F. (1959). *Individuals: An Essay in Descriptive Metaphysics*. London: Methuen.
——(1976). 'Entity and Identity', in H. D. Lewis (ed.), *Contemporary British Philosophy*. London: Allen & Unwin, 193–219.

Teller, Paul (1986). 'Relational Holism and Quantum Mechanics'. *British Journal for the Philosophy of Science*, 37: 71–81.

——(1989). 'Relativity, Relational Holism and the Bell Inequalities', in J. Cushing and E. McMullin (eds.), *Philosophical Consequences of Quantum Theory*. Notre Dame: University of Notre Dame Press, 208–23.

Thomason, Richard (1982). 'Identity and Vagueness', *Philosophical Studies*, 42: 329–32.

Thomson, Judith Jarvis (1983). 'Parthood and Identity Across Time'. *Journal of Philosophy*, 80: 201–20.

——(1997). 'People and their Bodies', in J. Dancy (ed.), *Reading Parfit*. Oxford: Blackwell, 202–29.

——(1998). 'The Statue and the Clay'. *Noûs*, 32: 148–73.

Tooley, Michael (1988). 'In Defense of the Existence of States of Motion'. *Philosophical Topics*, 16: 225–54.

——(1997). *Time, Tense and Causation*. Oxford: Clarendon Press.

Tye, Michael (1990). 'Vague Objects'. *Mind*, 99: 535–57.

——(1994*a*). 'Sorites Paradoxes and the Semantics of Vagueness'. *Philosophical Perspectives*, 8: 189–206.

——(1994*b*). 'Vagueness: Welcome to the Quicksand'. *Southern Journal of Philosophy*, 33 (suppl.): 1–22.

van Inwagen, Peter (1980). 'Philosophers and the Words "Human Body" ', in P. van Inwagen (ed.), *Time and Cause*. Dordrecht: D. Reidel, 283–99.

——(1981). 'The Doctrine of Arbitrary Undetached Parts'. *Pacific Philosophical Quarterly*, 62: 123–37.

——(1988). 'How to Reason about Vague Objects'. *Philosophical Topics*, 16: 255–84.

——(1990*a*). 'Four-Dimensional Objects'. *Noûs*, 24: 245–55.

——(1990*b*). *Material Beings*. Ithaca, NY: Cornell University Press.

Weingard, Robert (1972). 'Relativity and the Reality of Past and Future Events'. *British Journal for the Philosophy of Science*, 23: 119–21.

Wiggins, David (1967). *Identity and Spatio-Temporal Continuity*. Oxford: Basil Blackwell.

——(1980). *Sameness and Substance*. Oxford: Basil Blackwell.

——(1986). 'On Singling Out an Object Determinately', in J. Pettit and J. McDowell (eds.), *Subject, Thought and Object*. Oxford: Oxford University Press, 169–80.

——(1996). 'Replies' in S. Lovibond and S. G. Williams (eds.) (1996).

Williams, Bernard (1956–7). 'Personal Identity and Individuation'. *Proceedings of the Aristotelian Society*, 57: 229–52.

——(1970). 'The Self and the Future'. *Philosophical Review*, 79: 161–80.

——(1973). *Problems of the Self*. Cambridge: Cambridge Unversity Press.

Williamson, Timothy (1986). 'Criteria of Identity and the Axiom of Choice'. *Journal of Philosophy*, 83: 380–94.

Williamson, Timothy (1990). *Identity and Discrimination.* Oxford: Blackwell.
—— (1994). *Vagueness.* London: Routledge.
Wright, Crispin. (1976). 'Language-Mastery and the Sorites Paradox', in Gareth Evans and John McDowell (eds.), *Truth and Meaning.* Oxford: Clarendon Press, 223–47.
Yablo, Stephen (1987). 'Identity, Essence and Indiscernibility'. *Journal of Philosophy,* 84: 293–314.
Zimmerman, Dean W. (1995). 'Theories of Masses and Problems of Constitution'. *Philosophical Review,* 104: 53–110.
—— (1997). 'Immanent Causation'. *Philosophical Perspectives,* 11: 433–71.
—— (1998). 'Temporal Parts and Supervenient Causation: The Incompatibility of Two Humean Doctrines'. *Australasian Journal of Philosophy,* 76: 265–88.
—— (1999). 'One Really Big Liquid Sphere: Reply to Lewis'. *Australasian Journal of Philosophy,* 77: 213–15.

Index